A Still More Excellent Way

SCM RESEARCH

A Still More Excellent Way

Authority and Polity in the Anglican Communion

Alexander Ross

scm press

© Alexander John Ross 2020

Published in 2020 by SCM Press
Editorial office
3rd Floor, Invicta House,
108–114 Golden Lane,
London EC1Y 0TG, UK
www.scmpress.co.uk

SCM Press is an imprint of Hymns Ancient & Modern Ltd
(a registered charity)

Hymns Ancient & Modern® is a registered trademark of
Hymns Ancient & Modern Ltd
13A Hellesdon Park Road, Norwich,
Norfolk NR6 5DR, UK

British Library Cataloguing in Publication data

A catalogue record for this book is available
from the British Library

ISBN 978 0 334 05932 5

Typeset by Manila Typesetting Company
Printed and bound by 4edge Limited, UK

Contents

Foreword

by the Rt Revd Rowan Williams

St Augustine famously introduces one of his most original philosophical reflections by noting that we all know what 'time' means until someone asks us to define it. Anyone who has had anything to do with the institutional life of the Anglican churches in the last couple of decades will recognize the problem. A generation had grown up happily and rather vaguely talking about the Anglican Communion as a fellowship of local churches loosely bound together by connection with the See of Canterbury, a bit like the British Commonwealth and the Queen. But suddenly the pressure was on to define – to define limits and disciplines, structures, loyalties and priorities in ways that had never been articulated before. And the question was not a matter of benign interest from theologians exploring the nature of the Church in general; it was being asked by exasperated ecumenical partners, baffled congregations, irate hierarchs and unsympathetic journalists and commentators. We thought we knew – or at least we thought there were questions from which we were perhaps exempt. Not so.

Of course the idea that there was once a golden age of Anglican practice, in which hard questions about the limits of diversity and the nature of authority never arose, is a fiction (though still a popular one, not least in the Church of England); even a passing familiarity with the history of the last few centuries will show the vigour and variety of argument about these things. But it is not an accident that the development of a received wisdom about global Anglican identity emerges roughly in step with the post-war transformation of Empire into Commonwealth. The idea of a federation of local/national polities, united in cordial diplomatic relations under the aegis of a symbolic British institution, played a significant role in shaping what seemed to be common sense in the understanding of the Anglican family. Increasingly, Anglican life outside Europe was organizing itself not only in the traditional shape of 'provinces' led by metropolitans, but in 'national churches', whose operational independence was largely taken for granted, though moderated by the growth (through the latter part of the twentieth century) of various cross-national forums and consultative bodies – which again reflected a characteristic post-war cultural style.

Is it enough to think of the Anglican Communion – or indeed any global Christian body – as essentially a 'commonwealth' of national churches? What has made the question acute is a set of debates about one very specific ethical issue, the theological reassessment of same-sex partnership. But the high profile of this has sometimes drawn attention away from the more basic and more difficult question of what sorts of interchange – what sorts of 'porosity', you might say – are needed for the Church of God to be more than an ensemble of separate local congregations. It has been recognized for a good many years now that the appeal to sovereign 'autonomy' as a self-evident and overriding good is ambiguous, whether for individuals or for communities; but anything resembling centralized executive power has understandably been resisted. How is it possible for local Christian bodies to express their interdependence, their accountability to one another, their commitment to converging goals in witness and mission? How is it possible to shape an 'ecology' of church life in which, without coercion from a supreme court, communities can find ways both of supporting one another and of calling one another to account, while sharing significant resources and genuinely ministering the gospel *to each other* as well as to the wider world?

Alex Ross's groundbreaking and profoundly illuminating study grows out of a dissatisfaction with the simple repetition of mantras about autonomous national churches; but it is certainly not a plea for any kind of ecclesiastical superstate. On the healthy assumption that we have actually *learned* what we take for granted, he carefully traces the ways in which the early and mediaeval Church began to create vehicles for interaction and interdependence through 'metropolitical' structures, provinces whose composition might vary but which were seen primarily as a way of securing effective episcopal partnership and collegiality; and we see how aspects of this tradition proved helpful in the climate of the Reformation era and immediately afterwards, as a ground for resisting claims for a single universal jurisdiction in the Church. We see also how, already in the eighteenth and nineteenth centuries, Anglicans were thinking hard about the nature of the Church's global identity and interaction: in particular, how the experience of the planting of new Anglican entities in non-Western contexts generates some creative new perspectives. The steady drift towards a norm of national Anglican provinces led by primates (with or without 'internal' provinces as well) is tracked through the later part of the twentieth century, along with the new significance given to the Primates' Meeting as an 'Instrument of Unity' in the Anglican world. There is a really enlightening discussion of the very idea of nationhood in cultural modernity, and its impact on these developments, from the Victorian period onwards. And we are finally given a glimpse of how the non-national province can in fact work as (it seems) it was originally meant to – as an effective embodiment of shared learning and co-ordinated and responsible action; a reminder that the model of the national church is far from the only or the best way of thinking about convergent and mutually nourishing relations between local churches.

This is a book that fills a serious gap in Anglican studies, and indeed in ecclesiology more generally. It demonstrates wide and deep historical scholarship and keen theological insight, and is written with clarity and (sometimes refreshingly subversive) wit. It is an indispensable point of reference for any future work on Anglican doctrines of the Church, and makes a substantial and enormously creative contribution to the ongoing debates about unity and diversity within the Anglican family.

The Rt Revd Rowan Williams,
Cambridge May 2020

Methodological Introduction

> The discussion in the afternoon bored me stark.
> It dealt with the multiplication of Provinces in
> the Anglican Communion.
> I deserted and went to the Athenaeum.
> - Hensley Henson on the
> Lambeth Conference of 1920.[1]

Sustained theological reflection on questions of Anglican ecclesial polity, let alone provincial jurisdiction and metropolitical authority, may not always have commended itself for creative engagement by the church and academy. Even that great progenitor of theological reflection on the ecclesiastical polity of the English church, Richard Hooker, concedes the task might seem, at times, 'perhaps tedious, perhaps obscure, dark, and intricate.'[2] The pressing crises of each age, whether represented by John Colenso in a previous generation or Gene Robinson in our own, seem to make the most urgent calls on the Communion's finite resources for reasoning and reflection. However, there is an increasing awareness within Anglicanism that beneath these 'flashpoint' issues lie foundational questions of authority and constitution. The examination of metropolitical authority within Anglicanism, and negotiation within it of provincial relationships, demonstrates intrinsic and important aspects of a polity which not only values and holds itself accountable to the inheritance of its tradition but also makes a commitment to look beyond the local through the formalisation of relational structures. This 'key relational dimension' provides for 'patterns and models for personal and group interaction and channels of mutual fidelity.'[3] Such a commitment is particularly relevant for the Anglican Communion, where the consideration of polity must grapple with the reality that it is not a single 'church' with a uniform interior ordering and juridical framework but, rather, an association of extra-provincial dioceses, provinces, multi-province national churches and multi-national provinces all with diverse polities of their own. Furthermore, the Communion claims an existence that is not simply the sum of its parts but points toward the intensification of relationships 'in communion' as a model for its own belonging within the church catholic, and to this end it has developed tangible signs of its own corporate life through the 'Instruments of Communion' (the Lambeth Conference, the Primates' Meetings and the Anglican Consultative Council, with the Archbishop of Canterbury acting as a 'Focus of Unity') and the coordination through its central secretariat of a number of other commissions, networks and dialogues.[4]

Successive reports of the Inter-Anglican Theological and Doctrinal Commission (IATDC) have attempted to expound different aspects of a distinctly 'Anglican' mode of being church. The 1986 report, *For the Sake of the Kingdom*, locates Anglicanism within the tensions inherent between Christian identity and its contextualisation in particular political situations, defining itself as both 'belonging' and 'not belonging' to inherited and adopted political and social contexts. In 1996 *The Virginia Report* drew on an increasingly popular trend of applying Trinitarian discourse to ecclesiological reflection, largely prompted within Anglicanism by the influence of Orthodox theologian John Zizioulas' development of *communio* ecclesiology to inform Anglican self-reflection on the nature of its own ecclesial 'communion' in the context of disagreement about the ordination of women. The 2007 report, *Communion, Conflict and Hope*, develops this exploration of *communio* ecclesiology but, rather than highlighting shared commonalities within the Communion through the accidents of history, language and Reformation heritage, instead takes seriously the creative opportunity of conflict within the church and the vocation of Anglicanism to engage with its own brokenness.[5] Eclipsed and overshadowed by the publication of the *Windsor Report*, the fruit of the independent but concurrent Lambeth Commission on Communion which eventually sought implementation in the proposed Anglican Covenant, *Communion, Conflict and Hope* is perhaps most interesting of the IATDC reports in that it challenges the equivalence of 'communion' with uniformity, and proposes conflict as the positive (albeit painful) context in which the church discerns its vocation:

> *Communion, Conflict and Hope*, the only report to emerge out of the ecclesiological controversies within the Anglican Communion that puts the communion ideal into conversation with the inevitability of conflict and the eschatology of hope, makes precisely this di cult and messy point — and has been ignored on account of it.[6]

Ecumenical dialogues have also attempted to engage with questions of polity, particularly the structuring of ministry and the nature of episcopal, conciliar and synodical authority, born out of the historical debates and disagreements which have divided the Christian churches.[7] Nevertheless, the extent of theological reasoning made possible and presentable through committee reports, not to mention their reception, is necessarily and unavoidably limited. More probing academic enquiry has begun through the expanding exchange of ideas in a number of new and established academic journals, as well as more substantial publications concerning both polity and canon law.[8] Nevertheless, there remains a perception that the consideration of ecclesial polity concerns itself more with institutional 'navel-gazing' than theological engagement with the nature of the Christian church as embodied and expressed through culture and context. At the press conference following the 2016 Primates' Gathering, Archbishop of Canterbury Justin Welby when asked by a journalist whether the meeting had considered proposed changes to the Communion's self-ordering and self-imagining, as had been widely anticipated, responded dismissively that:

> Frankly, talking about the refugee crisis with 60 million refugees, talking about religiously motivated violence, with over half the Communion suffering from it in one way or another, for some strange reason that seemed slightly more important than dealing with issues of internal organization.[9]

However, the dismissal of the theological merits of polity is increasingly being challenged within both the church and academy, as a sophisticated and contextual approach to the formal study of ecclesiology is being developed. In a critique of the methodology behind the Church of England's programme of *Reform and Renewal*, Dean of Christ Church Oxford, Martyn Percy, decries the rise of 'an alloy of executive-managers and episcopal-enforcers' at the expense of a theological 'point of origin for addressing and transforming the church' as leading, inevitably, to a 'vacuous polity.'[10] Perhaps less polemical, but nevertheless as pertinent, is a recent editorial by Paul Avis in the journal *Ecclesiology* which calls for a re-examination of the importance of polity as the outworking of applied ecclesiology:

> Ecclesiology is frankly helpless without polity. It lacks purchase and efficacy. It is not enough for a church or a communion of churches to have, and to own, an ecclesiology. A church or a communion of churches also needs a polity, an order or structure that facilitates its work. Polity has to do with the distribution and exercise of authority, the exercise of oversight, the making of policy and the resolving of disputes. Polity enables discernment of God's will . . . [it is] essentially the outcome of applied theology, a salient example of *praxis*.[11]

This study is an effort to respond to this call for careful theological attention to questions of ecclesial polity, and particularly the place of provincial polity – and metropolitical authority – within the Anglican Communion. Considerations of polity are intimately connected with questions of authority and its exercise within the church; however, understanding polity to be properly a sub-discipline of ecclesiology allows these questions to be framed theologically rather than through a purely pragmatic or circumstantial lens. This theological perspective allows for 'the systematic analysis, evaluation and development' of 'structures and legal relations within churches, as well as their mutual relations' which is rooted in the fundamental ecclesiological concern of how the Christian community is to faithfully give expression and articulation to its vocation to herald and witness to God's Kingdom and to steward the mysteries of Sacrament and Scripture by which God's purposes are revealed and carried forth.[12]

Discerning the Anglican 'Character'

Paul Avis proposes a largely deductive relationship between polity and ecclesiology – whereby the practicalities of polity are derived from the theological principles of ecclesiology.[13] However, his initial call for a rediscovery of the importance of polity in ecclesiological enquiry is developed and nuanced in a more substantial article for the *Ecclesiastical Law Journal* in which he acknowledges that the 'traffic . . . is not all one way' in the interrelationship of ecclesiology, polity and the codification of legal principles in ecclesial jurisprudence.[14] An interrelated approach to the interplay between inductive and deductive methodologies, where polity is seen as both informing ecclesiological reflection as well as being itself thus formed, offers a more dynamic framework in which to explore the historical development as well as the contemporary incarnation of provincial polity within Anglicanism. Although respecting Avis' concern that polity must be rooted in fundamental ecclesiological convictions rather than arbitrary pragmatism, and that therefore 'it is not for us to invent, re-invent or dream up a blueprint for polity, or to play around with a received form of polity simply because we have had a few bright ideas,' even a cursory survey of the development of polity within Anglicanism exhibits both changes and continuities which are not merely pragmatic compromises but have fed back into discernment of Anglican self-identity and ecclesiological definition. This is a contemporary reality as much as a historical one, where – prompted by reflection on present experience – the particulars

4

of Anglican polity call into question the ecclesiological commitments of Anglicanism itself:

> Is it any wonder that it is so challenging to state with final clarity what Anglicanism is? The truth of its life is a work in progress and is subject to a number of recurring distortions that diminish its capacity to be the fellowship of churches it aspires to be. In this respect Anglicanism eschews rigid forms of top down control and is equally wary of practices that exclude (both overtly and subtly) rather than include people in conversations, listening and reform of practice. Both of these are distortions of the Anglican idea of the church. And both of these ways of handling conflict and resolving matters of dispute transpose truth seeking into a question of power.[15]

Anglican identity, and the ecclesiological commitments which are fundamental to its character, remain still very much contested. The beginnings of the Anglican Communion's modern and recognizable polity may clearly be traced to the emergence of distinct and quasi-independent churches by the various efforts of missionary and colonial endeavour beginning in the early nineteenth century. However, an exclusive emphasis on its codification in the nineteenth century neglects the emergence in the wake of the Reformation and into the eighteenth century of the episcopally ordered churches in Scotland, Ireland and the United States, tracing a familial descent, even if not formal association (with the exception of Ireland), from the Church of England. The influence of Episcopalians in the United States was central to the vision of a 'communion' with visible markers of an organic union of churches, predicated on a hopeful vocation to precipitate further Christian unity.[16] The phrase 'Anglican Communion' itself emerged sometime in the early nineteenth century to describe what were considered the two (and sometimes three, when Scottish Episcopalians were included) branches of the Anglican family in England and the United States.[17] Recently, the seventeenth and eighteenth-century emergence of 'Anglicanism' as an ecclesial style, method and temperament has been helpfully distinguished from the Reformation origins of the Church of England: allowing for a more fluid and organic definition of Anglican identity that isn't tied to the ecclesiological struggles of any particular era but is instead marked out by principles such as compromise, accommodation and communality.[18] The capacity of these principles to constitute any kind of institutional reality, let alone unity, among the member churches of the Communion has been tested, as Anglicans have been faced with an even more fundamental existential dilemma: does the Anglican Communion exist and, if so, what is it?

Does the Anglican Communion Even Exist?

In 1998 the then Joint Registrar of the Diocese of Oxford and Legal Advisor to the Anglican Consultative Council, John Rees, submitted a 'deliberatively provocative' article to the Ecclesiastical Law Journal entitled, 'The Anglican Communion: does it exist?'[19] A decade later the Yale Professor of History, Frank Turner, submitted an article to the online news service, Episcopal Café, with an equally provocative title, 'The imagined community of the Anglican Communion.'[20] The two papers, and their authors' approach to the question of Anglicanism's existential angst, couldn't be more different. Rees, perhaps unsurprisingly, attempts to chart some legal and structural coherence in a polity which notoriously 'lacks all the classic jurisprudential marks of authority.'[21] He settles for an exposition of the four 'Instruments of Communion' – the Archbishop of Canterbury, the Lambeth Conference, the Primates' Meetings and the Anglican Consultative Council – as together constituting a 'multiplicity of unifying bodies' which reflects an Anglican penchant for 'dispersed' decision making and authority, both in the formulation of its theology as well as the embodiment of its relationships and structures.[22] Now, twenty years later, Rees' somewhat institutional approach seems conservative and (perhaps uncharitably) unimaginative, certainly less provocative than his title suggests. However, it does represent an important move toward finding some tangible representation of an ecclesial reality binding the churches of the Communion together; a visible expression of a shared inhabitation of the Church's vocation and participation in God's mission which might be identified as characteristically 'Anglican'.

By contrast, Frank Turner's article reflects a growing sense of disillusionment with the 'Instruments' as cumbersome and unfit for purpose.[23] With particular reference to a perceived trend toward centralised authority, played out in the dispute over a proposed 'Anglican Covenant' by which the Communion's relationships might be ordered, Turner decries any effort to establish normative grounds of authority in anything that might represent a global, institutional 'Anglican Communion':

> The good that the Archbishop of Canterbury seeks to achieve is the unity of an imagined Anglican Communion that has virtually no existence in reality . . . For the sake of unity of a communion that does not really exist, he has (perhaps unwittingly) fostered turmoil, dissension, and schism.[24]

In fact, for Turner and those who would follow him, the existence of the Anglican Communion itself is an entirely novel and constructed myth; it 'does not really exist but must be forcibly drawn into existence [with reference here to the Covenant], Radical innovation rather than tradition drives the process.'[25] At this end of such a reductionist Anglican ecclesiology, the only ecclesial realities exist at the level of self-sufficient, self-governing and autonomous provincial – or national – churches. To seek any further reality in their interrelatedness is to stray dangerously into the realm of 'imagined community' whereby, following that concept's original conception by Benedict Anderson and its application to the rise of twentieth-century nationalism, the inevitable result is an ecclesial version of nationalistic jingoism (albeit operating inter-nationally, or inter-provincially) with the attendant outcome of the eventual persecution of minorities.

Promoting an Appreciation of Polity within Anglican Studies

In response to this challenge to the Communion's own *esse*, and in an effort to negotiate the definitional boundaries of the Communion and the assumptions of Anglicanism which undergird it, this research seeks to avoid too much legalism in over-identifying the Communion with the Instruments, secretariat, and even personalities which serve it, while still affirming the reality of an evolving global institution constituted of provinces and national churches with a common heritage variously connected with English Christianity and a shared cognition of how that heritage has shaped distinctively Anglican characteristics, relating to liturgy, doctrine, theological method and, most importantly for our purposes, polity.

The role of polity within this discernment of identity is not simply to give expression to ecclesiological principles unconnected to the Anglican experience, but to provide the source and substance for formative reflection on how Anglicanism has taken shape through varying contexts in faithfulness and obedience to its ecclesial vocation. The task of asserting normative and generalised patterns of behaviour and belonging which might be found within all Anglican churches has recently been taken up with enthusiasm: from the distillation of distinctly Anglican principles for reading Scripture, to commonalities across the Communion in Canon Law.[26] Other systematic attempts to locate a singular Anglican identity have characterized it as embodying in itself a theological, or more precisely an ecclesiological, method:

On this interpretation, the distinctive identity of Anglicanism is located in the sphere of theological method, in the understanding of authority that informs it, and in the way that authority is exercised . . . what is distinctive about Anglicanism lies not in its substantive affirmations, the content of its teaching, but in its method, spirit or approach to Christian faith and life.[27]

Examination of ecclesial polity is the theological process by which a Church's ecclesiology is understood to take form as a visible society, enabling its mission in the world.[28] The theological content of ecclesial polity, then, derives from both the ecclesiological assumptions and assertions which underpin it as well as the task of theological reflection whereby the resources of Christian faith are brought into conversation with the reality, and ideals, of the Church's ordering. The nature of this ordering has classically been understood within the Anglican tradition to be 'porous, less circumscribed and not entirely self-defining.'[29] This reflects something of an eschatological ecclesiology, whereby Anglicanism is understood to exist not for its own sake but rather as a particular and provisional means by which the church might point to and, ultimately, give way to the Kingdom of God which is the 'perfection of relationality as the eschatological culmination of God's work in creation.'[30] Former Archbishop of Canterbury, Robert Runcie, described this as the 'radically provisional character which we must never allow to be obscured.'[31] The challenge to the embodiment and implementation of an eschatological ecclesiology and a provisional polity is greatest in times of institutional stress:

> Where anxiety and fear impel theologians and church leaders to seek security and certainty through control and the supposed neatness of uniformity, eschatological assertions of partialness and provisionality are given over in favour of immediate surety, relationality is hierarchized and the otherness of diversity is limited, and the acceptable range of authentic Christian practice is reduced.[32]

The current climate of Anglican disagreement calls, more than ever, for purposeful theological analysis and critique of the place of metropolitical authority and provincial polity. Archiepiscopal authority naturally inclines itself to the appropriation of a 'vertically' structured hierarchical ecclesiology. While the 'vertical' dimension of ecclesial polity is not without its place, without theological reflection it risks neglecting the inherent relationality and 'horizontal' interconnectedness which is proper to provincial polity. Theological reflection, therefore, and a commitment to the theological content that underlies the examination and extrapolation of polity, is at the heart of any attempt to 'embrace the political, pastoral and administrative structures of a church and to determine its organizational shape.'[33]

The recent and renewed attention to the study of ecclesial polity involves not just an evaluation of its inductive and deductive interplay with ecclesiology, and an appreciation of its own theological integrity and content as it seeks to express ecclesiological principles, but also its potential ecumenical impact. The impact of ecumenism, particularly in the second half of the twentieth century, has 'softened' some of the hard edges of differences in polity between the churches.[34] Ecumenism likewise faces the challenge that the fruits of its dialogues too quickly turn to idealised and aspirational statements of ecclesiology which find no translation into polity as an 'agenda for action.'[35] Avis cites the agreed statement of the second Anglican-Roman Catholic International Commission, *The Gift of Authority*, as a 'partial exception,' presumably given its bold proposal, among others, that the primacy of the Bishop of Rome could 'be offered and received even before our churches are in full communion.'[36] However, the reception and rejection of *Gift of Authority*, at least among the churches of the Anglican Communion, has demonstrated just how contentious proposed changes to polity can be, particularly where they seem to touch on the foundational and constitutional understandings of episcopal, primatial and even papal authority.

Reflecting on Norman Doe's extensive effort to formulate a body of legal principles common to the Christian churches, and the opportunity to advance ecumenism through a common understanding of ecclesial jurisprudence, Leo Koffeman has likewise highlighted the possibility of polity to 'open up new horizons' in ecumenical dialogue.[37] Although this study of metropolitical authority and provincial polity is confined to their distinctive expression within global Anglicanism, it also inevitably has an ecumenical dimension as the polity is itself 'part of our inheritance from the pre-reformation' Western Church with parallels, though again distinctive, in the Eastern and Oriental Orthodox communions.[38] The third, and current, dialogues of the Anglican-Roman Catholic International Commission have engaged with questions of local and regional primacy, albeit leaving alone as 'unhelpful' the proposals raised by *Gift* of universal primacy, and explored a shared commitment within the two communions to 'sustaining a variety of 'levels' of differentiated unity.'[39] This ecumenical work may also offer insights and resources within Anglicanism, particularly in bringing into focus the implications of its own provincial polity.

Chapter Outline

This examination of Anglican polity involves significant engagement with the historical narrative of its evolution and development. A historico-critical approach to church polity complements the methodology of applied theology in providing for a 'critical conversation between the past and the present . . . [allowing] an even more nuanced approach to theological interpretation of particular events in the present.'[40] Through this historical survey of the development of a particular polity, certain themes and problems are brought more clearly into focus, providing the prompt for further sustained theological reflection in succeeding chapters. Engagement with Anglican self-reflection on its own polity draws out how questions of authority, interdependence and autonomy have been posed in the past and continue to have relevance in the current climate of perceived crisis and disunity. Historical enquiry, then, provides the context out of which key issues may be explored. A 'thick description' by means of a diachronic historical analysis of the development and nature of provincial polity and metropolitical authority as it has developed within Anglicanism in itself makes a new contribution to understanding a little-studied aspect of Anglican polity.

A broad historical survey of the nature of provincial polity and metropolitical authority as it has developed and is understood within Anglicanism is undertaken in Part One, through three chapters. Chapter One outlines the early origins of provincial polity in the Early Church and its introduction to the British Isles at the beginning of the seventh century through Augustine's mission to Canterbury, while charting some of the historiography of metropolitical authority within England and its appropriation and application to the questions of Anglican comprehensiveness arising in the late-seventeenth and eighteenth centuries. The chapter concludes with the establishment of the Royal Supremacy, through the English Reformation and Elizabethan Settlement, as providing the 'coping stone' by which the provincial polity of the English church was held together.

Chapter Two explores the very early development of distinctively 'Anglican' expressions of being church outside England: in Scotland, the United States of America and Ireland. This chapter is not intended to provide a comprehensive history of this development, but rather to explore how provincial polity and metropolitical authority was adapted (as in Scotland), asserted (as in Ireland, albeit unsuccessfully, in defining itself within a 'United Church') and abandoned (as in the United States).

Chapter Three follows the birth in the nineteenth century of the modern institution discernible as today's Anglican Communion. This involved the establishment of the first colonial bishoprics, based on the authority of royal Letters Patent, which provided the legal foundation for the exportation of metropolitical authority throughout the British Empire. This chapter tells the story of the first metropolitical see to be erected among the Anglican churches since Augustine's mission to Canterbury over a millennium earlier, at Calcutta, and the subsequent growth of a provincial polity within the colonial dominions of Australasia, Canada and South Africa. Questions of authority and legitimacy which challenged the legal and ecclesial foundations of this metropolitical authority, such as were played out in South Africa in the notorious 'Colenso Affair', led to an increase in the assertion of provincial autonomy and an eventual settlement influenced largely through the efforts of the colonial bishops, including George Augustus Selwyn of New Zealand, Robert Gray of Cape Town and William Grant Broughton of Sydney. Broughton's influence, particularly, requires reassessment as his impact has been largely neglected and overshadowed by the notoriety of Gray and the Colenso controversy, and the charisma of Selwyn. The settlement achieved in this critical period came to be codified through the early Lambeth Conferences and continues to influence contemporary understandings of Anglican polity.

Parts Two and Three bring into focus some of the key ecclesial questions regarding provincial polity within Anglicanism which have been drawn to the surface through the contextual and historical narrative of its development in Part One. Part Two explores the emergence of a 'national church' polity, the twentieth-century successor to the 'contained catholicity' of the English Reformation, and the failure of provincial polity to take hold along anything other than national lines in Scotland, the USA and Ireland. Chapter Four contains a critique of this 'national church' polity, and its pretension to be the ideal form of a complete and self-contained constituent component of the Communion, as deficient in its claim to catholicity. While the experience of Anglican colonial expansion in the nineteenth century had witnessed a resurgence in ecclesiological reflection on the place of the province and the nature of metropolitical authority in Anglican polity, this creative and dynamic framework for building a true communion of churches was replaced in the twentieth century by the façade of the 'national church'. This development is traced through the language of Lambeth Conferences between 1920 and 1948, the broader ascendency of the 'nation state' in dominating the geopolitical landscape and some reflection on how current trends in the field of International Relations might inform and nuance the ecclesial appropriation of concepts such as sovereignty, legitimacy and recognition.

Chapter Five continues this reflection on the 'national church' through a close reading of the constitutions of the member-churches of the Communion. This research demonstrates that there is typically some nascent articulation of relationality with other parts of the Communion, and the Archbishop of Canterbury, built into the constitutional foundations of member-churches as well as some level of consistency with regard to the definition and exercise of metropolitical authority within those churches. This latter feature is a result of a resolute effort from within the Anglican Communion Office in the 1960s and 70s to promote the independence, self-sufficiency and self-determinism of member-churches in response to perceived inequalities in the relational dynamic based on both the historical circumstances of colonial inheritance as well as the directional flow of missionary aid and resources. It is this development which has directly given rise to what former Archbishop of Canterbury, Robert Runcie, decried as the 'shibboleth of autonomy' as a maxim of Anglican polity. However, the internal consistency evident within provincial constitutions regarding metropolitical authority, including a marked shift from the personal to its corporate and synodical expression, is not matched by any commensurate reckoning of how churches might relate inter-provincially within the Communion.

Instead this work has been taken up by the Primates, themselves personally representative of the autonomy of member-churches while increasingly assuming through their 'Primates' Meetings' an executive and magisterial authority which usurps the authority represented through the collective and collegial discernment of the other 'Instruments of Communion': the Anglican Consultative Council and Lambeth Conferences. Part Three follows this exploration of the developing role of primacy within Anglicanism. Through this exploration it becomes apparent that the increasing assertion of primatial authority within Anglicanism is not in fact an answer to the 'shibboleth of autonomy' but is instead the natural extension of a 'national church' polity being played out at the level of the international Communion. Accordingly, the Primates have become the personification of single national ecclesial units, all but obliterating the nuanced and complex relationships of a properly provincial polity.

Chapter Six will proceed with some brief discussion of the background and development of primacy in the Anglican tradition, sketching the concept's origins as part of the varied and complex degrees of ecclesiastical honours and papal preferment in the Western Church and its distinctively Anglican evolution both within the British Isles and beyond. Some key manifestations of the problem of primacy, which emerge from this history and continue to have a bearing on the Anglican experience of the concept, will be explored: the problematic appropriation of patristic sources and terminology such as *prima sedes* (Council of Nicea 325) and 'primacy of honour' (Council of Constantinople 381) to legitimate a particular understanding of primacy within Anglican polity, as well as the haphazard development during the eleventh and twelfth centuries of the distinct office of 'Primate' in the Western Church, not least in the British

Isles, and its questionable continuity with its current Anglican incarnation. The central problem which emerges from this discussion is whether primacy is in any way related to any formal jurisdiction or authority, or whether it is a purely honorific 'dignity' which commands nothing more than esteem.

This will lead to a more extended examination in Chapter Seven of the contemporary conceptualisation of primacy within the Communion, by means of a narrative account of the increasing international prominence of the Primates as they have gathered, since the 1970s, in the regular Primates' Meetings. This has been the principal forum through which the Primates have forged a greater self-awareness and articulation of their identity and role in Anglican ecclesial polity.

Finally, this chapter's exploration of the nature of primacy within Anglicanism will conclude with some evaluation of the January 2016 Primates' Meeting at Canterbury, the first convened by Archbishop Justin Welby and widely reported as a potential turning point in Anglican ecclesiology. Increasingly the ministry of the Primates is standing in for metropolitical authority within international Anglicanism and there is apparent an emerging trend away from institutional metropolitical jurisdiction in favour of a personal and pastoral primacy.

Part Four completes the context-reflection-action process through the practical application of this reflection on provincial polity to the case study of the Anglican Church of Australia and, within it, the role of the Province of Victoria in responding to issues of Professional Standards and Safeguarding most recently brought to public scrutiny by the Royal Commission into Institutional Responses to Child Sexual Abuse. The Anglican Church of Australia is often cited as analogous to the Communion: having a loose federal system where individual dioceses have considerable autonomy.[41] The Australian experience offers insights not only for the reassertion of a provincial polity within the international Communion but also within the existing structures of multi-province national churches.

Chapter Eight will explore more deeply the claim that the Australian context represents a microcosm of the Communion. This exploration will take account of the formal constitutive elements of the Anglican Church of Australia, the structure of its national institutions, its written constitution and system of tribunals, as well as the reality of a strong 'diocesanism' within the church's polity which marks it out as somewhat unique among the churches of the Communion. The origin and development of this 'diocesanism' will be briefly surveyed, along with some assessment of its interaction with the ecclesial province and the 'national church'.

Chapter Nine will examine how the dysfunction of the 'national church' within Australia, and the problems posed by 'diocesanism', have been brought sharply into focus through the recent Royal Commission into Institutional Responses to Child Sexual Abuse.[42] The provinces within the Australian church, however, have emerged as having potential to drive a response to the concerns of the Royal Commission in implementing a regime for Professional and Episcopal Standards which co-ordinates dioceses in a consistent and clearly defined scheme which does not impinge on their autonomy but expresses a 'whole-church' commitment to seeking justice for all those impacted, as well as strategies for prevention and accountability. The ecclesiological implication of this is that here, as a concrete and clearly defined example, a provincial polity is proving to offer a vision of Anglicanism which can make claim to an identity, though not exclusively so, as One, Holy, Catholic and Apostolic. The Australian example exemplifies the potential of provincial polity to be a paradigm for international Anglicanism, offering it a theologically robust and credible ecclesiology into the twenty-first century.

It will become apparent that the definitional boundaries of provincial polity and metropolitical authority within the Anglican Communion have been, and continue to be, subject to constant evolution. However, it is understood here as a fluid yet ordered ecclesial system, both hierarchically and horizontally governed, laying emphasis on relationships with and recognition of the other, as the people of God shepherded by their bishop around the risen Christ, find their own identity in the church catholic only by looking beyond and recognizing the marks of the risen Christ outside their own bounds too. This reciprocity is mediated at every level, institutionally and personally, but particularly through the ministry of bishops and, within and between provinces, the metropolitan. It is a polity which is constantly being negotiated, stretching always beyond itself, and never complete.

It is perhaps then no wonder that a report prepared by the Anglican Executive Officer on 'Provinces and Dioceses: their Creation and Division,' in preparation for the first Anglican Consultative Council meeting in 1971 declared:

It is a mistake to suppose that one knows what is a Province of the Anglican Communion. An investigation of the matter cannot be very brief . . .[43]

Notes

1. Henson 1950, 2:7
2. McGrade 2013, 1:43

3. Avis 2015, 286

4. Avis 2016, 10

5. The reports of the IATDC can be found by searching the 'Document Library' of the Anglican Communion website, http://www.anglicancommunion. org. The influence of John Zizioulas at the 1988 Lambeth Conference is noted by the Doctrine Panel of the Anglican Church of Australia in their response to the *Virginia Report*. They note the impact of his 1985 book, *Being as Communion*, as well as a full plenary presentation he gave at the Conference as the catalyst for applying a popular reading of the 'social Trinity' to an ecclesiological framework. Colin Gunton offers a classic articulation of this trend, describing the church as a 'finite echo or bodying forth of the divine personal dynamics,' see Gunton 1991, 74

6. MacDougall 2015, 201

7. See for example the 1981 *Final Report* of the first Anglican-Roman Catholic International Commission as well as the 1982 Faith and Order 'Lima Text' of the World Council of Churches, *Baptism, Eucharist and Ministry*.

8. See for example, Avis 2016; Koffeman 2015; Percy 2013; Driver 2009; Doe 2008; Percy 2004; Doe 1998; Rees 1998; see also Martyn Percy's ecclesiology trilogy: Percy 2005; 2010; 2012

9. *Press Conference Following Primates' Gathering* 2016. The Archbishop's response would have been more convincing if it had been clear that these were the substantive issues discussed by the Primates, rather than the proposed 'consequences' to The Episcopal Church which dominated the Primates' Communique.

10. Percy 2016a

11. Avis 2015, 285

12. Koffeman 2014, 3

13. Avis 2015, 285

14. Avis 2016, 5

15. Pickard 2013, 237

16. Chapman 2013a; Bosher 1962, 19

17. An excellent summary of the development of the nomenclature is given in Cameron 2013, 11–12

18. McCullough 2014, 327ff

19. Rees 1998

20. Turner 2009

21. Rees 1998, 14

22. Rees 1998, 17

23. For an account of this critique, and an excellent reappraisal of the role of the 'Instruments' and the nature of instrumentality itself in relation to the Communion, see Pickard 2013

24. Turner 2009

25. Turner 2009

26. *Deep Engagement, Fresh Discovery: Report of the Anglican Communion 'Bible in the Life of the Church' Project* 2012; Doe 2008

27. Avis 2007, 35. Avis qualifies his own approach, which follows this line but does not go so far as to assert that Anglicanism is itself devoid of distinctive doctrines or beliefs.

28. Avis 2016, 11

29. Avis 2016, 9

30. MacDougall 2015, 258

31. Runcie 1989, 7
32. MacDougall 2015, 59–60
33. Avis 2016, 4
34. Avis 2016, 3
35. Avis 2016, 5
36. Avis 2016, 5; Anglican-Roman Catholic International Commission 1998, para. 60
37. Doe 2013; Koffeman 2015, 193
38. Hamid 2002, 357
39. Moxon 2016
40. Brandt 2011, 374
41. Tolliday 2008
42. See Royal Commission into Institutional Responses to Child Sexual Abuse 2013a, para. 16
43. *ACC-1 Limuru, 23 February to 5 March 1971: Preparatory Documents Circulated* 1971, 303. Note that records of these and all similar documents can be consulted in the Catalogue Index of the Archives of the Anglican Communion Office.

Part One

The Pedigree of a Polity

The use of the term *province* for the member bodies of the Communion seems to have crept into Anglican discourse partly by accident. In Anglican ecclesiology the so-called *provinces* are more properly understood as churches. There are exceptions and anomalies: there are provinces that are made up of more than one particular or national church; some churches consist of more than one province; and some member churches of the Communion are legally styled *the Province, etc.* Nevertheless, the important point is that they are *churches*, with all the privileges and responsibilities of churches.[1]

The province has crept, like a kind of ecclesiological critter, behind the Communion cupboard to nest in our Anglican polity. That, at least, seems to be the understanding of the Inter-Anglican Standing Commission on Unity Faith and Order (IASCUFO)'s summative report, *Towards a Symphony of Instruments*, as it attempts to account for the confusing and conflicting use of the term within Anglicanism, particularly since the rapid establishment and growth of provinces in the second half of the twentieth century. At the very least, this somewhat dismissive assessment of the province within Anglican polity highlights not only the confusion around which the term is used and understood, but also the contested nature of Anglican ecclesiology itself as it struggles to convincingly articulate and locate the relationship between its own structures with the correlating theological reality of the Christian *ecclesia*.

Through an exploration of the development of the province within ecclesiology, beginning with its relationship to the geographical demarcation of the Roman Empire and its gradual consolidation alongside the codification of metropolitical authority and culminating in a study of the development of a distinctly Anglican provincial polity through the long eighteenth century and colonial era, the following three chapters will demonstrate that the province has a greater pedigree within Anglican polity than IASCUFO imagines and that, while the use of the term has become confused, a rediscovery of our provincial polity would not only be beneficial for the future of Anglicanism but also faithful to its history and development.

Note

1 Inter-Anglican Standing Commission on Unity, Faith and Order 2012, para. 1.18.

I

'A Glorious and Salutiferous Œconomy': Provincial Polity Established

The origin of provincial boundaries and the locus of metropolitical authority developed in the Early Church largely alongside the pre-existing political units of the late Roman Empire. During the Roman Tetrarchy, civil administrative provinces were subdivided into smaller units and organized under thirteen *dioceses* which themselves formed an intermediate level of governance below the Praetorian prefecture.[1] These provincial boundaries were taken over into the ecclesiastical polity by the end of the fourth century, and the major *dioceses* were largely reflected in the development of patriarchates and exarchates.[2]

An interest in chronicling the development of this provincial polity within the Church, and its relationship to provincial boundaries in the late Roman Empire, was sparked in continental Europe during the sixteenth and early seventeenth centuries. In particular this is illustrated in Charles Vialart's 1641 *Notitia Ecclesiae*[3] and Guido Pancirolus' commentary on the fifth-century Roman manuscript, *Notitia Dignitatum*, which set out in detail the organizational units of the Roman Empire in both the East and West.[4]

This scholarship was taken up within England in the early eighteenth century. Roger Altham, Archdeacon of Middlesex, employs these sources in a vigorous defence of the harmony between civil and ecclesial polity in a published address to clergy attempting to establish that 'Provincial Authority was the first Settled, External Authority in the Church of Christ.'[5] The context for the Archdeacon's addresses was the heated conflict at the time concerning the relationship between civil and ecclesiastical authority, following the deprivation of the nonjuring bishops after the Glorious Revolution of 1688 and the tumultuous controversy between the High Church and Erastian parties which was brought to a head in the Bangorian Controversy of 1716 to 1721.[6]

In his pamphlet Altham claims to be arguing for a mediating position between what he characterizes as, on the one side, the Erastian and Whig position, 'that there are no Powers in the Church, but what are deriv'd

to it by the Civil Authority,' and on the other side the High Church
Tory position espoused by the dismissed Convocations of Canterbury
and York, which would not meet again until the mid-nineteenth century,
that, as Altham asserts, 'affirm such an independent Power to the Church
as does necessarily interfere with the Divine Commission granted to the
secular Magistrate.'[7]

As it turns out, Altham's position is not a mediating one at all but
comes down strictly in favour of the Erastian party. In support of this he
makes the extraordinary claim that the purpose of the 'glorious and salu-
tiferous œconomy,' a phrase he uses to refer to the Incarnation of Christ,
was the reformation 'of the Sacred Polity only,' presumably meaning the
prevailing structures of first-century Jewish authority and administration,
so that it may be totally conformed to the civil administration of the
Roman Empire by the establishment of a provincial polity.[8] In pushing
forward his argument, Altham draws heavily on both Pancirolus and
Vialart, as well as the works of Italian Cardinal Robert Bellarmine and
Archbishop of Paris Pierre de Marca.[9]

Joseph Bingham and the Origines Ecclesiasticae

However, the most comprehensive and significant account written in
English of the development of provincial polity within the Early Church is
contained within the extensive work of Joseph Bingham. In 1695, following
a sermon on the Trinity which was deemed 'false, impious and heretical,'
Bingham was forced to resign his fellowship at University College, Oxford
and retreated to a parochial living near Winchester.[10] He devoted much of
his remaining life to scholarship and, between 1708 and 1722, produced
a ten-volume history of the Church, *Origines Ecclesiasticae*, intended to:

> . . . give such a Methodical Account of the Antiquities of the Christian
> Church, as others have done of the Greek, and Roman, and Jewish
> Antiquities; not by writing an Historical, or continued Chronological
> Account of all Transactions, as they happened in the Church . . . but
> by reducing the antient Customs, Usages and Practices of the Church
> under certain proper Heads, whereby the Reader may take a View at
> once of any particular Usage or Custom of Christians, for four or five
> of the first Centuries.[11]

Translated into Latin after his death and running through various reprints, abridgements and translations in German and Dutch,[12]
Bingham's work was again rediscovered in the mid-nineteenth century

having been republished in nine volumes together with sermons and other personal papers by his great-grandson Richard Bingham. This act of great-grandfilial piety was perhaps not entirely selfless, Bingham Jr notes in his introductory life of the author:

> Here I hope I may be allowed to observe, how frequently it occurs, and how encouraging it is to reflect, that the merits of an eminent ancestor are productive of honour or emolument to their posterity.[13]

Nevertheless, Joseph Bingham's contribution is certainly comprehensive and has recently been described as 'unsurpassed,'[14] although this may euphemistically reflect something of an unwillingness or neglect in recent scholarship, particularly within Anglican studies, to examine issues of provincial polity.[15] Although Bingham has been relatively well researched in relation to his part in the controversy over lay baptism in the seventeenth century,[16] a rediscovery of his work on the development of ecclesial polity is essential for constructing a coherent narrative of provincial ecclesiology and metropolitical authority as it has emerged and continues to function within Anglicanism.

The earliest origins of provincial polity are difficult to pinpoint. Although it has been asserted that it may reach back as far as the end of the second century, this is difficult to substantiate convincingly.[17] With reference to Eusebius and Chrysostom, Bingham points to the superintendency of Timothy and Titus in Ephesus and Crete as an early precursor to metropolitical authority among the episcopate.[18] Particularly, Bingham refers to Eusebius' brief mention within his *Church History* to:

> Timothy, so it is recorded, was the first to receive the episcopate of the parish in Ephesus, Titus of the churches in Crete.[19]

and also to Chrystostom's homily on Titus:

> Titus was an approved one of the companions of Paul; otherwise, he would not have committed to him the charge of that whole island, nor would he have commanded him to supply what was deficient, as he says, 'That thou shouldest set in order the things that are wanting.' He would not have given him jurisdiction over so many Bishops, if he had not placed great confidence in him.[20]

Even Bingham must concede that this does not constitute the most conclusive of evidence on which to presume a 'General Settlement of Metropolitans in every Province' at the time of the Apostles or shortly thereafter.[21] He does, however, outline a tendency toward the evolution of metropolitical authority through the first three centuries:

> If we ascend higher yet, and look into the 2nd Century, there are some Foot-steps of the same Power, though not so evident as the former [discussion of Nicea]. Lyons in France was a Metropolis in the Civil Account, and Irenaeus who was Bishop of it, is said to have the Superintendency of the Gallican Paroeciae, or Dioceses, as Eusebius words it. Philip Bishop of Gortyna in Crete, is stiled by Dionysius of Corinth, Bishop of all the Cretian Churches. Polycrates Bishop of Ephesus presided in Council over all the Bishops of Asia Palmas Bishop of Amastris over the Bishops of Pontus, and Theophilus of Caesarea with Narcissus of Jerusalem, over the rest of the Bishops of Palestine . . . 'Tis true indeed, none of these are expressly called Metropolitans : For that Name scarcely occurs in any ancient Record before the Council of Nice : But they were at first termed πρῶτοι and κεφαλαὶ, chief Bishops, and Heads of the Province, as the Apostolical Canon stiles them.[22]

Bingham's leaning on the Canons of the Apostles for some earlier authority for metropolitans, albeit under a different name, seems somewhat tendentious given what is largely considered to be a later date for their authorship than even Nicea.[23] Futhermore, the text of Canon 35 to which Bingham refers does not use the terms πρῶτοι and κεφαλαὶ substantively as he seems to infer, as if parallel to metropolitan as a title or style, but rather uses them simply as descriptive of the relationship of some bishops with others. This is not to discount, however, that herein lies something of a precursor or reflection of metropolitical authority.[24]

Provincial Polity in the Canons of the Early Church

At the very least, it seems apparent that by the Council of Nicea in 325 a structured system of metropolitical authority and a provincial polity had become normative and justified according to ancient custom:

> [Canon 4] It is by all means desirable that a bishop should be appointed by all the bishops of the province. But if this is difficult because of some pressing necessity or the length of the journey involved, let at least three come together and perform the ordination, but only after the absent bishops have taken part in the vote and given their written consent. But in each province the right of confirming the proceedings belongs to the metropolitan bishop.[25]

While this may not reflect a fully developed metropolitical jurisdiction by the time of Nicea, it does indicate that already the bishop of the metropolis is exercising some primacy of honour, if not greater authority. So, Canon 6 of the Nicene canons acknowledges, as well established custom, the patriarchal primacy of the bishop of Alexandria over Egypt, Libya and Pentapolis.[26] The Canons of Antioch, traditionally dated to 341 although recent scholarship suggests they may originate in an earlier synod of 338,[27] demonstrate an already established provincial polity and go further to explicitly set out and attempt to regulate the nature of the relationship between bishops and their metropolitans:

[Canon 9] It behoves the bishops in every province to acknowledge the bishop who presides in the metropolis, and who has to take thought for the whole province; because all men of business come together from every quarter to the metropolis. Wherefore it is decreed that he have precedence in rank, and that the other bishops do nothing extraordinary without him, (according to the ancient canon which prevailed from [the times of] our Fathers) or such things only as pertain to their own particular parishes and the districts subject to them. For each bishop has authority over his own parish, both to manage it with the piety which is incumbent on every one, and to make provision for the whole district which is dependent on his city; to ordain presbyters and deacons; and to settle everything with judgment. But let him undertake nothing further without the bishop of the metropolis; neither the latter without the consent of the others.[28]

There is much in this canon that is resonant with current supposed 'hallmarks' of Anglican ecclesial polity. There seems to be an early acceptance of something like subsidiarity; where each bishop is left to exercise authority in 'such things as have reference to the diocese of each.'[29] The emphasis of the canon, however, remains on the authority of the metropolitan and their particular ministry of responsibility 'to take thought for the whole province,' thereby calling for a kind of canonical obedience as might be understood today.

Furthermore, this metropolitical authority is not absolute, but is instead balanced by the conventions of a consensual collegiality with the other bishops. Elsewhere, the canons of Antioch strongly condemn the practice of bishops attempting to exercise jurisdiction, particularly by ordaining persons to ministry, outside the boundaries of their own province (Canon 13), and envisage the settlement of disputes and exercise of discipline among bishops to be undertaken within their own provinces; unless there is disagreement in which case the metropolitan looks to the opinion of the neighbouring provinces (Canon 14).[30]

Augustine of Canterbury and Provincial Polity in the British Isles

The nature and development of the earliest ecclesial polity in Britain is more difficult to discern. It is evident that British bishops were present at the Council of Arles in 314; Eborius and Restitutus from York and London respectively and a third, Adelphius, who may have been from Colchester.[31] Athanasius counts Britain among those places which have accepted the Nicene position against the Arians, and his distinction between the churches of Spain, Gaul and Britain suggests some separation of ecclesial organization which may perhaps reflect an independent ecclesial province in Britain by the mid-fourth century.[32]

Nevertheless, the state of Christianity in Britain at this time is not likely to have been prosperous, evidenced at the Council of Rimini in 359 where three British bishops 'were driven to accept the imperial offer of money to pay their expenses, though all the other bishops present had refused to do so in order to preserve their independence.'[33] However, the influence and character of Christianity in Britain would undergo a major shift following the decline of Roman influence which precipitated the 'collapse and abandonment of towns and villas' as well as a 'drastic reorientation from eastern to western Britain, prompted by the Anglo-Saxon raids.'[34]

This disruption did not annihilate Christianity from Britain, but the influence of Anglo-Saxon paganism and the dismantling of any kind of organizational unity based on the Roman province, situated in urban centres, caused a distinctive polity to develop responsive to local conditions. The increasing uptake of a monastic ecclesial model, following the Irish experience, suited this locally based polity but was not entirely divorced from the wider influence of Roman Christianity as particularly expressed in Gaul:

> By the sixth century there was thus a Christian social nexus operating against the background of contacts with the eastern Mediterranean, Gaul, and the developing churches in Ireland. In this nexus monasticism, which had arisen in the eastern Mediterranean in the years around 300 and was practised in Gaul by the late fourth century, was known and becoming increasingly important . . . Monasticism was all pervasive in the sixth-century Church, and coexisted with continuing episcopal power – most conspicuously in Gaul, where bishops were the main agents for spreading it. The aspect of the 'Celtic Church' myth which pictures an idiosyncratic all-monastic culture, isolated both from its Roman background and from mainstream aspects of Church governance, is thus fundamentally misleading.[35]

Despite some measure of continuing ecclesial organization under these conditions through the joint influence of monastic and episcopal structures, the fractious nature of authority and power across the kingdoms of post-Roman Britain makes it difficult to discern any clear scheme of ecclesial polity. This is not to assert that such a scheme was absent; there is some intriguing evidence from Northumbria, the west midlands and Wessex that pre-Augustinian British Christianity was organized, complex and mobilised for evangelism.[36] This does not cohere, however, with Bede's 'project to construct a new English Christian identity, founded on Gregorian Rome, which encouraged a British cultural amnesia and cold-shouldered any help – if in fact there was any – on offer from the learned and well-organized Churches of western Britain.'[37] Bede's assessment of the British bishops upon the arrival of Augustine, therefore, is necessarily low and chief among his accusations is:

> that they never preached the faith to the Saxons, or English, who dwelt amongst them. Nevertheless, the goodness of God did not forsake his people, whom he foreknew, but sent to the aforesaid nation much more worthy heralds of the truth, to bring it to the faith.[38]

A further distinction is made by Gregory in a letter to Augustine distinguishing between the British bishops and those of Gaul under the authority of the Bishop of Arles. While Augustine was to respect the metropolitical independence of the Gauls – 'because the bishop of Arles received the pall in ancient times from my predecessors, and we are not to deprive him of the authority he has received' – with respect to 'all the bishops of Britain, we commit them all to your care, that the unlearned may be taught, the weak strengthened by persuasion, and the perverse corrected by authority.'[39] Augustine's approach, however, was not to assimilate into the pre-existing polity, but rather to impose a new provincial structure, under the authority of Pope Gregory, and the creation of new bishoprics which would for a time sit alongside, and eventually supersede, the native church of the Britons.

The establishment of provincial polity under the explicit patriarchal authority of the Bishop of Rome was brought to England with Augustine's arrival in 597 and his subsequent consecration as Archbishop and Metropolitan in 601. Correspondence between Pope Gregory and Augustine, reproduced in Bede's *Ecclesiastical History,* details the mechanics of establishing a new province born out of Augustine's early missionary success:

> because the new Church of the English is brought to the grace of Almighty God by the bounty of the same Lord, and by your toil, we

grant to you the use of the pall in the same to perform the solemnities of masses only, so that in several places you ordain twelve [several] bishops to be under your authority so far as that the bishop of the City of London ought always hereafter to be consecrated by his own synod and receive the pall of honour from this holy and Apostolic See which, by God's authority, I serve.[40]

The granting of the pall symbolically bestowed metropolitical authority upon Augustine and his successors; whom it was intended thereafter would base their see in the more prominent city of London rather than Canterbury, which had served as a convenient base for Augustine's early missionary work but was likely deemed inferior to the dignity of a metropolitan.[41] Augustine was also charged to consecrate other bishops under him, and so in 604 he laid hands upon Mellitus (London), Justus (Rochester) and, somewhat irregularly as it was during his own lifetime, Laurentius to succeed him at Canterbury.[42] As well as these, Gregory further envisaged the creation of another British province with its metropolitical see based in York; the important capital of the former Roman province *Britannia Inferior*:

Moreover we will that you send a bishop to York, whom you shall have seen fit to ordain – yet only so that if the same city shall receive the word of God along with the neighbouring places, he himself also ordain twelve bishops, and enjoy the honour of metropolitan, because if our life last we intend, with the Lord's favour, to give him also the pall. But we will that he be subject to your authority, my brother, and that after your decease he should preside over the bishops he has ordained, but without being in any wise subject to the Bishop of London.[43]

Not all was to go exactly to plan. Augustine and Gregory both died in 604, and the passing of metropolitical status from Canterbury to London never eventuated owing to a cocktail of political and social upheavals which left the see vacant between 617 and 654. Canterbury, therefore, retained the primacy within the province and the fourth incumbent of that see, Justus, consecrated Paulinus as first bishop of York following his successful mission to Northumbria in 625.[44] Claims to rightful status as metropolitan were made occasionally by bishops of London: Anselm, in a letter to Pope Paschal II in 1108 which principally concerns the unwillingness of the new Archbishop of York to declare obedience to Canterbury thus delaying his consecration, urges against granting a pallium to the bishop of London; presumably refuting a request by the incoming bishop of that see, Richard de Belmeis:

Hoc ipsum et eodem affectu suggero reverentiae vestrae de Lundonia, si eius episcopo pallium petitur, quod numquam habuit, ut scilicet ad hoc nullatenus assensum praebeat.[45]

There is some irony to Belmeis' claim as he was himself a key proponent of securing York's submission to Canterbury and, following Anselm's death in 1109, consecrated Thomas as Archbishop of York.[46] However, he maintained a claim to primacy over Thomas during the vacancy of the see of Canterbury.[47] A generation later the successor to Belmeis' nephew, also Bishop of London, Gilbert Foliot, would renew this claim to metro-political status and independence from Canterbury.[48] Refusing to accept his excommunication by Thomas Becket, he based this claim upon the historically spurious assertions of the 'past glories of the see' recounted in Geoffrey of Monmouth's *Historia Regum Britanniae*.[49]

These claims were never realized. Hence there would be two ecclesial provinces in Britain, according to Gregory's original design, although the see of Lichfield briefly enjoyed a short lived elevation to the dignity of metropolitan in the late eighth century owing to the rise of the Kingdom of Mercia.[50] Despite the seemingly clear intentions of Gregory, there would persist an ambiguity and dispute over the equivalent status and relationship between the primatial sees of Canterbury and York until its distinctively 'Anglican' settlement in the fourteenth century.[51]

This survey of the earliest development of provincial polity and its establishment in England is not simply of historical interest but rather has a direct relevance to questions of contemporary Anglican polity, not least by establishing the foundation for the structures which are still in place both in the Church of England and throughout the Communion and which continue to be replicated. Furthermore, it is evident that the province has an authentic and integral place within Anglican polity and one which predates a 'national church' model. Fundamental to provin-cial polity is the balancing of both independence and interdependence, as it is based on an essentially relational ecclesiology which eschews both isolationist self-sufficiency and overly-constrictive centralism. An early distinction is also evident between metropolitical authority and primatial precedence. The nature and scope of primatial authority, as will be explored further in Chapter Six and Chapter Seven, continues to be contested and misunderstood within Anglicanism. The negotiation of a shared primacy in England – a model also followed for similar rea-sons in Ireland – demonstrates the relational tension inherent in holding together rival centres of authority. Furthermore, an unhelpful emphasis on 'national church' governance obscures the legitimate role of metro-political authority and the province and, in the contemporary Anglican

Communion, the crude assertion of primatial authority has come to replace it. This infatuation with the 'national church' model was to take root at the English Reformation and put in motion a perpetually problematic Anglican polity.

An Ecclesial 'Coping Stone': The English Reformation and the Royal Supremacy

The Henrician Reformation in England marks a fundamental and decisive shift away from the inherent relationality of provincial polity to the self-sufficiency of the particular church bounded within the Realm by the Royal Supremacy. The English Church was henceforth to define itself fundamentally as a national church, and this nationally based ecclesiology has become a mantra of Anglicanism:

> The idea of a 'national church' belongs to the essence of historical Anglicanism and is integral to the Anglican understanding of the Church. I would say that the dominant concrete form of the Church recognised by historical Anglicanism is the national one.[52]

This assertion that a national ecclesial polity is of the *esse* of Anglicanism extends not only to England but makes a claim to be foundational to the very 'existence of the worldwide Anglican Communion.'[53] The veracity of this claim in relation to contemporary Anglicanism will be tested in following chapters; it is sufficient here to give some accounting for its genesis in the settlement which emerged out of the English Reformation.

The positive formulation of the English Church as 'national' naturally stands in contradistinction to that which, in both an ecclesiological and juridical sense, is 'foreign'. The characterization in England of papal authority as a 'foreign jurisdiction' during the sixteenth century creates the legal framework for both spiritual and temporal independence within the Realm.[54] That legal framework was itself predicated on the claim, articulated in the Ecclesiastical Appeals Act of 1532, that 'this Realm of *England* is an Empire, and so hath been accepted in the World, governed by one supreme Head and King, having the Dignity and Royal Estate of the Imperial Crown of the same.'[55] Although codified in the 1532 Act, there had been a growing movement in the attempt to find a resolution to Henry's 'great matter' to promote and substantiate this assertion that the English Crown rightfully laid claim to an imperial status – thereby according it complete sovereignty in matters both spiritual and temporal without recourse to papal, or any other, appeal.[56] The most crucial collection of evidence prepared in pursuit of this constitutional claim to ecclesial autonomy was the exhaustive *collectanea satis copiosa*.

The significance of the *collectanea satis copiosa* has only come to be appreciated in studies of the Henrician Reformation relatively recently.[57] The original manuscript exists in a series of folios held at the British Library and includes a number of collected materials and annotations by the King.[58] It was likely put together through a committee of scholars and presented to Henry around 1530, and would form not only the basis for the assertion of the Royal Supremacy but also put forward arguments for the independence and self-sufficiency of the 'national church'.[59] The *collectanea* was later revised by Edward Fox for public consumption and published as his *de vera differentia*, which was in turn translated into English by Henry, Lord Stafford.[60] The *collectanea* also seems to have been the basis for various other pamphlets of royal propaganda, including the 1532 publication *A Glasse of the Truthe*.[61]

It is Fox's *de vera differentia* that gives the most systematic account of the growing consensus in support of the royal position concerning the English church's autonomy by virtue of the King's imperial authority. The argument proceeds by means of an assault on two broad fronts: first, that the authority of the king should be distinguished and absolute from the influence and interference of the clergy and, secondly, that the particular claim of the Bishop of Rome to a universal primacy was neither consistent with the primitive practice of the church nor supported by any convincing Scriptural warrant that might provide it with some mandate. On the first point, the independence of the civil authority is upheld with frequent reference to Jesus' words in John 18:36, 'My kingdom is not of this world':

> What thynge could more playnely declare that bysshopes and prelates shulde not intermedle with Empire or Dominion than those words of chryst in the Evaungeliste John. My kingdome is not of this worlde. That is to saye, after the commen glose, I am not to rule or raygne as with temporall dominion, for that is the office of kynges . . .[62]

Interestingly, in the understandable polemic against a universal primacy claimed by the papacy there is a reassertion of the independence of the patriarchates one from each other:

> If one by the lawe of god is father of fathers and al moust be reduced into a unite whye by the worde patriarke whiche is halfe greke, halfe laten are there rekned foure patriarkes that is to say foure fathers of fathers whiche be joined together by no mutual relation . . . other, but

as thoughe they by diversite of power were rulers of othere men and they subject to no man. And in that order the bishop of Rome is hinder most.[63]

De vera differentia frequently makes such appeals back to the polity and practice of the 'prymative churche', with particular reference to the first Council of Nicea and its canons concerning the privileges of metropolitans.[64] These appeals support the view that although the Royal Supremacy would eventually mark a radical departure from accepted constitutional norms regarding civil and ecclesiastical authority, initially, and despite the political expediency given the question of Henry's divorce, what was being claimed was not so much an absolute abrogation of papal influence in the Western Church, but rather its correction to a more primitive polity which prevents any kind of universal primacy.[65] This is certainly the position put forward in the 1532 Henrician propaganda pamphlet *A Glasse of the Truthe*.[66]

The *Glasse*, which takes the form of a dialogue between a lawyer and a divine, puts forward a number of arguments in support of the dissolution of Henry's marriage to Catherine of Aragon. The tract begins with an appeal to the interests of the stability of the Realm and the lack of a male heir before pursuing three broad lines of argument to substantiate the King's case: a lengthy exegesis of the disputed Levitical and Deuteronomic texts along with some hermeneutical discussion of their proper interpretation, a defence of the independence of ecclesiastical provinces in settling disputes without recourse to any other authority, and, finally, some speculative enquiry into the veracity of Catherine's claim that her marriage to Henry's brother, Arthur, was never consummated. It is the second of these arguments which is of interest here as, along with the *collectanea satis copiosa* and the *de vera differentia* and finally culminating in the Ecclesiastical Appeals Act, it is illustrative of a trajectory in ecclesiological reasoning which would eventually emerge as the Royal Supremacy, based on the core ecclesial proposition that the province ought to enjoy freedom of autonomy in the determination of its own disputes and laws. The *Glasse*'s 'lawyer' character expounds this in his introductory remarks:

concernynge the kynges separation fro the queen. It is tossed and tourned over the hye mountaynes, laboured and vexed at Rome, from judge to judge, without certayne ende or effecte: beinge very perillous for his hyghnesse, and moche more daungerous (if god helpe not) for us his poore and lovinge subjectes. Whiche if it had ben ordeined in the right and due cours, that is to saye within the realme, and so by the metropolitane examined and discussed, as lawe and reason wolde it shulde have ben, there had ensued in this ryght way or this tyme an honorable ende and purpose: to the great welthe of this realme and quietnes of christendome.[67]

This appeal to the necessity of disputed matters to be heard within their own provinces is then substantiated with reference to various authorities of the Early Church, including Canon 6 of the Nicene Council which is quoted in full and the determinations at Constantinople and Chalcedon, concluding that 'by this it may well appere, that there is or ought to be a special jurisdiction or power within every province: in ecclesiasticall observations and deciding of causes.'[68] The power and authority of the Pope to contradict these councils is challenged; drawing on the fruits of the conciliar movement a century earlier which imagined the church as 'the perfect example of a community understood as a *societas*,' with authority exercised through '. . . the consensus of many wills. No one person, not even the pope, can impose his will on that of the others.'[69] The *Glasse* shows its further indebtedness to the conciliar movement in quoting from the controversial pronouncement of the Council of Constance, *haec sancta synodus*, that 'every man of whatsoever state or dignite that he be, ye though he be the pope: is bounde to obey the generall counsell.'[70]

This insistence on the English church's freedom from the Pope's authority, that he is just one patriarch among many, is undermined by the simple fact that the provinces of Canterbury and York form part of the patriarchate of Rome and, further, that the English church has by convention enjoyed a particular and abiding relationship with Rome since Gregory the Great's mission to the Anglo-Saxons.[71] The claim that provinces (i.e. Canterbury) ought to be independent in their determination of local disputes ignores the external and outward relationality of provincial polity, except insofar as provincial diversity is quashed by the Royal Supremacy and substituted within the Realm by the 'national church'.

The Reformation argument against the Pope's universal jurisdiction obscures the inconvenient truth that the Bishop of Rome may still claim a particular patriarchal jurisdiction over the English provinces. In establishing the imperial independence of the English Crown, what effectively emerges is a patriarchate without a patriarch: the Royal Supremacy is to fill the gap. The Elizabethan period saw an effort to smooth the inconsistency of this assumption through an interest in the historical retrieval of the English church's continuity with the Christianity of the Britons which preceded Augustine's arrival. Elizabeth herself claims 'Joseph of Arimathea to be the first preacher of the Word of God within our realms,' before commending the vitality and integrity of the church of the Britons.[72] Matthew Parker and John Jewell also provide their own apologetic contribution to the rediscovery of the English church's pre-Augustinian heritage.[73]

Of course, a 'patriarchate' of only one Realm is fairly limited and so what is really established is a polity affirming the self-sufficiency of the 'national church'. This Reformed ecclesial vision still understands itself to be part of a wider movement or 'fellowship' of the 'Protestant International' but without any claims to jurisdiction beyond the borders of the Realm. This is challenged, however, as Anglicanism moves outside these borders: whether by finding itself abruptly and unwillingly cut out of Establishment and cast out into a place of sedition and suspicion (as in Scotland), or having to accommodate and adapt to a revolutionary expansion of national vision and consciousness (as in the United States of America), or (as in Ireland) surrendering to disestablishment after failing to account for the integrity of provincial interdependence and the potential for its conciliar expression.

Ultimately, the inadequacy of the Royal Supremacy to provide the 'coping stone' for Anglican polity would be proved through the experience of the colonial churches in the nineteenth century, particularly in Australia, New Zealand and South Africa, as the national incarnation of the church in England becomes the truly international 'Anglican Communion'.

Notes

1   Lenski 2010.
2   J. Bingham 1726, 1:ix, 341–44.
3   Vialart 1641, 9, 15.
4   Pancirolus 1608.
5   Altham 1721.
6   Starkie 2007, 74.
7   Altham 1717, 5–6.
8   Altham 1721, 10.
9   Altham 1721, 13–14.
10   Handley 2004.
11   J. Bingham 1726, 1:iii.
12   Yudha 2006, 179ff.
13   R. Bingham 1834, 1:xxi.
14   Humphries 2006, 246.
15   Paul Avis has recently written of the need to take seriously issues of ecclesiastical polity alongside ecclesiology as an outworking of the more recent discipline of Applied Theology. See Avis 2015.
16   Yudha 2006.
17   W. Smith and Cheetham 1875, 473.
18   J. Bingham 1726, 1:59.

19 McGiffert 1995, 136.
20 Schaff 1995, 519.
21 J. Bingham 1726, 1:59.
22 J. Bingham 1726, 1:60.
23 For a further discussion of the origins of the Canons see the introductory note in Coxe 1995, 388–89.
24 W. Smith and Cheetham 1875, 117.
25 Tanner 1990, 7.
26 Tanner 1990, 9.
27 Stephens 2015, 15.
28 Percival 1995, 113.
29 Ancient Epitome to Canon 9, Percival 1995, 113.
30 Percival 1995, 115.
31 Moorman 1980, 4.
32 Frend 1968, 39.
33 Moorman 1980, 5.
34 Blair 2005, 10.
35 Blair 2005, 18.
36 Blair 2005, 30–32.
37 Blair 2005, 33.
38 Sellar 1907, bk. 1, chap. 22.
39 'Answers of Gregory the Great to St Augustine of Canterbury,' reproduced in Gee and Hardy 1896, 9.
40 Gee and Hardy 1896, 9.
41 Delivré 2008, 394.
42 Stubbs 1858, 1.
43 Gee and Hardy 1896, 10.
44 Stubbs 1858, 1.
45 'As regards London, I propose to Your Reverence the same thing, in the same spirit – that is that, if there is a request for a pallium for its bishop, which he has never had, there should be no kind of consent given to this,' Schmitt 1968, 2:399.
46 Mason 2004.
47 Eyton 1855, 2:197.
48 Knowles 1970, 160.
49 For further discussion of the influence of Geoffrey of Monmouth on various claims to metropolitical authority see Brooke 1958, 203.
50 Story 2012, 818. For further evaluation of the evidence for the establishment of a metropolitan see at Lichfield see Brooks 1984, 118–27.
51 See Chapter 6, page 128ff.
52 Avis 2002b, 112.
53 Avis 2002b, 112.
54 Doe 2002, 80; see also, Doe 1996, 25.
55 *Ecclesiastical Appeals Act* 1532.
56 Rex 2006, 7.
57 See Nicholson 1977.
58 For a detailed discussion of its compilation see Nicholson 1977, 292.
59 MacCulloch 1995, 147.
60 Nicholson 1977, 61, 117.

61 Nicholson 1977, 111.

62 Fox 1548, fol. xxxiiii.

63 Fox 1548, fol. xxiiii.

64 Fox 1548, fols xxvii–xxviii.

65 Rex 2006, 7.

66 Richard Rex convincingly argues for a later publication date of 1532, see Rex 2003, 16–27.

67 Henry VIII 1532, emphasis added.

68 Henry VIII 1532.

69 Randall 2008, 31.

70 Henry VIII 1532.

71 A detailed account of this relationship in the century preceding the break with Rome is given in Harvey 1993.

72 Harrison 1968, 30; quoted in Chapman 2013b, 414.

73 Parker's 1572 work, 'De antiquitate Britannicae ecclesiae,' and Jewell's 'Apology' of 1562. See Chapman 2013b, 414, 418.

2

The Mean Between the Streams: Provincial Polity Adapted and Abolished

The Anglican Communion brought together churches whose understandings of church governance differed markedly. The United Church of England and Ireland had continued the episcopal structure inherited from the Western Church, albeit now subject to royal, rather than papal, supremacy. The Scottish Episcopal Church was a tiny minority church in a largely Presbyterian country, formed in defence of hierarchy by High Churchmen who remained loyal to Scotland's bishops when episcopacy was abolished there in 1690. By contrast, the 'polity' of the Protestant Episcopal Church in the United States of America, which was formed in Philadelphia in 1789, after the American Revolution, reflected a democratic and egalitarian ecclesiology . . . These, then, were the two streams that coalesced in the mid-nineteenth century and definitively in 1867 to form the Anglican Communion. On the one hand, there was the western catholic tradition, inherited by the United Church of England and Ireland and the Scottish Episcopal Church, of episcopal governance . . . On the other hand, there was the novel democratic, republican polity of the Protestant Episcopal Church in the United States of America.[1]

Anglicans love to juggle: the art of keeping in fleeting contact with two balls while a third dances elusively above their head. And it is that third, elusive, ball upon which they fix their eyes. Because, not trusting what can be too easily grasped, it is in the suspension of that third ball between the other two that they locate their identity. So begins the quest for the fabled *via media* – the middle way – the mean betwixt extremes – as Anglicans attempt to sit, despite the wonky rock, on their uneven three-legged stool.

This penchant for negotiating the dichotomies in Anglicanism is taken up again by Colin Podmore in his exposé of the 'two streams' in Anglican ecclesial polity which he characterizes, broadly, as ancient and apostolic on the one hand and novel and democratic on the other. In Podmore's development of this thesis, these 'two streams' have their fount in 'A Tale of Two Churches', an article published in both the Ecclesiastical Law Journal and the International Journal for the Study of the Christian Church in 2008, which compared the ecclesiology of both the Church of England and The Episcopal Church, concluding that a fundamental and dividing difference existed in regard to both churches' understanding of episcopacy:

> The Episcopal Church is essentially a congregational church with bishops, rather than an episcopal church as that term is understood in the Church of England – a church which has 'taken episcopacy into its system' but perhaps not fully digested it.[2]

This chapter is intended to assist that digestion with an emphasis less on episcopacy but, more specifically, the place of provincial polity and metropolitical authority and jurisdiction. In his reply and critique of Podmore's analysis, Bishop Pierre Whalon, Bishop in Charge of the Convocation of Episcopal Churches in Europe, identifies a divergence in the nature and exercise of metropolitical functions between the two churches as a more significant difference than in their episcopacy.[3] Furthermore, this chapter will unpack some of the assumptions behind the democratic 'New World' and hierarchical 'Old World' dichotomy through an exploration of the development of a shared, collegiate episcopate in the Scottish Episcopal Church and their rejection of a traditional metropolitical office in favour of a nominal 'Primus', a move which was more innovative than Podmore concedes. The impact of this distinctive Scottish settlement on the formation of The Episcopal Church will be evaluated with reference to the relational ideals expressed by both Seabury, in his correspondence with the Scots and consecration at their hands, as well as White's vision for an American church outlined in his 1782 pamphlet, *The Case of the Episcopal Churches in the United States Considered*. Finally, contrary to the case which Podmore makes for a seamless adherence to the 'western catholic tradition,' the example of the union of the churches of England and Ireland in 1801 displays a failure to impose a clear hierarchy within the newly created ecclesial body as pre-existing provincial structures were not brought into any practical or organic unity. What emerges, instead, are ignored Irish calls for a Convocation, or General Synod, of the whole united church which even envisaged the participation of the laity. This enquiry into the life of the other churches of the British Isles during the long eighteenth century fills out a little more of the complexity and depth of this period as elements of the English church are exported and contextualised.

Anglicans Abroad: From 'National' to 'International'

Despite the political, social and religious upheaval of the Henrician Reformation, the provincial polity of the church in England remained largely intact with the most significance change being the replacement of Rome's patriarchal authority with the Royal Supremacy.[4] The Elizabethan Settlement would forge a strong national identity for the church, uniting both its provinces, through the Act of Uniformity (1559) and Act of Supremacy (1558), under the authority of the 'Supreme Governor'. However, this clarity would not always be available or apparent outside England in the churches which would come to identify as Anglican.

In Scotland, scruples of conscience over the authority of the 'Supreme Governor' – and, more particularly, to whom that allegiance was due – proved the catalyst for disunity which caused those of the 'episcopal persuasion' to be cast not in the fair weather, as members of a protected and established ecclesial society, but instead under a cloud of suspected sedition and disloyalty. In this stormy climate the old provincial polity which had existed, gathered around the two archiepiscopal sees of St Andrew's and Glasgow, would be swept away, while episcopacy itself would only survive by scrambling aboard the inflatable life-raft which was the interim College of Bishops. The presbyters of the 'episcopal persuasion' were no less persuaded, it seems, by some of the principles and practices adopted by their brethren in the established kirk, and were themselves a significant force in carving out a new episcopal polity which balanced the bishops' oversight with presbyteral rights. The bishops, for their part divided on the question of whether to reintroduce diocesan organization, settled for a revised adaptation of the former provincial polity which abandoned the former two provinces and the metropolitical jurisdiction of the archbishops and instead invested authority 'for presiding and convocating only' in an elected 'Primus'.

In what would become the United States of America the redefinition of the established episcopal polity following American independence was influenced by two distinct visions of episcopacy for a 'national church'. The first, represented by Samuel Seabury, with an emphasis on episcopacy (to be acquired from Scotland) as fundamental to the primitive and pure polity of any authentic church; the second, represented by William White, with an emphasis on the church's organization 'from the ground up' through conventions of clergy and laity with the episcopate marking the final, though not fundamental, guarantor of this essentially democratic order. In both cases, however, ecclesial emphasis was given to the attributes of freedom and independence from the civil magistrate and the divestment of any temporal authority among its prelates. This common aversion to attribute anything other than 'spiritual authority' to its bishops, stemming from a general indisposition to the idea of any authority being exercised personally and not corporately, naturally led to an even greater distrust of any kind of metropolitical authority within the American church. The later establishment of a provincial polity was resisted on the grounds that it might threaten the unity of the national whole, capped by the General Convention, and although a kind of internal provincial structure was eventually adopted it was hardly, if at all, recognizable as in continuity with provincial polity and metropolitical authority elsewhere.

In Ireland the Royal Supremacy, as originally enacted under Henry VIII, would have much the same impact on the four Irish provinces as it did for those in England; albeit with considerably more conservative resistance to reform, notably from the Irish Primate of All Ireland and Archbishop of Armagh, George Cromer.[5] Under the Royal Supremacy, the Church of Ireland would develop a precarious claim to national establishment representing only a fraction of the Irish population and although its liturgy and ecclesial hierarchy was drawn largely from English sources, its four provinces would nevertheless constitute an independent church in Ireland until the formation of the United Church of England and Ireland in 1801. The formation and ultimate failure of the 'United Church' is important for our understanding of the place of the province within Anglicanism as it represents the first significant effort to unite two independent national churches. The failure of the ecclesial union and Irish Disestablishment in 1871 resulted at least in part from an unwillingness to account for the distinctive place of the provinces, and their convocations, within Anglican polity as well as the missed opportunity for promoting their inter-relationship amidst Irish calls for a 'General Synod' following the revival of the Convocations of Canterbury and York with deliberative authority by means of Royal Licence.

The examples of Scotland, the United States and Ireland demonstrate the first moves toward an Anglican identity developing outside England which was pressed to negotiate an ecclesial polity that in some cases incorporated an inherited provincial organization, though without clear provision for how they might be bound together, and in other cases adapted or entirely abandoned it.

Preserving the 'Episcopal Persuasion': Provincial Polity in Scotland

Two provinces had existed in Scotland, with their metropolitical sees based at St Andrews and Glasgow, since the mid-fifteenth century. Prior to this the place of the Scottish dioceses had been disputed, with the Archbishop of York claiming a tenuous jurisdiction. This had been settled by the end of the twelfth century, when Pope Celestine III made Scotland a 'special daughter of the Holy See' directly under papal oversight.[6] Under this arrangement, until St Andrew's was made a metropolitan see in 1472, the Scottish bishops had no clear superior among themselves, instead electing a 'conservator of the privileges of the Scottish Church' from among their number who would convene their provincial councils.[7]

Despite a popularly repeated assertion that the eighteenth-century tradition of a Primus for 'convocating and presiding only' is a reflection of 'the papal enactment of 1192,'[8] there is no evidence that the College of Bishops were particularly mindful of this early precedent and, if they were, even less reason to believe they would consciously model their own polity on a papist pronouncement of the past.

Instead the unique episcopal settlement which emerged in the eighteenth century was much more a result of high church conscientiousness in preserving a native Scottish episcopal succession; the lack of any meaningful exercise of the Royal Supremacy by the exiled Jacobite Pretender; an underlying national ambivalence around the nature and need for episcopacy in Scotland; and, the assertion – even among Episcopalians – of the rights of the presbytery in calling their own bishop and deliberating together in assembly.

The influence of two significant events has had an enduring, if underappreciated, impact on shaping the identity and polity of the Scottish Episcopal Church in the formative years following the death of Bishop Alexander Rose of Edinburgh in 1720, the last of the pre-Revolution bishops: the election of Rose's successor by the presbyters of Edinburgh and the emergence of the office of 'Primus'; and, as will be subsequently explored in relation to the development of The Episcopal Church of the United States, the involvement of the Scottish bishops in the consecration of Samuel Seabury.

Despite the official suppression of episcopacy following the 1688 'Glorious Revolution', the deprived bishops continued to exercise a 'caretaker' ministry over those nonjuring clergy and congregations who became referred to as of the 'episcopal persuasion'. Conscious of their own mortality, these bishops resolved to consecrate others in order to maintain a native episcopal succession 'and thereby preserve the Church of Scotland from the necessity . . . of applying to foreign assistance for a regular and valid Episcopacy.'[9] At the death of Bishop Rose, there was a 'college' of six new bishops; all without diocesan authority or jurisdiction.[10] Following their nonjuring brethren in England, the Scottish bishops were generally reluctant to impinge upon the royal prerogative to fill vacant sees, and so the 'college' served not only to maintain the succession but also as symbol of transience and provisionality; a 'stopgap' measure in sanguine expectation of the Jacobite restoration.

The traditional provincial polity whereby the Scottish church was organized into two ecclesial provinces headed by two metropolitan archbishops had existed in Scotland for over two centuries and managed to persevere through the disruptions of the Scottish Reformation and eventual Presbyterian Settlement; albeit if only eventually recognized internally and somewhat informally by those of the 'episcopal persuasion'. By the time of Bishop Rose's death this polity had succumbed to a natural attrition whereby despite the episcopal succession being maintained, which was the preoccupation of the bishops, the polity which they had previously inhabited had all but collapsed. Their task, therefore, was to discern how they might reimagine and rebuild their ecclesial structures to give expression to the priority of episcopacy in their polity, yet apart from any royal authority which they could not in conscience accept. The product of this discernment continues to mark out the identity of the Scottish Episcopal Church in the context of the contemporary Communion, with its uniquely adapted provincial polity emphasising the collegiality of the episcopate gathered together by a 'Primus' rather than a metropolitan.

Eastern Gentlemen and Western Conventions: Provincial Polity in the USA

As in Scotland a century earlier, those of the 'episcopal persuasion' in the newly independent American colonies, who 'some from conviction, and others from the influence of ancient habits, [did] entertain a preference for their own communion,'[11] sought to establish an episcopal polity locally adapted to the particularity of their late eighteenth-century context. Two schools in the discernment of a distinctly American episcopacy, and ecclesial polity more generally, may be identified; broadly characterized in the first instance as Latitudinarian and Whig, with its heartland in Philadelphia and led by William White, and, in the second instance, the High-Church Tory party based in New England (the 'eastern gentlemen' as White referred to them) and championed by the Connecticut minister Samuel Seabury:

> For White and the churches in the south episcopacy was the coping stone which set off the democratic edifice of the church . . . Seabury and his supporters saw the office as the foundation stone of the church and resisted an understanding of the church that gave no distinct role to its bishops.[12]

The perceived convergence of these two influences has been instrumental in forging within The Episcopal Church an identity which attempts to balance catholicity with autonomy. The Episcopal Church's own hagiography neatly demonstrates the relative emphases on White and Seabury's respective legacies. The Collects and short biographies contained in the accompanying resource to the American Prayer Book's Calendar, *Holy Women, Holy Men: Celebrating the Saints*, single out White's characteristic 'wisdom', 'patience' and 'reconciling temper' as he 'steered the American Church' whereas Seabury is noted for his 'perseverance' in renewing the 'Anglican inheritance in North America.'[13] The dual remembrance of White as the architect of the church's Constitution and steady-handed steward of its General Convention alongside Seabury as the audacious acquirer of episcopal order has informed much of The Episcopal Church's self-identification:

> The result of this eighteenth-century process was an American Church in which we address differences through an unusual mix of episcopal authority and democratic deliberation. This particular construction of church polity has marked an American approach to reconciliation and institutional unity in profound ways, especially in the conviction — never easily achieved — that unity in mission need not require uniformity of belief in all matters.[14]

More recently, the synthesis of these two traditions has been challenged in an effort to determine which has had a greater formative influence on the current polity of The Episcopal Church. The impetus for this revision has undoubtedly been an attempt to explain the source of contemporary tensions and controversies concerning authority within The Episcopal Church itself, and across the Anglican Communion, as well as to claim something of an Anglican 'norm'.[15] The emergence of a distinctively American approach to provincial polity and metropolitical authority, however, has only been noted without much further exploration.[16] Both Seabury and White favoured the establishment of an episcopal organization; however, White felt that the immediate challenge of current circumstances, 'an instance, extraordinary and unprovided for,'[17] warranted a provisional approach which prioritized the formal incorporation of the church through assemblies prior to the procurement of a local episcopate:

> The other part of the proposal was an immediate execution of the plan, without waiting for the episcopal succession. This is founded on the presumption that the worship of God and the instruction and reformation of the people are the principal objects of ecclesiastical discipline;

if so, to relinquish them from a scrupulous adherence to episcopacy, is sacrificing the substance to the ceremony.[18]

Seabury had been party to calls for an American episcopate as early as 1766. An address by the clergy of New York, subscribed by Seabury, to the Society of the Propagation of the Gospel implores the establishment of a local episcopate chiefly to mitigate against heavy loss of life among candidates sent back to England to obtain ordination, the rate of loss being around a fifth at that time.[19] However, it was White's move to push on with incorporating The Episcopal Church without an episcopate, a proposal which the clergy of Connecticut decried as 'if it be not a contradiction in terms, would, however, be a new thing under the sun,' which gave occasion and momentum to Seabury's quest to obtain consecration for the benefit of the American church.[20] The circumstances which surrounded Seabury's sojourn in Britain for this purpose were shrouded in secrecy, Seabury and his supporters being fearful that its publicity might scupper their efforts and revive suspicions of imperial prelacy at home. The ten Connecticut clergy who met in Convention in March 1783 kept no minutes of their deliberations, nor did they initiate any laity into the particulars of their scheme.[21]

Two clergy were elected as suitable candidates to seek consecration in England, Jeremiah Leaming and Samuel Seabury, and, the former having declined due to age and infirmity, Seabury set off with letters testimonial and introductions to the Archbishops of Canterbury and York, as well as the Bishop of London, from the Clergy of Connecticut, through Abraham Jarvis the Secretary of their Convention, as well as other prominent clergy including Leaming himself and the Rector and Assistant Minister of Trinity Church, New York.[22] The story of Seabury's efforts to obtain consecration at the hands of the English bishops, their reluctant refusal, and his subsequent success in Scotland has been well rehearsed; particularly, it seems, in an effort to establish an authentic Anglican inheritance independent of the Church of England.[23] Seabury's recourse to the English bishops in the first instance was driven largely by a sense of loyalty to the 'venerable Society' (the Society for the Propagation of the Gospel) which provided missionary funding to the clergy in Connecticut, an indebtedness which he acknowledged in a letter to Myles Cooper, President of Kings College in New York, a year after landing in Britain, faced with the realization of the necessity of turning to the Scottish bishops, having abandoned any hope of procuring consecration in England:

On this ground it is that I apply to the good bishops in Scotland, and I hope I shall not apply in vain. If they consent to impart the Episcopal succession to the Church of Connecticut, they will, I think, do a good work, and the blessing of thousands will attend them. And perhaps for this cause, among others, God's providence has supported them, and continued their succession under various and great difficulties; that a free, valid, and purely ecclesiastical Episcopacy may from them pass into the Western World. As to anything which I receive here, it has no influence on me and never has had any. I indeed think it my duty to conduct the matter in such a manner as shall risk the salaries which the missionaries in Connecticut receive from the Society here as little as possible, and I persuade myself it may be done so as to make that risk next to nothing. With respect to my own salary, if the Society choose to withdraw it, I am ready to part with it.[24]

The eventual approach to the Scottish bishops was neither an afterthought nor a last resort but, rather, had been prepared for from a variety of quarters well in advance of Seabury's departure to Britain. The Connecticut clergy had instructed Seabury from the beginning that he should pursue the Scottish connection if he had no success in England, and there had been independent correspondence to the same effect for two years between George Berkeley, whose own father and namesake had unsuccessfully attempted to establish an Episcopal college for the training of ministers in Bermuda, and John Skinner, Bishop of Aberdeen, who would eventually consecrate Seabury.[25] Just as William White had correctly predicted the impossibility of obtaining episcopacy from England, writing that 'it is generally understood that the succession cannot at present be obtained. From the parent church it most unquestionably cannot; whether from any is presumed to be more than we can at present be informed,'[26] so too in New England was there a realistic pragmatism of the likely difficulties they might encounter in England and a clearly developed contingency plan which looked to Scotland as the obvious alternative. While much has been made of the differences in ecclesiological vision for the American church epitomised by both White and Seabury, there is also significant convergence relating to the nature of the episcopacy they sought and, particularly, its place within their ecclesial polity.

White's manifesto for an American church, *the Case of the Episcopal Churches in the United States Considered*, promotes an episcopate which disassociates itself as much as possible from its counterpart in England. Particularly, White argued for an episcopate which was responsible and answerable to the clergy and laity constituted in convention, having no connection with monarchy nor empowered with any civil jurisdiction, looking to Hooker and Hoadly and their advocacy of *liberty* in ecclesial polity in cases of *necessity*.[27]

Conversely, and yet complementarily, the New England clergy's pursuit of a 'free, valid and purely ecclesiastical episcopacy' which could be obtained only at the hands of the nonjuring bishops of Scotland, who by then had long abandoned any allegiance to the Jacobite pretence, similarly envisaged an episcopate that was independent of the civil magistrate (free), consonant with the church's tradition given expression in the apostolic succession (valid), and having no temporal authority to rival or challenge the integrity of the newly independent American states (purely ecclesiastical).[28]

Although motivated by widely different ecclesial and political perspectives, one High Church and Tory and the other Latitudinarian and Whig, and despite disagreement on the nature of episcopal authority and its necessity and expediency in the newly independent Episcopal Church, the commitment of both Seabury and White to an episcopate which modelled itself on the 'primitive model,' in Seabury's words, and 'independent of state establishments,' White's own expression, lent itself to emulate much more the polity which had been settled, in quite different circumstances, in Scotland than that which existed in England.

The later development of The Episcopal Church's polity and Constitution displays a significant resistance to establishing internal provinces with metropolitical oversight. A question put by the House of Deputies at the 1868 Convention asked whether the meaning of the term Presiding Bishop of this Church, contained within Section 3 of the Constitution, 'be that which stands upon the face of it, and is in the literal sense; and if we have actually and legally a Presiding Bishop in the sense of Primus, Metropolitan, or Patriarch.'[29] The result was to strike the words 'of this Church', clarifying the limited scope of the Presiding Bishop's function as President of the House of Bishops only. Despite a resolution of the 1865 Convention advocating the establishment of provinces, concrete proposals from the 1870s to establish territorially defined provinces with their own synods met with considerable opposition and fears that it would:

> . . . dismember this Church, and out of this now compact and united body, create five or seven or ten separate Churches. The ties which might at first unite them would grow weaker and weaker . . . No evidence has yet been furnished by experience of any action or want of action by the General Convention . . . which requires any large surrender or delegation of its powers to provinces or groups of Dioceses representing only separate portions of the Church.

> Any such surrender, practically establishing independent Churches, must eventually and inevitably operate to undermine and overthrow

the paramount authority of General Convention, vitally necessary for preserving the unity of the Church.[30]

Although a provincial organization was eventually adopted in 1913, it was with very limited powers and continued to maintain the precedence of the General Convention while also prohibiting provincial synods 'to regulate or control the internal policy or affairs of any constituent diocese. . .'[31] An attempt at the 1919 Convention to increase the powers of the provincial synods was resisted and the profile of provinces within The Episcopal Church today remains limited.[32] Archiepiscopal authority is not exercised through the provinces, and since 1979 the president of the provincial synod need not be a bishop:

> The impetus for this change was apparently the understanding that the role of the provinces with the Episcopal Church is one of information and education rather than one encompassing authority.[33]

Provincial organization within The Episcopal Church, therefore, is comparable to the traditional provincial makeup of England and Ireland only in so far as it gathers contiguous dioceses together, although since 1964 the Ninth Province has held together The Episcopal Church's overseas and missionary districts.[34] Instead, a strong unitary polity is provided for by the dominance of the General Convention and the submission of the dioceses, and provinces, to the Constitution.[35] Just as the Royal Supremacy provided the 'coping stone' for the 'national church' in England, so too does the General Convention 'cap the edifice' of The Episcopal Church's national polity.

Cracks in the Coping Stone: Provincial Polity in Ireland

Whereas the Scottish Episcopal Church and the Protestant Episcopal Church of the United States of America respectively adapted and abandoned any traditional provincial polity in favour of a much more unitary national church, the Church of Ireland demonstrates a much closer parallel with the English church and, in the union of both kingdoms and churches in 1801, represents the first attempt to draw together two national churches into a corporate unity as opposed to the much looser associational 'brotherly fellowship' envisaged between the Scottish Episcopal Church and the church in Connecticut following Seabury's consecration.

Ireland was provincially organized like England, albeit with four provinces centred at Armagh, Dublin, Cashel and Tuam, and even went through the same competitive squabbling over primacy between Armagh and Dublin as between Canterbury and York.[36] This was resolved in 1353 with the same creative solution as in England: Armagh would hold the primacy over 'All Ireland' while Dublin merely over 'Ireland'; albeit a distinction which in modern times might seem less diplomatic! Henry VIII elevated the status of Ireland to a Kingdom at the Reformation, an act which had less to do with Irish dignity and more to do with repudiating a long-held papal claim to Irish sovereignty which delegated 'lordship' to the English monarch but no more.[37]

That the Royal Supremacy would come to replace papal authority – or rather, that it would resume its rightful pre-eminence over supposed papal usurpation – would become a key tenet in later historiography of the Church of Ireland as it sought to discover the nature of its independence in the face of both its union with the Church of England in 1801 and, as that century progressed, the looming prospect of its disestablishment and, seeming, disinheritance. Richard Mant's 'useful, if biased, account'[38] of the history of the Church of Ireland, published in 1830, demonstrates this enthusiasm for the Royal Supremacy:

> Upon the difficulties arising from the circumstances of the country it is not proposed to dwell: but as to the sentiment of the English sovereignty [over Ireland] being derived from a foreign source, it may be briefly remarked, that the claim of the kings of England to the dominion of Ireland was independent of any Papal authority.[39]

Despite the polemic, or perhaps aided by it, Mant articulates the key belief that in Ireland, as it was in England, the Royal Supremacy had displaced any patriarchal claim of jurisdiction on the independence of the provinces. Not only did the Supremacy stand in for the loss of patriarchal authority, but it also served to further unite both the English and Irish provinces into respective national churches.[40]

Thus Ireland, as in England, saw the formation of a more tightly bounded 'national church', governed by the Royal Supremacy, and the subsequent suppression of a more outward and relational provincial polity. This would be tested, however, during the nineteenth century in the failed experiment of ecclesial union which was the creation of the 'United Church of England and Ireland' in 1801.

The creation of a 'United Church' seemed to flow necessarily from the political creation of a 'United Kingdom' of Great Britain and Ireland by means of independent legislation passed through the respective parliaments of each. Despite considerable debate and discussion of the details, the eventual polity which emerged was ambiguous: neither a complete assimilation and incorporation into the Church of England on the one hand, nor, on the other, the maintenance of full independence and distinctiveness in parallel to the Church of England in a united ecclesial structure. The Church of Ireland was not simply subsumed into the Church of England but rather kept its existing provincial structure and local identity without subordination to Canterbury or any other jurisdiction. However, through the Fifth Article of the Acts of Union, the two churches were brought together into a unity of 'doctrine, worship, discipline and government [that] shall be, and shall remain in full force for ever, as the same are now by law established for the Church of England.'[41] This somewhat vague mandate would serve to unite the two churches at least in name, even if the nature of their provincial relationality was left unspecified, untested and unclear.[42] This tenuous polity would need a test case to prove the true strength of its ecclesial union. Such a test case would arise following the revival of the Convocations of Canterbury and York in 1852 and 1861 respectively, and the failure of the Irish bishops to convince the Liberal government to condone the calling of a 'General Synod' of the English and Irish provinces together or, at least, the Irish convocations in like manner as the English.[43] This failure to account for the underlying provincial polity in the union of both churches would be its undoing.

The revival of convocations, whether in England or Ireland, threatened to dislodge the traditional role of the Royal Supremacy in checking the assertion and exercise of corporate metropolitical authority. This hesitancy and reluctance to call and trust in synods was also felt in the colonies,[44] though perhaps in their case greater ambiguity enabled more audacity in experimentation.[45] Supporters of an Irish Convocation, however, were happy to explicitly draw out the connection between provincial polity and synodical authority in the absence of a patriarchate:

> In connexion with this subject, it is essential to consider that in Churches of Provincial organization (such as that of Ireland) which are autocephalic, i.e., which do not owe obedience to a Patriarchate or an Exarchate, Provincial Synods are the ultimate authorities in doctrine subject only to an Oecumenical Council.[46]

The proposal for a 'General Synod' of the United Church of England and Ireland, which might have provided a 'coping stone' to draw together and 'set off' the unity of its provincial polity, instead, by its failure to convince, exposed the weakness of the grand pretentions, but vague aspirations, of the Fifth Article of Union. When tested, the unity of the established churches of England and Ireland proved to be only a façade. The Irish bishops, in calling for a united Convocation, sought to express the inherent relationality and ecclesial coherence which an appreciation of their provincial ecclesiology promised, as two national churches were made one. However, national identities die hard – in things spiritual as well as temporal – and the bonds would come unstuck by the failure to discern beyond the old structures the promise of something new.

Notes

1 Podmore 2010, 14, 20.
2 Podmore 2008, 143.
3 Whalon 2011, 8.
4 Avis 2007, 159.
5 Jefferies 2004.
6 B. Smith 2013, 442.
7 B. Smith 2013, 443.
8 B. Smith 2013, 443.
9 Skinner 1788, 2:602.
10 Bertie 2000, 515.
11 W. White 1782, iii.
12 Thomas 2004, 17.
13 *Holy Women, Holy Men: Celebrating the Saints* 2010, 466–67, 678–79.
14 *To Set Our Hope on Christ: A Response to the Invitation of Windsor Report 135* 2005, 34.
15 See for example Podmore 2010 which emphasizes the influence of White; an account of the critique of the Seabury/White 'synthesis' within recent historiography of The Episcopal Church is made by Brittain 2015a, 23ff.
16 Whalon 2011, 8.
17 W. White 1782, 21.
18 W. White 1782, 19.
19 Beardsley 1881, 463.
20 Beardsley 1881, 99.
21 Beardsley 1881, 78.
22 The full correspondence is reproduced in Beardsley 1881, 80–95.
23 The English bishops' inability, or unwillingness, to consecrate Seabury has not been forgotten: the recent response of The Episcopal Church to the Windsor Report describes the 'quest for an American bishop' as 'temporarily thwarted by the refusal of English bishops to ordain Samuel Seabury,' see *To Set Our Hope on Christ: A Response to the Invitation of Windsor Report* ¶135 2005, 33.
24 Beardsley 1881, 137.
25 For evidence that the 'Scottish option' was part of Seabury's original instructions see the correspondence between Boston clergyman Samuel Parker and Daniel Fogg, who had been present at the Woodbury convention, reproduced in Beardsley 1881, 104; for an account of the elder George Berkeley's aspirations for a local centre of Episcopal training in the Americas see Strong 2007, 77; an account of the correspondence between the younger George Berkeley and Bishop John Skinner is given in Mather 1992, 121.

26 W. White 1782, 16–17.

27 W. White 1782, 29–30.

28 The phrase 'free, valid and purely Ecclesiastical Episcopacy' is used repeatedly by Seabury in his correspondence with the Scottish Episcopal Church. The term was also incorporated into the preamble of the Concordat signed between Seabury and the Scottish bishops following his consecration in 1784. See Beardsley 1881, 135–54.

29 E. A. White and Dykman 1997, 1031.

30 Report of the 1874 committee on amendments to the Constitution, reproduced in E. A. White and Dykman 1997, 107.

31 E. A. White and Dykman 1997, 334.

32 E. A. White and Dykman 1997, 338.

33 E. A. White and Dykman 1997, 339.

34 E. A. White and Dykman 1997, 338.

35 Whalon 2011, 3; on this point, and in drawing the correct distinction between the nature of provinces within The Episcopal Church and the Church of England, Podmore and Whalon are in agreement. See Podmore 2008, 64.

36 The provinces of Cashel and Tuam were incorporated into Dublin and Armagh, respectively, under the 1833 Church Temporalities (Ireland) Act.

37 Maginn 2018.

38 Gordon 2004.

39 Mant 1840, 1:109.

40 This development of national ecclesial structures outside the British Isles is discussed more broadly with reference to territoriality and the Reformation in Cranmer 2002, 157.

41 Union with Ireland Act (1800).

42 S. J. Brown 2001, 2.

43 For the content of these debates see House of Commons' Paper 1863. Also, Hansard HC Deb 7 May 1863, vol 170, col 1299; Hansard HL Deb 19 May 1863, vol 170, col 1944; Hansard HC Deb 9 June 1863, vol 171, col 653; Hansard HL Deb 15 July 1864, vol 176, cols 1544–1545.

44 Strong 2007, 251–78.

45 See Chapter 3.

46 Joyce 1869, 30.

3

Colonial Communion:
Provincial Polity Exported

With the disappearance of traditional colonial empires (though not the world which they helped create), formerly subject peoples are rediscovering and reasserting their own political, economic, and cultural integrity. They seek, both at a domestic and an international level, to reverse the political and economic injustices which in part are the legacy of the colonial era. By the same token, they seek to reaffirm their cultural identities - to re-appropriate, where necessary, the customs, values, and insights that belong to their local or regional ways of life . . . The setting of these efforts to achieve integrity and justice . . . also concern the Anglican churches, which first became a world-wide communion, and only later discovered themselves as such, in the course of the movement of colonial expansion and its aftermath.[1]

The origins of the Anglican Communion are obscure. It has no founding document or inaugural event to mark its birth, and instead a number of contenders emerge in the development of its conception. This development, as has been charted through the preceding chapters, is tied up with the evolving nature and place of provincial polity within Anglican ecclesiology. A line up of these contenders might include Augustine's arrival in 597 and the establishment of two provinces at Canterbury and York, where an acknowledgement of the primacy of Canterbury, and communion therewith, continues to shape and define membership of the Anglican Communion.

A case could also plainly be made for the Reformation, not only in forging the Church of England's identity as both catholic and reformed, but also in the fundamental reorientation from the papacy to the Royal Supremacy. The Elizabethan Settlement established the Royal Supremacy as a unifying force not only within England but also between the independent churches of England and Ireland, as the six ecclesial provinces were united in communion across national boundaries.

Likewise, the developments in Scotland following the Glorious Revolution of 1688 saw the birth of a characteristically 'Anglican' episcopal church outside England; albeit one which lived under a cloud of seditious suspicion and suffered a problematic relationship with its Established southern counterpart. If this was not the beginning of the Anglican Communion, it might at least be the beginning of 'impaired communion'.

Finally, the special relationship established between the Scottish Episcopal Church and the Church of Connecticut, and the subsequent creation of The Episcopal Church in the United States of America, marks out a pivotal moment in the formation of a global Anglican identity adapted to local and national contexts.

By the end of the eighteenth century these Anglican expressions were bound together by little more than a vague family resemblance. Moreover, a variety of disparate polities had emerged, ranging from the traditional metropolitical provincial polity in England and Ireland, inherited from the western catholic church and adapted in the sixteenth century to accommodate the Royal Supremacy although otherwise largely unreformed, to the adapted provincial structure of the Scottish Episcopal Church carried over from the influence of the collegiate system in place in the early eighteenth century with diocesan but no metropolitical authority, as well as the democratically based structure of national and diocesan Conventions adopted in the United States based upon representation of laity as well as clergy.

The Uneasy Legacy of Colonialism

It was only with Britain's rapid expansion of empire in the nineteenth century, accompanied by a commensurate missionary effort supported by agencies and private philanthropy, that the United Church of England and Ireland (as it was from 1801) benefited from the global reach of colonialism. It was also the colonial period which, at least at first, encouraged a more coherent provincial and metropolitical structure to take shape in the new colonial lands: an inheritance which persists in the Communion's contemporary polity. This coherence, however, would prove only to be a pretence as the authority on which it was largely predicated, the royal Letters Patent, broke down through a series of legal disputes as well as a push from the colonial churches themselves for local self-determination and greater autonomy. As the first report of the Inter-Anglican Theological and Doctrinal Commission observes, at the head of this chapter, these challenges remain contemporary for the Communion as it comes to terms with its colonial legacy in a post-colonial world.

Colonialism enjoys something of a status as a 'dirty word' in current political discourse, no doubt justifiably, with its connotations of subjection, exploitation and hegemony. The twentieth-century critique of colonialism has tended to emphasize either the 'prima facie claim to self-determination' of national and cultural groups, or the attachment between sovereignty and the indigenous occupation of geographical territory.[2] A third objection may be made, particularly relevant to the development of provincial autonomy within the Communion during the nineteenth century, which is 'the creation and upholding of a political association that denies its members equal and reciprocal terms of cooperation.'[3]

Nevertheless, colonization within Anglicanism has also been motivated by a missional and evangelical theological imperative whereby 'empire' has been understood to be the providential circumstance by which God's mission might be furthered into the new world.[4] The Society for the Propagation of the Gospel in Foreign Parts, established in 1701, did much to establish this missionary discourse which further provided a theological basis to British imperialism into the nineteenth century, when it was joined by other voluntary subscription agencies such as the Church Missionary Society.[5] Similarly, the establishment of ecclesial provinces through colonial expansion was motivated not simply by a conformity of ecclesiastical structures to the growing British Empire, but by the missionary opportunities and challenges, and increasing calls for their own self-determination, experienced by the early colonists.

Cold Baths and Hot Sunbeds: the Establishment of the Metropolitical See of Calcutta

The first colonial bishopric established outside of the British Isles but within the Crown's dominion was at Nova Scotia in 1787.[6] Effected by Letters Patent, the Bishop of Nova Scotia was made 'subject and subordinate to the archiepiscopal see of the province of Canterbury . . . in the same manner as any bishop of any see within the province of Canterbury . . . is under the authority of the aforesaid archiepiscopal see of Canterbury,' except insofar as the Archbishop of Canterbury, or the ecclesiastical courts, held no appellate jurisdiction.[7] The first colonial see to be established was, therefore, part of the Province of Canterbury and under the metropolitical jurisdiction of the Archbishop of Canterbury, except that jurisdiction in matters of ecclesiastical law on appeal from the bishop bypassed the provincial Court of Arches to be settled directly by commissioners of the Crown sitting as the Court of Delegates. Similar Letters Patent issued in 1793 carved out the Diocese of Quebec from Nova Scotia and in 1814 created the Diocese of Calcutta, incorporating all of the lands held by the East India Company. The 1814 Letters Patent creating the see of Calcutta, within the metropolitical jurisdiction of Canterbury, also conform to its Nova Scotia precedent in bypassing the Archbishop of Canterbury and the provincial ecclesiastical courts in matters of appeal from the bishop of Calcutta but goes further to nominate the local Judges of the Supreme Court of Judicature and Members of Council at Calcutta to be the Commissioners Delegate to determine all matters of final appeal.[8] Even at this early stage an increasing tendency toward self-determination and local autonomy in ecclesiastical affairs within the colonies is beginning to take shape. The Bishop of Calcutta remained 'subject and subordinate to the archiepiscopal See of the province of Canterbury.' However it is unclear how, in practice, this might have been expressed.[9]

Two further dioceses were created in 1824, according to a similar form, in Barbados and Jamaica. However, the Diocese of Calcutta deserves fuller exploration as in 1835 it was reconstituted into a metropolitical see with oversight of the newly created suffragan dioceses of Madras and, from 1837, Bombay. This is the first creation of a new metropolitical see to be established within the dominion of the British Crown since the High Middle Ages.

Formal legislative proposals to establish Calcutta as a metropolitical see were made in 1833 as part of wider parliamentary revisions to the East India Company's charter.[10] The East India Company's Court of Directors received correspondence in June 1833 from Charles Grant, President of the Board of Control, mooting the appointment of suffragan bishops in both Madras and Bombay to relieve the bishop of Calcutta.[11] The catalyst for this proposal was the unfortunate and untimely demise of the previous four bishops of Calcutta who, it was supposed, had all died as a result of the extreme conditions and vast expanse of their diocese.[12] Less than a year before he died, Bishop Turner had drawn up proposals for the establishment of more bishoprics in India by the addition of a new Diocese of Madras to encompass the presidencies of Madras and Bombay.[13] Interestingly, this plan envisaged that the other colonial possessions (the Cape of Good Hope, the Isle of France, Ceylon, New South Wales, Van Dieman's Land and any other settlements being established on continental Australia) should come 'under the joint superintendence and authority of the two Indian bishops,' one or other of which should visit each colony once in three years.[14] Turner's proposals for effectively shared metropolitical jurisdiction in the colonies went no further, and the enquiries of the Select Committee on the Affairs of the East India Company focus more on the question of whether a second bishopric was expedient or necessary rather than how they might be ecclesiastically ordered. In any case, if the need for an additional bishopric was predicated on the difficulties and dangers of travel within India, surely Turner's proposal that two bishops should between them visit colonies as far apart as South Africa and New South Wales was ambitious. It does seem, however, at least an attempt to bring the churches in the colonies into a more coherent scheme for ecclesiastical establishment, as thereunto there had existed only chaplaincies under the ordinary jurisdiction of the Governor, outside of any diocesan or provincial structure. This tension between the ordinary jurisdiction of the colonial executive over its chaplains and the assumed authority of the bishops, imparted by Letters Patent, would later cause conflict in Tasmania and further press the question of what ought to be the proper sphere of the bishop's authority in relation to colonial governments, particularly in the context of a substantially sectarian society.[15]

The status of the Bishop of Calcutta as metropolitan would be decided by Parliament as part of a broader restructuring of governance in India through the St Helena Act of 1833. When the matter was debated late in the evening, approaching midnight, on Wednesday July 17th 1833 there was little to no discussion of the ecclesial novelty of creating an additional metropolitical see, and discussion largely concerned the financial implications objected to by the East India Company as well as sectarian considerations concerning favouring one establishment at the expense of others (such as the Presbyterian, as advocated by Scottish MP George Sinclair, or the Roman Catholic, as championed by Irish emancipationist Dan O'Connell), or else objection to establishment in India at all.[16] Nevertheless, the proposals passed and the wording of the final legislation was mirrored in the 1835 Letters Patent which created the bishopric of Madras and consequently elevated Calcutta to metropolitan status. These Letters Patent only vaguely outlined the newly acquired metropolitical jurisdiction of the Bishop of Calcutta as having 'full power and authority to perform all functions peculiar and appropriated to the office of Metropolitan,' although noting that in particular this did include 'full power and authority to visit once in every five years, or oftener if occasion shall require . . . for correcting and supplying the defects of the said Bishop of Madras and his successors, with all and all manner of visitorial jurisdiction, power and coercion.'[17] This visitorial jurisdiction was similarly reiterated in the creation of the bishopric of Bombay in 1837, again explicitly stipulating the metropolitan's authority 'to inhibit . . . the exercise of all . . . ordinary jurisdiction of the said Bishop of Bombay . . . [as] shall seem expedient . . . [and] to exercise . . . such powers, functions, and jurisdictions . . . as the said Bishop of Bombay might have exercised if he had not been inhibited from exercising the same.'[18] The newly created Bishop of Madras, Daniel Corrie, would swear an oath of obedience only to the 'Metropolitan Bishop of Calcutta and his successors' but be consecrated by the Archbishop of Canterbury.[19]

The Letters Patent establishing the metropolitan jurisdiction of the Bishop of Calcutta contained the proviso that he should be 'subject nevertheless to the general superintendence and revision of the Archbishop of Canterbury for the time being,' in the same manner by which he had been 'subordinate to the Archiepiscopal See of the Province of Canterbury in the exercise of all Ecclesiastical jurisdiction and powers which, previously to these our Letters Patent, were vested in the said Bishop.'[20] This effectively created a tripartite provincial scheme, whereby the metropolitical organization of one province subsisted under the authority of another. Autonomous, but not autocephalous, the first creation of a metropolitan see outside the British Isles also marks a move toward what might crudely be described as the 'Patriarchate of Canterbury'. This move was at best tentative, as the somewhat vague and ill-defined phrase 'general superintendence and revision' suggests, and it would not be long before this emerging polity would be tested and found seriously wanting.

The Uncertain Authority of Royal Letters Patent

Episcopacy and, later, a modified form of provincial polity, whereby metropolitans remained subject to the superintendence of the Archbishop of Canterbury, had been established in the wake of British colonial expansion through the authority and legal instrument of royal Letters Patent. However, the question of where authority lay within the church, and how it related to the civil authorities locally and 'at home', came to be the fundamental concern of the colonial churches from the mid-nineteenth century onward. The authority of Letters Patent had been challenged in Tasmania as early as 1837 when William Broughton, Bishop of Australia, had sought to protect one of his chaplains from being required to participate in a trial of the Executive Council prosecuting an accusation of fraud, insisting instead that 'the Bishop of the diocese is the only proper organ for securing the discipline of the clergy . . . manifest from the terms of the Letters Patent under the Great Seal, by which the see is constituted.'[21]

Tasmania again became the centre of troubles when its first bishop, Francis Nixon, revoked the licences of two chaplains: the first, Gregory Bateman, who had ceremonially washed his hands over the body of an executed convict after performing his burial and then declared himself 'innocent of the blood of this man,'[22] and the other, Thomas Wigmore, the 'bane of Bothwell' who, with his 'litigious and unhappy temper' had not only alienated all his parishioners but abandoned 'that part of his ordination vow which binds him to maintain . . . quietness, peace and love.'[23] Bishop Nixon proposed to establish a consistory court in order to exercise the ecclesiastical discipline assumed inherent in his Letters Patent, but was met with much resistance from the Lieutenant-Governor as well as deputations from the Congregational, Baptist and Presbyterian clergy.[24] Nixon begrudgingly acknowledged the Crown lawyers' judgement on the 'virtual invalidity of a portion of my Letters Patent' (the portion relating to the exercise of his jurisdiction to visit and discipline his clergy) and, eventually, accepted a revised form.[25]

The entire legal basis upon which the colonial bishoprics and, from 1835 in India and 1847 in Australia, provincial and metropolitical authority rested – that of Letters Patent – had been shaken. It would take until 1863, and the notorious controversy between the bishops of Cape Town and Natal, before the arrangement would be entirely abandoned. In the meantime the colonial churches felt a pressing need to overcome what was repeatedly referred to as the 'embarrassment' of their situation by agitating not only for some surety of legal security in their own establishment, but also a greater degree of self-determination in their organization and governance. In 1849 a proposed meeting of the five Canadian bishops was reported on enthusiastically by the *Colonial Church Chronicle* which articulated some hope that 'perhaps something in the shape of general rules or Canons for the government of the Church in their several Dioceses may be agreed upon.'[26] However, it was in Australia and New Zealand that the boldest efforts were first made to make this a reality. Whereas there had been very little conscious reflection on the significance of elevating Calcutta to the dignity of a metropolitan see, in Australia and New Zealand the opposite was true. The first bishop of New Zealand, George Augustus Selwyn, would greatly influence the settlement of a synodical polity for the colonial churches, a trait which continues to mark out Anglicanism as distinctive. However the role of Australia's first bishop, William Grant Broughton, has not yet been fully appreciated or developed. His leadership, up until his untimely death in 1853, did much to shape the direction of provincial independence and autonomy, necessitated by the particular challenges faced in the colonial churches as the authority of the Royal Supremacy, the legitimacy of Letters Patent and the reliance on the church 'at home' could no longer be assumed.

Australia and the Legacy of William Grant Broughton Re-Evaluated

The Letters Patent of 1835, which had dissevered Madras from Calcutta, had also released the far-off Archdeaconry of New South Wales from the

Bishop of Calcutta's jurisdiction, which it had been under since 1824. This took effect on the 10th October 1835, and in mid-January 1836 fresh Letters Patent were issued erecting the Bishopric of Australia and appointing its first bishop, William Grant Broughton. This new see, much like the Canadian and other colonial dioceses outside the newly created metropolitical bounds of India, was placed directly in relationship with the 'archiepiscopal see of Canterbury . . . in the same manner as any bishop of any see within the province of Canterbury . . .'[27]

Following the further expansion of colonial settlement in Australia, Broughton was made Metropolitan when his vast diocese was divided into the sees of Sydney, Melbourne, Newcastle and Adelaide in 1847. The Letters Patent which brought this into effect, taking much the same form as those that had achieved the same for Calcutta, also brought the sees of Tasmania and New Zealand under the bishop of Sydney's metropolitical oversight. However, this was not merely an unthinking replication of what had been done in India a decade earlier. Whereas in the case of Calcutta there had been very little, if any, reflection on the ecclesiastical significance of establishing new metropolitical provinces, in Australia there was a greater degree of readiness, certainly by Broughton, to reflect ecclesiologically on how the colonial Church of England might mature to greater independence within a global Anglican communion.

In his friendship with Joshua Watson, the influential high-churchman and member of the Hackney Phalanx, Broughton also had an influential ally. Watson was well established as a staunch supporter of the colonial churches, and particularly the establishment of bishoprics through his financial leadership of the SPG and support of the Colonial Bishoprics Fund. Writing to Broughton about how he might be styled as metropolitan, the title of Archbishop being contentious, he articulates a growing concern to hold together the Anglican churches in the colonies in particular relationship with the Church of England as they moved toward greater self-determination:

Patriarch was obviously the fitting thing, ecclesiastically speaking. But this involved, in my opinion, a sovereignty of its own; and by cutting off all particular relation to the Church in England, would have made the patriarchate of Australasia in no greater degree related to the untied Churches of England and Ireland, than to Sweden or Denmark; provided, that is, that the succession in these has been preserved. And to such absolute independence in matters ecclesiastical, I expected the most decided objection from our statesmen at home, from its loosening the best bond of colonial allegiance to the mother country under circumstances in which, with half the world between them, they could ill afford to let go any hold of connection. From the first, therefore, I have pressed for a patent raising the present see into a metropolitancy, with jurisdiction over the new sees absolutely, and over the old sees conditionally (i.e. upon surrender of their present patent of exempt jurisdiction by the actual incumbents) and hereafter peremptorily in the letter of the succeeding patents. All this I thought might be now settled, at once and for ever, by a patent creating you in that manner Metropolitan of Australasia.[28]

It's not clear entirely how serious Watson was being in suggesting the title of 'Patriarch' for the Bishop of Sydney – the title would seem rather grand, there being only eighteen clergymen and twelve parishes in the whole of Australia when Broughton arrived as Archdeacon; albeit the number of clergy had risen, by Broughton's own count, to three hundred by 1853.[29] What is interesting is that Watson seems to claim some personal agency in influencing the establishment of a metropolitical establishment in Australasia. Watson, and his associates in the Hackney Phalanx and the SPG, certainly had a close connection with Broughton and the other High Church Australian bishops, including William Tyrell, bishop of Newcastle, among whom he seems to have acted as something of an intermediary:

With Bishop Tyrell in particular he had enjoyed some very gratifying intercourse, from which he felt assured of the mutual comfort which the Suffragan and the Metropolitan would find in each other.[30]

Even in this early correspondence with Watson, Broughton expresses an aversion to the suggestion that a metropolitan of Australasia should remain nevertheless subject to the Archbishop of Canterbury, particularly if it were motivated – as Watson suggests – out of the political expediency of maintaining and strengthening the bonds of the British Empire. Broughton recalls, as a dangerous possible precedent to this proposed new jurisdiction of the Archbishop of Canterbury, the synod at Rome in 378 where Pope Damasus was exonerated against his Arian rival, Ursinus, and under the Emperor Gratian 'given that universal jurisdiction . . . by making him the centre of all appeals.'[31] Broughton articulates his concern that:

If our Primate [the Archbishop of Canterbury] have a corresponding privilege, it will be difficult to make the world comprehend that we mean it to be only *ordine ecclesiastico*, and not *jure divino*.[32]

The Bishops' Conference of 1850

Broughton would take a similar stance at the Bishops' Conference of October 1850 which met in Sydney and was attended by all the bishops of the province of Australasia under Broughton's metropolitical jurisdiction: Francis Nixon of Tasmania, William Tyrell of Newcastle, Charles Perry of Melbourne, Augustus Short of Adelaide and George Augustus Selwyn of New Zealand. The 1850 Bishops' Conference has become the subject of a substantial body of literature chiefly concerned with the development of synodical government and the constitutional framework of Australian Anglicanism. Three significant Australian accounts, all written in the 1920s during a period of constitutional clarification[33] for Australian Anglicans, have proved formative in appreciating the significance of the 1850 Conference on synodical development, and particularly the participation of the laity: Philip Micklem's *Principles of Church Organization* in 1921, Henry Lowther Clarke's *Constitutional Church Government* in 1924 and Robbie Giles' *Constitutional History of the Australian Church* in 1929.[34] More recently, Bruce Kaye has helpfully critiqued an assumption perpetuated by this historiographical legacy that characterized churchmanship, Tractarian and Evangelical, as the driving force behind the resulting ecclesial foundations within colonial Anglicanism based, on the one hand, through the authority of the local legislature (as in Victoria, New South Wales, Tasmania and Canada) and, on the other, of 'consensual compact' (as in Adelaide, New Zealand, and South Africa).[35] Discussion of constitutional development and the rise of synodical government has tended to eclipse the important place of the 1850 Conference for the evolution of metropolitical authority within Anglicanism, and particularly Broughton's own understanding of his role as Metropolitan of Australasia. Charles Perry, Bishop of Melbourne, kept detailed notes of the Conference proceedings in his diary and records Broughton's strong calls for provincial independence, his assertion that the Royal Supremacy had no bearing on church affairs in the province, and that authority for electing, consecrating and confirming bishops for Australia and New Zealand lay entirely within the jurisdiction of the province rather than with either the Crown or Archbishop of Canterbury:

> Now that there is a Province of Australasia and Metropolitan of Sydney, the nomination and consecration of Bishops within the Province by the See of Canterbury is irregular, and in fact a 'Papal' assumption of power.[36]

True to his convictions expressed to Watson eleven years earlier, Perry's notes reveal quite candidly Broughton's continued opposition to maintaining the Oath of Supremacy following the establishment of a new ecclesial province:

> The Queen's Supremacy restricts the power of consecration inherent in Metropolitan and Comprovincial Bishops. The time is good for Recommendation, and it is not good to wait for a 'casus belli' to declare our independency of State fetters; rather that we be ready and prepared; so that when they drop off (as they must ere long) we may be found in possession of a system of acting, and not having one to seek.[37]

Broughton's readiness to shake off the claim of the Royal Supremacy is perhaps surprising for a man of a definite High Church persuasion of the pre-Tractarian ilk, although his assertion of an inherent ecclesial authority proper to the local adaptation of the episcopate and its provincial organization under metropolitical jurisdiction is faithful to his underlying Tory principles.[38] Broughton's strong language even goes so far as to assert that the Church of England has departed from 'the primitive Church system in that one Metropolitan interferes with another's functions,' presumably a reference to his own subjection and subordination to the Archbishop of Canterbury.[39] In a final question which he poses to his fellow bishops and which is left hanging as the final entry for that day in Perry's diary, discussion being adjourned until the following week, Broughton asks:

> Would it not be well, should it be found that the act authorising the Queen to create Colonial Dioceses . . . is illegal! Consequently the Provincial Synod possesses its inherent power of subdividing Dioceses and consecrating through their Metropolitan?[40]

Selwyn makes reference to Joseph Bingham's work on provincial polity as it was developed and understood in the Patristic period, a clear example of Bingham's early eighteenth-century work of antiquarian history directly informing a rethinking of metropolitical authority within the emerging polity of what was already being called the 'Anglican Communion'. Interestingly, Perry records Selwyn's use of the term 'Patriarch' to describe the Archbishop of Canterbury's place within this polity.[41] Complementing this, Tyrell and Short employ arguments from the examples of the episcopal churches of Scotland and the United States to further assert the independence of the ecclesial province.[42] The Bishop of Adelaide, perhaps optimistically, notes that in the current circumstances there exists a harmony between the interests of state and church, with the former pursuing the interests of the latter on its behalf.

Therefore the provincial synods had no need to overreach in their claim for an inherent ecclesial authority:

> Under existing circumstances, the [intention] of the State being to extend the Colonial Episcopate, as wanted by the Church, he [Short] did not think it incumbent upon the Provincial Bishops to exert their independent Ecclesiastical Functions. Such a necessity must arise, but need not be anticipated. At present to recommend what was wanted, and needful for the order and effectiveness of one Church would be enough.[43]

Perry, however, is keen to maintain the connection with Canterbury in order to safeguard doctrinal orthodoxy, likening it – perhaps extraordinarily as an Evangelical – to the universal jurisdiction of the Pope: 'Romish provincial bishops refer in all proceedings to Rome – so we should to Canterbury.'[44] The *Minutes of Proceedings* of the 1850 Conference reflect something of a compromise between these two visions of provincial independence. They propose the organization of the Australasian province into provincial and diocesan synods (composed of bishops with representatives of the clergy, the laity being involved in decision making over church temporalities by means of concurrent diocesan and provincial conventions), with authority to subdivide dioceses and to recommend episcopal appointments. However, they implicitly acknowledge – if somewhat begrudgingly – their uncertain standing with regard to the church 'at home'.[45]

Whereas the establishment of metropolitan jurisdiction was given very little reflection and thought when first initiated by the division of the Diocese of Calcutta, being it seems an entirely pragmatic solution to problems of local ecclesial administration in a vast – and, to English sensibilities, harsh and uncompromising – foreign land, Bishop Broughton did much to promote the comprehensive establishment of a provincial polity among the colonial Anglican churches, and to assert their autonomy from Canterbury and, most particularly, from the Crown as it became increasingly clear that the Royal Supremacy meant very little at all in the ecclesiology of Empire.

The 'Colenso Affair': Provincial Autonomy and the Royal Prerogative

If Broughton and his contemporaries began this process of ecclesial reflection around the place of metropolitical authority and provincial polity in the burgeoning Communion, it was the fallout to the notorious 'Colenso Affair' that dominated the 1860s which finally occasioned the necessity not only for clarity concerning the legal and ecclesial relation of the colonial churches to England, but also forced the question of where and how Anglican authority was to be grounded: in the Crown, or consensual compact. The Colenso controversy is itself fairly well-known, and has become something of a fabled forerunner, a 'myth of origin' for the emergence of a global 'Anglican Communion' in the context of international conflict and controversy.[46] Its significance is principally linked with the calling of the first 'Lambeth Conference' in 1867, although this vastly oversimplifies both the contributing causes which led to the 'Pan-Anglican Synod' as well as the impact of the Colenso case on its agenda.[47] The 2004 *Windsor Report* utilises the Colenso case as an example of political manoeuvrings to influence the agenda at Lambeth, 'a foretaste of what would follow in international gatherings of Anglicans, when controversial topics arise.'[48] Colenso has been held up as an archetype for theological liberalism within Anglicanism, as well as a champion of missionary enculturation.[49] In the current context of conflict and controversy within Anglicanism, commentators have not failed to notice something of an irony in the contemporary reversal of the nineteenth-century contest between the theological liberalism of a bishop and diocese in Africa and calls, particularly from the United States and Canada, for a measure of doctrinal discipline to be exercised through the instrument of an international synod of bishops, to become the Lambeth Conference.[50] Despite the frequent citations of the Colenso case, there has been little deep engagement with its implications for Anglican ecclesiology.[51] Colenso has been variously, and sometimes dubiously, appropriated and the Communion would benefit from a richer, and less polemical, understanding of his legacy and a more systematic account of the ecclesial implications of the controversy itself, a project which falls outside the scope of this study.[52]

However, the Colenso case does sharply bring into focus the muddled question of how the newly established ecclesial provinces in the colonies were to organize themselves and relate both with each other (as well as with the episcopal churches of Scotland and the United States) and with the church 'at home'. At last, pressed into action by a very public international controversy, the Anglican churches were forced to confront the problematic and haphazard nature of their polity, as it had emerged, and to engage in some more explicit reflection on the nature of a metropolitical polity in a global Communion.

Whatever might be made of the substantive issues causing contention surrounding the Bishop of Natal, the scandal of his biblical criticism and doctrinal doubts, at the heart of this controversy is a clash between two visions of emerging metropolitical polity for a global Communion: Colenso understanding his colonial episcopate to be no more than a relocation of the Church of England abroad, and acknowledging only the most limited formal association between his comprovincial (if that reality is even be admitted) bishops, and Gray seeking instead to build the structures of a self-sufficient and autocephalous ecclesial province with the Archbishop of Canterbury providing a quasi-Patriarchal oversight. Colenso rested his case on a strict, and wholly proper as the Judicial Committee confirmed, interpretation of the legal basis to his bishopric; alternatively, Gray – while justifiably following the provisions of his Letters Patent which he took to be legitimate – instead found greater justification in an appeal to the wider tradition and ordering of the church catholic. The novel appeal of this latter position is what seemed so incredible to Colenso:

> I have no concern with, and do not in any manner recognize, the pow-
> ers of a Metropolitan, as they may have existed at some time or other in
> the ancient Catholic Church, or as they may now exist 'in the Churches
> of the Roman obedience,' . . . I recognize them only so far as they exist
> in the 'United Church of England and Ireland, as by law established,' in
> which, as is well known, the supreme powers, usurped by the Pope in
> the Roman Church, are restored by the Constitution to the Crown.[53]

Although Colenso held the secure legal ground he stands as something of an obstinate figure, stubbornly upholding an ecclesiological position which is remarkably conservative in its imperialist assumptions, while the sands of ecclesial change shift fast beneath his feet. The tide was quickly turning to promote the establishment and independence of self-governing provinces *in communion* with the Church of England at home but not identical to it. There is no small irony in this, not least considering the far from conservative doctrinal and biblical positions espoused by Colenso, but also in that Gray has traditionally been characterized as legalistic and rigid in his prosecution of Colenso.[54]

In fact, Robert Gray was extremely *avant-garde* in asserting his own metropolitical jurisdiction, despite its dubious legal position, and in pursuing Broughton's earlier vision of independent ecclesial provinces, brought together under a kind of personal patriarchate of the Archbishop of Canterbury. Finding little support in legal instruments, an important tool in establishing legitimacy for this new paradigm was an appeal to 'catholic order' and the employment of antiquarian sources as author-itative witnesses to tradition. This was of course just one example of a wider shift occasioned by the Oxford Movement to locate an eccle-sial authority inherent to the church's own order and ministry: 'Magnify your Office!' was John Henry Newman's rally for apostolic authority which commenced the first of the Tracts for the Times.[55] Proponents for this new provincial polity, considering that the colonial churches have been 'thrown back upon the primitive precedents of the second and third centuries of the Christian era,' look again to works such as Bingham's *Origines Ecclesiasticae* and sources such as de Marca and Cyprian's letters to reimagine their constitution and establish ecclesial authenticity which is independent of the Royal Supremacy and, even more so, the Judicial Committee of the Privy Council.[56]

Successive Lambeth Conferences of the second half of the nineteenth century further codified this movement with an emphasis on the development of provincial polity as a mark of ecclesial maturity. The first gathering of bishops at Lambeth in 1867 committed consideration of the nature and extent of metropolitical jurisdiction to a committee comprising the colonial bishops, the bishops of London, St David's and Oxford, as well as seven others from among their number 'to consider the constitution of a voluntary spiritual tribunal, to which questions of doctrine may be carried by appeal from . . . each province of the colonial Church.'[57] In fact, the 1867 'Pan-Anglican Synod' which would become the Lambeth Conference was notable for doing little more in its 'resolutions' than committing a series of questions for the consideration of committees.[58]

The subsequent report of the relevant committee on metropolitical jurisdiction, issued in December 1867 and chaired by the Bishop of Montreal and Metropolitan of Canada, urged the establishment of provinces where this had not already taken place, calling for a coordinated effort between the Archbishop of Canterbury, 'to whom the Bishops of the Dioceses that are at present extra-provincial have taken the oath of canonical obedience,' and the dioceses themselves.[59] The language of the Committee is strong, asserting provincial polity to be not only 'in accordance with the ancient laws and usages of the Christian Church,' but in fact, 'essential to its complete organization.'[60]

An appeal was again made to ancient use in 1878 when the bishops' letter which was issued from that Conference (there being again no formal resolutions but rather an encyclical comprising the various committees' reports) repeated calls for 'those dioceses which still remain isolated [to] . . . associate themselves into a province or provinces, in accordance with the ancient laws and usages of the Catholic Church.'[61] The Conferences of 1888 and 1897, insofar as they dealt with issues of provincial polity, were concerned largely with the relative merits and appropriateness of allowing metropolitan bishops to be styled according to the dignity of 'Archbishop' – something which, although mooted as early as 1846 in Broughton's correspondence with Joshua Watson and moved upon formally in 1870 by the Provincial Synod of South Africa, was not enacted within individual provinces until after the 1888 Conference had commended the cautious report of the Committee on Mutual Relations of

Dioceses and Branches of the Anglican Communion which tentatively suggested that 'taking the question upon broad grounds and looking to the general interests of the whole Church . . . there are cases of important Provinces in which distinct advantage would result from adopting the ancient and honoured title of Archbishop.'[62] By the 1897 Lambeth Conference there were Archbishops of Ontario, Rupert's Land, Sydney, Capetown and the West Indies alongside the old established metropolitans of Canterbury, York, Dublin and Armagh.[63]

The following four chapters shall explore two problematic aspects of the exercise of metropolitical authority and provincial polity in the contemporary Communion which emerge from this historical enquiry, as they relate to the formal and recognized institutions and structures of Anglican polity. These are: the tension between a provincial polity, articulated and codified to varying levels of precision in provincial constitutions, with a 'national church' model which has come to be uncritically accepted as the ecclesial ideal within Anglicanism; and, the developing nature of primatial authority in the life of the Communion, as particularly expressed through the regular 'Primates' Meetings'. In confronting the problem of Anglican polity, it will be argued that what is needed is a richer and more nuanced, while also more precise, appreciation of the workings of metropolitical authority and the place of the province. While its complexity and plurality has been born out through this survey of its history and development, its specificity is best discerned not by sweeping generalisations nor 'lowest common denominator' ecclesiology but in finding the force of its challenge to our current polity.

The theological reflections of the following chapters, with their emphases on the principles of 'recognition' and a conciliar primacy, will draw out this challenge against the fundamentalism of the 'national church' as a unit of Anglican ecclesial polity, and against the magisterial individualism of the Primates. Indeed, only a recovery and reappraisal of the distinctive and enduring place of metropolitical authority and provincial polity, with its dual emphasis on the exercise of authority both internally and externally related, offers a sufficient and satisfactory imagining of Anglican ecclesial ordering that can hold together its devotion to the local enculturation of authority and autonomy with its commitment to catholicity and global communion.

Notes

1 Inter-Anglican Theological and Doctrinal Commission 1986, paras 46–47.
2 Ypi 2013, 158–60.

3 Ypi 2013, 158.

4 Heaney 2013, 726.

5 Recent research into the missionary consciousness of the SPG has challenged the prevailing historiography that eighteenth-century missionary societies were little more than organs of political imperial policy, and that true evangelistic missionary efforts did not begin until the beginning of the nineteenth century. See Strong 2007, 14.

6 'Letters Patent of the First Bishop of Nova Scotia, 1st August 1787' in Levi 1868, 4:343.

7 'Letters Patent of the First Bishop of Nova Scotia, 1st August 1787' in Levi 1868, 4:345.

8 Abbott 1845, xv.

9 Abbott 1845, xi.

10 Hansard HC Deb 17 July 1833, vol 19, cols 797–807.

11 'No. 72: Minute of a Secret Court of Directors, held on Friday 28th June 1833' in House of Commons' Paper 1833, 31.

12 This was, however, disputed by the directors of the East India Company, who attributed the deaths of Calcutta's first two bishops, Thomas Middleton and Reginald Heber, to 'a coup de soleil to which he unnecessarily exposed himself' and 'an improvident use of the cold bath' respectively. See 'No. 86: Letter from the Chairman and Deputy Chairman to the Right Honourable Charles Grant, dated 10th July 1833' in House of Commons' Paper 1833, 66.

13 House of Commons' Paper 1832, 810.

14 House of Commons' Paper 1832, 811.

15 A comprehensive narrative account of this episode is given in Border 1962, 108–42.

16 Hansard HC Deb 17 July 1833, vol 19, cols 801–802.

17 Abbott 1845, xxxiv.

18 'Letters Patent Disservering Bombay from the See of Calcutta,' 1st October 1837, 7 Will. 4 in Abbott 1845, liii.

19 'Letters Patent creating the Bishoprick of Madras,' 13th June 1835, 5 Will. 4 in Abbott 1845, xlii.

20 Abbott 1845, xxxiv.

21 'Copy of a Letter from the Bishop of Australia to Lord Glenelg, Sydney 12 December 1837,' in House of Commons' Paper 1850b, pt. 2:19.

22 House of Commons' Paper 1850b, pt. 1:2.

23 Correspondence from Nixon to Wilmot, 26 July 1844, in House of Commons' Paper 1850b, pt. 1:4.

24 The entire affair is recounted in detail in Border 1962, 122–43.

25 Letter from the Bishop of Tasmania to Earl Grey, 30 June 1847, in House of Commons' Paper 1850b, pt. 1:8.

26 *The Colonial Church Chronicle and Missionary Journal* 1849, 2, July 1848–June 1849:360.

27 'Letters Patent constituting the Episcopal See of Australia' in House of Commons' Paper 1850a, 2.

28 Correspondence between Joshua Watson and William Broughton reproduced in Churton 1863, 266–67.

29 *The Colonial Church Chronicle and Missionary Journal* 1853, 6, July 1852–June 1853:394; for purposes of comparison, in 1851 there were 17,621 clergy in

England and Wales and 160 clergy of the Episcopal Church in Scotland in 1856, see Currie, Horsley, and Gilbert 1977, 196–202.

30 Churton 1863, 267.

31 Correspondence between Broughton and Watson, reproduced in Churton 1863, 267.

32 Churton 1863, 267.

33 Writing as early as 1918, Clarke explains that the 'Legal Position of the Church of England in Australia has been defined in recent years by 'Opinions' obtained in England and Australia independently. These agree in saying that nothing has hitherto been done by any Synod in Australia to separate the Church from the Church of England, and that the legal status of the Church in Australia makes it still an integral part of the Church of England and not a Church in full communion therewith,' Clarke 1918, 23.

34 Micklem 1921; Clarke 1924; Giles 1929.

35 Kaye 2003.

36 Perry 1850; attention to Perry's diary, held at the archives of the Diocese of Melbourne, in relation to the 1850 Conference is first made in Kaye 2003, 183. I have since, however, obtained access to the diary entries and am able to quote more extensively from them directly, as they relate particularly to Broughton's understanding of developing metropolitical authority in the colonial churches.

37 Perry 1850.

38 For a more detailed analysis of Broughton's background see Kaye 1995; for a re-evaluation of Broughton's legacy in the historical record, and particularly his place within early colonial society, see also G. P. Shaw 1970.

39 Perry 1850.

40 Perry 1850.

41 Perry 1850.

42 Kaye 2003, 183.

43 Perry 1850.

44 Kaye 2003, 184.

45 The subsequent story of the 1853 Bill introduced by the Archbishop of Canterbury and passed by the House of Lords but rejected by the Commons, and its resurrection as the Church Act of 1854 passed by the Victorian legislature on the initiative of Perry, is well known. See, Sharwood 2004.

46 Calvani 2005, 148.

47 Prichard 2013, 93.

48 Lambeth Commission on Communion 2004, para. 100.

49 Presler 2013, 24; Sachs 2013, 37.

50 Doll 2012, 431.

51 For example, Colenso receives only one fleeting mention in Paul Avis' important attempt to give a systematic accounting of Anglican self-understanding, see Avis 2007, 52; quite bizarrely, Colenso has even been held up as a founding father in the early history of the 'alternative' Church of England in South Africa - a Reformed and Evangelical expression of Anglicanism ostensibly finding its origins in conflict with the Anglo-Catholic Robert Gray but only codifying its formal organization in 1938 with the assistance of the Diocese of Sydney, a relationship which has continued to prove controversial within the Communion and was criticised at the 1984 meeting of the Anglican Consultative Council (Res. 32). For an insider's account of this unlikely identification with Colenso see Hammond 1988, 256; even more

mainstream and current historiography of the Anglican Communion has made this identification with Colenso, see Battle 2015, 546.

52   For further reading relating to the historical treatment of Colenso over the past fifty years, see Hinchliff 1963; Guy 1983; Draper 2003.

53   Colenso 1864, 16.

54   Southey 1998, 19.

55   Avis 2002a, 106.

56   Wordsworth 1865, 9.

57   Lambeth Conference 1867, Resolutions 9 & 10.

58   Such an approach might be instructive for our current Lambeth Conferences where, with the exception of 2008, each resolution has been looked to for a definitive statement of the Anglican 'position' – whether reflective or not of the received 'mind' of the Communion.

59   'Report of Committee on Provincial Subordination' appointed by the Conference of 1867, in Davidson 1889, 129.

60   Davidson 1889, 128.

61   'Letter of the Bishops attending the Lambeth Conference of 1878, including the Reports adopted by the Conference,' in Davidson 1889, 167.

62   The Conference had been prompted to declare its opinion on the subject following a request from the General Synod of Australia. See Clarke 1924, 29. The full report of the Committee may be found at Davidson 1889, 321ff.

63   'List of the bishops attending the Lambeth Conference of 1897, arranged according to Provinces' in Davidson 1907, 19–24. It is notable that the arrangement is made by provinces, with the England and Irish sees also divided between Canterbury, York, Dublin and Armagh. The province clearly takes priority here over the 'national church'. The bishops of Calcutta and Auckland are also noted as metropolitans without the style 'Archbishop', and the Bishop of Brechin in the Scottish Episcopal Church is listed as 'Primus' whereas the bishops of the United States are listed simply in alphabetical order.

Part Two

The National Church

We still think, and rightly, of the Church of England as the 'National Church'; but the word *national* in this context can no longer mean what it once meant . . . I prefer to think of the Church as what I believe it is more and more coming to be, not the 'English Church', but national as 'the Catholic Church in England'.
T.S. Eliot, 1931[1]

What is the most fundamental and complete unit of ecclesial polity within the Anglican Communion? The Communion is described on its website as being constituted of thirty-nine 'autonomous national and regional Churches plus six Extra Provincial Churches and dioceses.'[2] While the website is certainly not a comprehensive source of Anglican self-reflection on its own ecclesiology, this formulaic emphasis on 'national' or 'regional' churches – not to mention their distinction from 'Extra Provincial Churches and dioceses' – as fundamental to the polity of the Communion is a familiar trope. This chapter will reflect theologically on the nature of the 'national church' within international Anglican polity, with particular reference to its emergence as a keystone in the 'contained catholicity'[3] of the English church at the Reformation and the problematic nature of balancing that catholicity with assumptions of national and ecclesial sovereignty within the international polity of the contemporary Communion.

The language of 'provincial' polity has become confused and conflated in Anglican ecclesiology with the emergence of the autonomous 'national church', providing a challenge for the Communion's embodiment of catholicity which the re-appropriation of a more properly 'provincial' polity has the potential to address. Discourse around the 'national church' has also tended to concentrate more on the relationships between church and state, particularly in the context of the Church of England's establishment, rather than its particularity as a unit of polity itself. There is a long tradition of reflection, at least since the twentieth century, on the nature of this relationship. It is the subject of a number of charges and addresses by

Bishop of London, Mandell Creighton, at the turn of the century,[4] while in the United States there was likewise, in a very different context, a conversation initiated by the prominent clergyman William Reed Huntington on the potential for The Episcopal Church to imagine itself as a 'national church' with an ecumenical vocation.[5] William Temple delivered the Bishop Paddock Lectures at the General Theological Seminary in New York on 'Church and Nation' at the beginning of the First World War,[6] and a defence of the 'national church' from a more Evangelical perspective was given by long-serving General Secretary of the Church Missionary Society, Max Warren, in three Advent lectures at Westminster Abbey in 1963.[7] Adrian Hastings, Roman Catholic theologian and historian, in his Gore Lecture at Westminster Abbey in 1991 offered a critique of Warren's 'unanalysed assumption' that the United Kingdom, and with it the established church, constituted 'the society of a nation,' instead asserting this to be 'profoundly damaging to the identity of minorities within the state – the smaller nations of which it consists, and of the smaller churches,' concluding that the idea of a 'national church' was nothing more than a 'theologically phoney category.'[8] More recently, a series of articles in the *Christian Law Review* has engaged ecumenically with the concept of a 'national church' both in England and in other parts of the British Isles.[9]

Fundamental to the definition of a 'national church', which has emerged over the past century, has been a commitment to integration and engagement with the 'nation', some degree of shared identity with the wider population, a commitment to maintaining a ministry and presence within the totality of geographic borders, as well as an approach to mission and membership which is invitational and 'inclusive' rather than strictly confessional.[10] Notwithstanding their usefulness, these markers all contribute to a picture of how the church relates to the nation, but do not necessarily speak to the polity of the church as predicated in some way on the priorities and characteristics of the nation-state. Such characteristics include sovereignty, defined geographical borders and legitimization by means of mutual recognition. Ecclesiological reflection on the nature of the 'national church' must engage not only with a church's sense of mission and vocation in and to the nation, but how they see themselves ordered and akin to the pattern of nation-states – each church itself a kind of ecclesial nation. It is this aspect of the 'national church', rather than its missional dimension, which proves problematic for Anglican polity. Within the Anglican Communion this notion of a 'national church' as a complete and fundamental unit of polity, not just a vocational descriptor of mission, has become accepted as a truism. However, the diversity and actual make-up of the churches which constitute the Communion, and the nations they exist within and across, makes this a dubious foundation.

Of the thirty-nine 'national and regional' churches of the Communion, twenty-five are predominantly co-terminous with national borders (including The Episcopal Church, although it has a wider international presence). Most churches comprise a single province, although seven contain more than one province within them: the majority being in the West (England and Ireland each have two, New Zealand has three, Canada has four and Australia has five) and the remaining two in Africa (the Church of the Province of West Africa having two, while Nigeria stands apart with an extraordinary fourteen provinces). There are also six 'extra-provincial' churches, five of which exist under oversight by the Archbishop of Canterbury (albeit entirely distinct from the Province of Canterbury and the Church of England) and the other (the Episcopal Church of Cuba) by a 'metropolitical council' comprising the Primate of Canada, the Archbishop of the West Indies and the Presiding Bishop of The Episcopal Church.

While the precise membership of the Communion, and who might be arbiters of that determination, remains contested and contentious, a satisfactory working understanding of how the Communion is constituted is given by the Constitution of the Anglican Consultative Council (being the 'Articles of Association' of a private company limited by guarantee under UK law).[11] The Constitution provides not only for plenary meetings of the Council, which are familiar as the Anglican Consultative Council meetings held every two or three years, but also for a Standing Committee (which recently has styled itself the 'Standing Committee of the Anglican Communion') and a Secretariat (styled the Anglican Communion Office) led by a Secretary General (to whose title the addendum 'of the Anglican Communion' is in practice applied). The Schedule to the Constitution also lists those churches which, while in communion with the Archbishop of Canterbury, compose the definition of a 'Member-Church' for the purposes of that document. Provision is made for the Standing Committee to alter this Schedule, subject to the concurrence of a two-thirds majority of Primates (five of whom sit as *ex officio* members of the Standing Committee).[12]

Therefore, while these structures do not formally constitute nor govern the membership of the Communion, they have come to stand in as representative signifiers of an assumed polity. Nevertheless, the six 'extra-provincial' churches of the Communion are not mentioned explicitly in either the Schedule or elsewhere and it can only be assumed that their personal communion with the Archbishop of Canterbury is claimed as sufficient grounds, at least in practice, to legitimate membership of the Communion.

The proposed Anglican Communion Covenant defined the Communion as a 'fellowship, within the One, Holy, Catholic and Apostolic Church, of national or regional Churches,' borrowing this statement from its original formulation at the 1930 Lambeth Conference, although the term 'national and regional' has replaced the Conference's own wording of 'dioceses, provinces, or regional churches.'[13] The 1930 Lambeth resolution has become a popular benchmark in attempts to draw close to a definition of the Communion's corporate identity. However, the ecclesiological weight which the otherwise fairly under-developed terms are asked to bear is not well supported and has encouraged a kind of laziness in thinking through how these ecclesial concepts, and units of polity, reflect the catholic order of the church as well as serve the Communion in its life and mission.

In fact, the geographic and sociocultural descriptors 'national' and 'regional' developed in tandem alongside the ecclesiastically more precise terms 'diocese' and 'province' as the Communion sought to articulate the shape of its relationships in the early twentieth century. The concept of a 'national church' was a familiar element of the Anglican inheritance from the Reformation experience of the Church of England, and was enshrined in the thirty-fourth of the Thirty-Nine Articles: 'Every particular or national Church hath authority to ordain, change, and abolish, ceremonies or rites of the Church ordained only by man's authority, so that all things be done to edifying.'[14] However, this was challenged as the clarity of the concept of a contained nation-state was muddied by imperialist expansion and, ecclesially, as colonial churches became self-governing and a provincial and metropolitical polity was rolled out. T.S. Eliot's reflections after the 1930 Lambeth Conference with respect to the 'national church' model, expressed in the epigraph to this Part, aptly articulate a shift in ecclesial emphasis from Anglican isolationism and self-sufficiency to the local contextualisation of a global Communion.

Notes

1 Eliot 1931, 25.
2 Anglican Communion Office 2016.
3 This is a term coined in M. Chapman 2010, 114 and expanded further in Chapman 2013a.
4 Creighton and Creighton 1901.
5 Huntington 1899; for a fuller treatment of Huntington see Chapman 2013a.
6 Temple 1915.
7 Warren 1984.
8 'Church and State in a Pluralist Society: the Gore Lecture, Westminster Abbey, 13 November 1991' in Hastings 1995, 116–17.
9 'Law & Justice: The Christian Law Review' 2002.

10   These markers of a 'national church' are identified and further articulated in Cranmer 2002, 169.

11   An emphatic statement was recently made by the Secretary General of the Anglican Communion, Josiah Idowu-Fearon, claiming that communion with, and recognition by, the Archbishop of Canterbury is the essential condition for membership of the Communion. See Idowu-Fearon 2017.

12   *Constitution of the Anglican Consultative Council* 2010, sec. 7.2.

13   Lambeth Conference 1930, Resolution 49.

14   Article XXXIV.

4

'Contained' or Compromised Catholicity: a Critique of the 'National Church'

The central tension inherent in a 'national church' polity is its compatibility with the church's claim to catholicity. At the English Reformation, as the autonomy and independence of the English realm was asserted in all things spiritual as well as temporal, the church faced a crisis in its self-conceptualisation: how could it be both catholic as well as self-contained? A European pan-Protestantism offered some sense of fellowship beyond the nation-state, providing a common identity forged more from a common opposition, Roman Catholicism, than a confessional unity.[1] This was given religio-political expression in the alliances which constituted the 'body of political organizers and religious heads who collaborated with each other during periods of relative peace and moved into action by mobilizing forces at other times,' a 'Protestant International' which gave political force to shared, albeit loosely defined, religious commitments.[2] Although a commitment to the 'Protestant International' ideal allowed for some understanding of the church's identity beyond the local, in the Church of England's assertion of its autonomy this was always subject to the supremacy of the Crown.[3] Mark Chapman has recently characterized this expression of the English church's understanding of itself as part of the church catholic as a 'contained catholicity' where catholic identity is expressed temporally, standing in continuation of the primitive church, rather than spatially:

> This meant that, despite the frequent attempts at continental alliances from Henry VIII onwards, as well as participation in doctrinal discussions, most importantly at the Synod of Dort in 1618–19, the teachings of such discussions were always trumped by the authority of the Crown. Consequently, although the Church of England considered itself catholic, its form of catholicism came to be expressed more 'temporally' in terms of its inheritance from the past, than 'spatially' through its relations with churches overseas. The reason for this was simple: such churches, even when they were in fundamental agreement

with the Church of England, were solely limited to the jurisdiction of their own territories. This de facto limitation of catholicity to history and to the primitive church rather than to relations across space led many apologists from the Reformation period onwards to defend the catholicity of the Church of England in terms of a continuity with the apostolic church.[4]

This 'contained catholicity' may have served the English church as it emerged from the Reformation, but it is unclear how it might operate within the context of a worldwide communion of churches which claim a closer relationship than the 'Protestant International' but still retain autonomy and sovereignty as hallmarks of their Anglican inheritance.[5]

'Nationality and Liberty': Provincial Polity Gives Way to the 'National Church'

As the Anglican Communion emerged out of the nineteenth century, the 'national church' principles which characterized the Church of England's self-understanding came to be applied to the newly defined provinces; the creation of which, in many instances, mirrored the gradual process of maturity to national sovereignty experienced by the former British colonial possessions. At the turn of the twentieth century this saw a fairly uncritical endorsement of the providential merits of the nation: Bishop of London, Mandell Creighton, in a collection of essays published at the turn of the new century, describes the 'differentiation of nations [as] part of that continuous revelation of God's purposes which is contained in history,' whereby liberty, ecclesiastical as well as political, is protected from tyranny (and herein is concealed his not so subtle anti-Roman Catholic bias).[6] Creighton follows the now familiar narrative of a 'contained catholicity' whereby catholic identity and legitimacy is expressed through fidelity to 'the Creeds of the Universal Church,' but nevertheless guarded from 'interference from outside, because experience had shown that that interference was a hindrance and not a help.'[7] Creighton's assessment of the triumph of the 'national church' over the universal is as instructive now, over a century later, as it ever was in considering the challenges which face the discernment of an ecclesiologically coherent global Anglican polity:

The idea of a Church, universal in its organisation, has been tried, and, as a matter of fact, has failed, because it could not make room for two forces which have been most powerful in shaping the modern world – the forces of nationality and liberty.[8]

The coalescence of these two forces proved most potent in the early decades of the twentieth century, as the ecclesial language of provinces within Anglicanism came to refer less to territories of metropolitical jurisdiction within a global Communion, but rather to sovereign churches in sovereign states. In his Paddock Lectures of 1914–15 delivered at the General Theological Seminary in New York, William Temple, sketches out something of what might be thought to be an early articulation of the vocation of international Anglicanism, as it was transplanting the ideals of the 'national church' to a global communion:

> The hope of the future lies in a truly international Church, which shall fully respect the rights of nations and recognise the spiritual function of the State, thereby obtaining the right to direct the national States along the path which leads to the Kingdom of God.[9]

The Language of Lambeth: 1920–1948

The development of this movement can be further charted through the language used in the reports of the Lambeth Conferences of this period, particularly from 1920 to the end of the Second World War. The 1920 Lambeth Conference makes a distinction between 'provincial' and 'national and regional Churches.' Resolution 44, which sets out the composition and clarifies the role of a 'Consultative Body' to act as a representative 'board of reference' for the Communion, contains references to this mixed ecclesial economy. The make-up of the Consultative Body contains representatives from the provinces of Canterbury, York and (the newly disestablished) Wales alongside single representatives of multi-provincial national churches such as Canada and Australia. This gives something of an interpretive key to the use of these terms elsewhere in the Conference's resolutions, where 'national and regional' paired with 'provincial' are not necessarily used as inter-changeable terms but are a 'catch-all' for what was a developing polity. Significant attention is made also to missionary districts and extra-provincial churches directly under the supervision of the Archbishop of Canterbury; further anomalies with which to prove the provincial rule.[10]

A desire to iron out these anomalies is evident in Resolution 43 of the 1920 Conference, which promotes the 'Development of Provinces' so that 'each newly founded diocese should as soon as possible find its place as a constituent member in some neighbouring province.'[11] The resolution sets down guidelines for the minimum number of dioceses (four) to be gathered into a new province, and the importance of bishops gathered together into a college to make allegiance to the metropolitan or 'other authority constitutionally appointed to receive it.'[12] This resolution was primarily influenced by a report drawn up by former Bishop of Tasmania, Henry Hutchinson Montgomery, which strongly advocated the systematic organization of the churches of the Communion into local provinces, as opposed to being somewhat artificially included within the Province of Canterbury if not completely isolated altogether.[13] This private paper for circulation among the bishops in preparation for the Conference provides a mix of both ecclesiological pragmatism as well as a more fundamental commitment to 'catholic order'. Chief among Montgomery's reasons for the implementation of provincial organization is as a 'safeguard against hasty action on the part of a Bishop or Diocese in any of the directions which obviously tempt at times the leaders of the Church' as well as providing something of a buffer 'between two separate questions, namely, whether a subject is merely local or Diocesan on the one hand, or whether it is a Catholic question and beyond the powers and scope of an individual Diocese.'[14]

By the Lambeth Conference of 1930 this emphasis on the place of provincial polity – which may or may not correlate with national boundaries and identities – had given way to an increasingly nationalist ideal for ecclesial organization. While the formation of provinces was strongly encouraged (this is reflected in a string of nine resolutions which expound the various practicalities), the governing principle is that provinces be subordinate to a 'national church' ideal, most succinctly expressed in the resolution which heads the Conference's discussion on the subject:

Saving always the moral and spiritual independence of the divine society, the Conference approves the association of dioceses or provinces in the larger unity of a 'national Church,' with or without the formal recognition of the civil government, as serving to give spiritual expression to the distinctive genius of races and peoples, and thus to bring more effectively under the influence of Christ's religion both the process of government and the habit of society.[15]

Like those of the 1920 Conference, the resolutions regarding provincial organization at the 1930 Conference closely reflect a private briefing paper circulated before the meeting and prepared by former Bishop of Bombay, Edwin Palmer. Palmer writes forcefully, explaining that his views are:

. . . stated here somewhat dogmatically for brevity's sake. The alternative procedure . . . gives the impression that the whole subject is a matter of uncertainty or 'in the melting pot.' The writer's belief is the opposite, viz., that our principles are ancient and well-founded and generally acknowledged.[16]

Palmer argues strongly for the local autonomy of churches as an expression of their 'spiritual individuality.'[17] While qualifying autonomy as not 'absolute autonomy . . . [but] autonomy of a member in a body,' Palmer identifies this characteristic of the Communion's polity with the 'purest traditions of the undivided Church.'[18] He lauds the particular assertion of provincial autonomy made by the Protestant Episcopal Church of America as providing a pattern and principle of autonomy to be followed by the other churches, even if it has 'been maintained at times in an exaggerated fashion, as, for instance, by the continued refusal to appoint representatives on the Central Consultative Body.'[19] Finally, Palmer sees in the Communion an ecumenical hope for a return to the 'primitive constitution of Christendom' which, along with the Eastern Orthodox Communion, 'would be pointing the one way to ultimate and all-inclusive unity.'[20] His vision for the Communion, then, is of a comprehensive manifestation of the church catholic owing some of its appearance and idiosyncrasies to its cultural inheritance in the Church of England, but not bound by this. Full communion with the Church of Sweden, for example, should see their own bishops represented at the Lambeth Conference, and provinces should not be established in 'countries where the Catholic Church is undoubtedly represented already by a Church which is the Church of the country,' regardless of whether they be in communion with Canterbury.[21]

The supreme marker of this 'national church' polity was autonomy, just as sovereignty would define the nation-state. By the 1948 Lambeth Conference the strongly nationalistic language had fallen out of favour, perhaps unsurprising given the recent and costly defeat of aggressive nationalist ideologies across Western Europe and East Asia. The text of all 118 resolutions of that Conference uses the word 'national' in reference to the churches of the Communion only once, whereas 'province' and its cognates, sometimes paired with 'churches' and 'dioceses', is used eighteen times.[22] However, despite the change in terminology, the usage closely follows the vision of autonomy set out by Bishop Palmer and aligned with the concept of a 'national church' in the 1930 Conference; the hard limits of autonomy which define the 'national church' masquerading under the language of provincial polity. Subsequent Lambeth Conferences use the language of provincial and 'national' or 'regional' churches interchangeably with little reflection on their distinction; laying the foundation for the current ambiguity in Anglican polity.

Ecclesial and National Polities

The emergence and dominance of the national church, which persists in Anglican ecclesiology, is closely related to the political emergence of the nation-state; and the attendant issues of sovereignty, nationalism and the challenge of globalization offer an important contribution to an ecclesiological appraisal of the national church, cast in conversation with the political sciences, as a unit of ecclesial polity. The relevance and endurance of the nation-state itself within the global geopolitical landscape is steadily being challenged.[23] In response to rapid advances in communication and connectivity, technology and travel, and the increasing exchange of economic and intellectual capital, the complex and intensified relational networks which govern, or at least impact, both the global collective as well as the local individual have tested the competence of nation-states not only to secure their own place within this volatile and quickly shifting system but to influence and shape it also, according to normative (and, then, not necessarily 'national') interests. The impact and influence of these international forces is seen by some as a *fait accompli* as the nation-state, which 'at one time guarded its territorial and social boundaries with a zeal bordering on the neurotic,' is subsumed by the wave of globalization.[24] Envisioning its collapse, Jürgen Habermas neatly articulates the crisis of confidence in the nation-state:

> The globalization of commerce and communication, of economic production and finance, of the spread of technology and weapons, and above all of ecological and military risks, poses problems that can no longer be solved within the framework of nation-states or by the traditional method of agreements between sovereign states. If current trends continue, the progressive undermining of national sovereignty will necessitate the founding and expansion of political institutions on the supranational level, a process whose beginnings can already be observed.[25]

This view is not, however, a consensus and there remains not only a clear dominance of nation-state polity within global politics, but a continuing awareness of its importance in setting fiscal and monetary policy agenda as well as a prevailing impulse to assert sovereignty against both internal and external pressures.[26]

Current Trends in International Relations for Ecclesial Reflection

The concept of nation-state sovereignty – with which we might draw parallels with the assertion of provincial autonomy within Anglicanism – remains a powerful construction within International Relations. While definitions of sovereignty may be contested, they broadly involve a state's claim of control over internal territory and population as well as independence alongside external 'peers'.[27] This internal and external dimension to sovereignty was codified at the end of the sixteenth century by the progenitor of modern understandings of sovereignty, French political philosopher Jean Bodin.[28] Accordingly, the primary actor on the international stage is the easily defined and identifiable 'nation-state', with the recognition of sovereignty supposedly providing a level playing field whereby the diplomatic game is played under the pretence that each discrete and independent political unit may relate on equal terms. Sovereignty is essentially self-serving: to play by the 'rules' on the international stage is to ultimately protect the domestic assertion of the state to exercise control over its own territory and people. Set in theological language, the critique of sovereignty is that it 'predicates of a created being – individual or collective – a divine attribute, namely total independence and self-sufficiency.'[29]

Because this polity of homogenized plurality cannot, by definition, be governed at a supranational level it relies on mutual recognition by states of the principles of non-interference in internal affairs and restraint in foreign policy to maintain the balance of sovereignty. Sovereignty is, then, essentially granted to states through this recognition by other states – rather than being an intrinsic quality of statehood itself:

> Sovereignty is not an attribute of the state, but is attributed to the state by other states or state rulers. Recent work, most notably by Robert Jackson (1990), is quite persuasive in demonstrating the state's dependence on other states for its authority. The modern state system is unique in that its members recognize one another as equal authority claimants . . . Each is recognized as having the final and exclusive authority to use coercion within its territorial borders. This recognition dimension of sovereignty entails two principal empirical questions: whose recognition is required?, and what are the criteria for recognition?[30]

Recognizability, as well as assessments of legitimacy, have emerged in International Relations discourse as a means of acknowledging that sovereignty isn't a wholly contained concept but that it relies on a balance of reciprocity and acceptability regarding the source and exercise of authority.[31] Legitimacy refers to the means by which sovereignty is incarnated in a particular political regime, as well as how political control is acquired, measured against 'socially accepted beliefs about the (1) rightful source of authority and (2) the proper ends . . . of government.'[32]

Recognizability refers to the necessity of a state's acceptance within the international community; that the mere self-declaration and identification as a nation-state does not in itself give adequate qualification. The appreciation of these two aspects of sovereignty, particularly since the end of the Second World War, has made possible the advancement and promotion of shared international norms, particularly in areas such as human rights.[33] Legitimacy itself may be said to have developed from recognizability, as states organically develop a normative picture among themselves of what might constitute grounds for equal participation in the community of nations. If recognizability is the making (or at least the confirmation) of sovereignty, then these mutually governed checks on sovereignty are less restraints and challenges occasioned by the rise of international organizations than the natural outworking of sovereignty itself as it self-regulates a system which understands individual interests best served in the mutual flourishing of the greater community: 'if interdependence is growing, it is a reflection of state power and interests.'[34]

This chiefly relational characteristic of sovereignty operates not only in the nation-state's external interactions but also in its internal dynamic whereby its legal and political elements, authority and power, are recast holistically as sovereignty is 'generated as a product of the political relationship between the people and the state.'[35] This represents a shift in imagining sovereignty's internal legitimacy as deriving from a kind of compact between the state and citizenry rather than invested (by divine providence?) in absolute monarchy.[36] Within our post-modern context there is perhaps more resonance with the political plurality of the pre-modern age where 'as a result of overlapping jurisdictions and a complex web of intermediary associations such as guilds and fraternities, political sovereignty tended to be dispersed and diffused.'[37] Sovereignty is, then, far from being an absolute property of any political entity, rather always in a continual process of negotiation both within the state, insofar as it is constituted, but also from outside, insofar as it is recognized.

To engage in this negotiation is the call of the body politic. Following the Second World War, in the first of a series of volumes seeking to put forward the positive rational and moral case for democracy to counter the claims of totalitarian political philosophies, French Roman Catholic philosopher Jacques Maritain draws a helpful distinction between the nature of a 'community' and a 'society'.[38] Maritain characterizes a 'community' as 'more nearly related to the biological' and a 'society' as 'more a work of reason, and more nearly related to the intellectual and spiritual properties of man.'[39] Maritain describes the 'nation' as a *community of patterns of feeling* rooted in the physical soil of the origin of the group as well as in the moral soil of history,' who are defined more by self-reflection on the 'accidents' of their shared circumstance than by self-conscious determinism:

> A nation is a community of people who become aware of themselves as history has made them, who treasure their own past and who love themselves as they know or imagine themselves to be, with a kind of inevitable introversion.[40]

The 'State' by contrast is identified with the work and output of reason, those institutions which together are 'concerned with the maintenance of law, the promotion of the common welfare and public order, and the administration of public affairs.'[41] These institutions which together make the State serve an instrumental purpose, and are not in themselves an end to be served:

> Putting man at the service of that instrument is political perversion. The human person as an individual is for the body politic and the body politic is for the human person as a person. But man is by no means for the State. The State is for man.[42]

This brief exposition of some current trends in the study of nation-states within International Relations cannot possibly do justice to that discipline itself, but, for our purposes, it does highlight some important concepts and considerations which have a bearing on discussion of the 'national church' polity which dominates international Anglican ecclesiology. Recognizability, legitimacy, negotiated sovereignty and the distinction between a community and a society all contribute to ecclesial reflection and offer a qualifying critique of the prevailing understanding of the 'national church' in global Anglican polity.

Recognition, Hegel and Rowan Williams

Within discussions of sovereignty and nation-state political systems, the concept of recognizability is perhaps most significant in referring to the acceptance that sovereignty – and, thereby, the existence and legitimacy of the nation-state itself – is not an inherent or given characteristic, but one which is bestowed through the diplomatic, economic and other relationships which encompass the international body politic. The concept has its roots in the philosophical struggle for self-consciousness and existential certainty expounded by Hegel in his *Phenomenology of Spirit*.[43] For Hegel, the reflective self – or self-consciousness – comes to know itself as self only in confrontation with the self-consciousness of an other.[44] The recognition of the other as not merely an object to be negated, or super-seded, in the agent's quest for self-surety, but itself also its own subject, thereby objectifying for itself that which objectifies it, is Hegel's masterful insight by which the essence of self is found not through introspection but mutual recognition:

> A self-consciousness exists for a self-consciousness. Only so is it in fact self-consciousness; for only in this way does the unity of itself in its otherness become explicit for it. The 'I' which is the object of its Notion is in fact not 'object' . . . A self-consciousness, in being an object, is just as much 'I' as 'object'.[45]

However, this confrontational realization – the inherent tension in the subjective and objective relationship – inevitably involves conflict and the struggle for domination as the subject asserts its subjectivity and neces-sarily binds itself to the object resulting in a state of lordship and bond-ship, the Master/Slave Dialectic for which Hegel is perhaps best known:

> This [final] outcome would seem to be satisfying for the master or lord, who is able to satisfy his desires through another person who recognizes him as superior (190). But this satisfaction turns out to be illusory. The superior master turns out to need the humble slave for his own sense of self (191–193), while the slave, seemingly condemned to life of meaningless labor (194), comes to recognize the true value of agency in work, through which human beings can transform the objects of the natural world into their own creations, the tangible and lasting expressions of their own agency (195).[46]

Hegel's ideas are dense and complex, and for our purposes there is no great need to go beyond this initial sketch of the dominant themes as they relate to the concept of 'recognition' in self-determination and existential discovery. But its application to ecclesiology provides for a new and revealing perspective on the nature of the national-church model within Anglican polity, the limits of autonomy and the Church's own constitution and 'self-consciousness'. There is a resonance too in Hegel's development of 'recognition' with the Trinitarian conception of God whereby, for Hegel, '. . . the relationships expressed by the economic Trinity are part of a process that God undergoes to properly *be* God.'[47] While Hegel's own formulation of Trinitarian doctrine might not con-form to the Nicaean norms of orthodoxy, rejecting as 'childlike and fig-urative' the conceptualisation of Father, Son and Spirit as 'persons',[48] his emphasis on the act of differentiation within the Trinity as self-revelation provides a model for its ecclesiological application:

> Hegel's emphasis on the Trinity's third hypostasis is therefore strictly connected with the mutual recognition between the individuals who form a community. In this context, the novelty of the Christian church, considered as a prototypical community, is its willingness to perform a twofold withdrawal that mirrors the Trinitarian dynamic: first, each individual surrenders her subjectivity to establish the community's intersubjectivity, and second, the community gives up its spirituality (the religious community's traditional spiritual component) to engage the world. Therefore, Hegel's account of the Trinity leads to the conclusion that God's essence, as long as it is Trinitarian, is intrinsically relational.[49]

The surrender of subjectivity is central to the identity of individual Christians, who understand themselves not only as objects of God's love, design and purpose but also, together, as interrelated members of Christ's body (Romans 12:5). Christian identity is found not just in the interrelationship and exchanges within the Christian community but in the negation of self-subjectivity, to be instead incorporated within the other in whom 'all things hold together' (Colossians 1:17). The application of this Hegelian dynamic to ethical discernment within the Christian community, and by extension to ecclesiology itself, has been a feature of former Archbishop of Canterbury Rowan Williams' legacy.[50] In an essay, while Bishop of Monmouth, on developing a New Testament ethic wherein ultimate existential identity is found 'in the world of exchange – language and interaction,' in response to a theological as well as philosophical trend to isolate out some kind of internalised *'authentic* self,'[51] Williams comments on the polarization of attitudes toward 'political correctness' (which might be 'curable,' he suggests 'by the digestion of more Hegel') in a way which illuminates his later development of Hegelian recognition to the polar extremes of disputes over Anglican polity and ethics:

> . . . on the one hand, the separatist moment is absolutised in an insistence that self-definition, definition 'from within', is the most fundamental moral need in a situation of manifest and continuing inequity; on the other hand, objectors fail to see the significance of the recognition entailed here that language and negotiation are about *power*, and that the bestowal of power on the powerless requires the most unsparing interrogation of the processes by which groups, persons and interests are in fact, historically and socially, defined.[52]

The complex dynamic of power, identity and socio-historical, as well as self-, definition is central to Hegel's portrayal of the self-conscious self's quest for existential certainty and free agency. Williams recognizes this, but adds an additional *a priori* affirmation which reconceives Hegel's zero-sum struggle for domination and submission as a more genuinely Christian discovery of identity given and secured *in Christ* from which freedom and distinctiveness is not threatened by the other but found in the common recognition of their equally secure standing before God.[53] Contra to Hegel's struggle, the 'given-ness' of the life-affirming relationship between God and the individual 'creates conditions for a noncompetitive community because one's belonging or being is not the result of any special action or ultimately threatened by the action of others.'[54] This 'noncompetitive community' is governed by the twin principles of Pauline 'edification' and the manifestation of the 'selfless holiness of God in Christ' witnessed in the Gospel narrative account of Jesus.[55] The ecclesiological implications of this Christian reformulation of the Hegelian encounter reach beyond shared ethical discernment to the task of evaluating polity itself and the shaping out, and negotiation of, a common Christian community:

> If there is no anxiety of rivalry in our ethical reflection, no anxiety about the possible ultimate extinction of our interest in the presence of God, it follows that every *perceived* conflict of human interest represents a challenge to work, to negotiate.[56]

The process of 'recognition' remains central and maintains its characteristic Hegelian double-effect: being the 'turning point'[57] where consciousness becomes self-consciousness, and Christians come to know the assurance of their own self loved, unconditionally, by God through the manifestation and edification of that love in and for the Christian community. Recognition, then, binds the ecclesial community together in the mutual acknowledgement of shared discipleship and a common journey through sin, repentance and grace filled transformation while also establishing 'markers of Christian identity' which regulate and guide the actions and relations of that community.[58]

The language of recognition features prominently in Williams' discourse around Anglican polity, attempting to mediate the ethical and doctrinal controversies which seem perpetually to precipitate schism. In his address to the Third Global South to South Encounter in 2005 he acknowledges that recognition is as much about the discovery of self as the objectification of the 'other' – and this must be particularly remembered in situations of conflict and the exercise of ecclesial discipline:

Our unity involves that also; that recognition is not the stranger on the other side of the universe – the sinner is me and my neighbour. And one of the hardest tasks we have when discipline is exercised, when discriminations are drawn, is how we remain in loving and prayerful fellowship with those who are our fellow sinners, not wholly strangers to us.[59]

The theme of recognition is continued elsewhere with some limited application to interfaith relations and dialogue,[60] but also particularly with reference to the primatial ministry as it might be imagined within both Anglican polity and ecumenically. Williams casts it as 'a sign of the continuing reality of active tradition' whereby the Primates collectively mediate the tradition between themselves as personal agents of their churches, embodying a process of mutual recognition as a marker of catholic authenticity amidst innovation and local development:

And a primatial initiative in challenging or seeking to limit local development on these grounds becomes intelligible as part of the service of the 'mother church' to the local – not ignoring or making light of local pressures and needs, but reminding the local assembly and its chief pastor that it must not lose its recognisability or receivability to other communities – across the globe and throughout history.[61]

The influence of this recognition discourse is evident in the 2004 report of the Lambeth Commission on Communion, established by Archbishop Rowan Williams at the request of the Primates, the *Windsor Report*. Many of the same themes of legitimacy and a tempered autonomy, bound by principles of interdependence, dominate the report. Mutual recognition of orders, and the recognition of Scripture as the cornerstone of authority within Anglicanism, are taken to be signs and markers of the outworking of communion, as in the former case, and, in the latter, of the norms by which we determine what might be recognizably faithful to the Anglican inheritance.[62]

The importance of recognition in the governing of mutual relationships and the developing definition of 'communion' for Anglicans is further articulated in a critical paragraph of that report:

Communion is, in fact, all about mutual relationships. It is expressed by community, equality, common life, sharing, interdependence, and mutual affection and respect. It subsists in visible unity, common confession of the apostolic faith, common belief in scripture and the creeds, common baptism and shared eucharist, and a mutually *recognised* common ministry. Communion means that each church *recognises* that the other belongs to the One, Holy, Catholic and Apostolic Church of Jesus Christ, and shares in the mission of the whole people of God . . . In communion, each church acknowledges and respects the interdependence and autonomy of the other, putting the needs of the global fellowship before its own.[63]

However Williams' promotion of recognizability for determining the boundaries of Anglican polity is perhaps most developed in his 2007 Advent Letter to the Primates, in part providing further reflection and elucidation on the Joint Standing Committee's reception of New Orleans Statement offered by the House of Bishops of The Episcopal Church (itself a response to the Windsor Report and the Communique of the Primates at their meeting in Dar es Salaam in February 2007). Here Williams casts the work of recognition as central to maintaining and promoting any constitutive unity within the Communion, acknowledging that as a 'voluntary association' there exist no instruments of central coercive jurisdiction nor an enforceable canon law.[64] In more closely defining this work of recognition, Williams explains:

. . . local churches acknowledge the same 'constitutive elements' in one another. This means in turn that each local church receives from others and recognises in others the same good news and the same structure of ministry, and seeks to engage in mutual service for the sake of our common mission.[65]

This recognition involves a threefold acknowledgement in the other of fidelity to the authority of Scripture, authenticity in the ministry of Word and Sacrament, and the priority of evangelism in the Church's mission. The tensions facing the Communion, according to Williams, are less about the presenting issue of human sexuality and more 'a crisis about whether we can fully, honestly and gratefully recognize these gifts in each other.'[66] Accordingly, this work of recognition is not reducible to a simple polarity over the 'right' and 'wrong' of a particular sexual ethic or biblical hermeneutic, which writes off a local church's ministry as 'completely defective' and seems to justify 'smaller and smaller groups taking to themselves the authority to decide on the adequacy of a neighbour's ministerial life or spiritual authenticity.'[67] However this leaves open and unanswered how the voluntary association which is the Communion might organize and legitimize the shared discernment necessary to test the recognizability of national churches 'behaving anomalously' and determine the appropriate implications for ecclesial communion and Anglican identity.

Nuancing National Polities: Opportunities for Further Ecclesiological Reflection

As has been explored, the strict demarcation of the 'nation-state' in International Relations is having to nuance itself in an increasingly globalized world. One such marker of nuance, recognition, has been explored with regard to both its Hegelian origins as well as its ecclesial translation as articulated by former Archbishop of Canterbury, Rowan Williams. The other markers, flagged previously as the distinction between 'community' and 'society' in understanding nationhood, and the impact of 'legitimacy' on bringing about a 'negotiated' sovereignty, also have some ecclesial application in assessing the place of the 'national church' ecclesiology which dominates international Anglican polity.

There is, for example, a significant pedigree of ecclesial reflection in imagining the church as 'society', with much the same meaning as Maritain (from his own Roman Catholic perspective) uses in relation to the nation-state. This 'society' is not the mere sum of the many and varied incidental, and accidental, associations of human existence, but rather the purposeful union of those who have been 'called out' and gathered to be, and to become, a particular kind of social organism.[68] Such a purposeful constitution of the church is, foremost, the good purpose of divine initiative and it is God's purposes which are worked through the society with the promise and assurance of its ultimate indefectibility. Nevertheless, it is the discernment of, and participation in, that purpose which exercises the faculty of reason in catholic continuity which is both spatial and temporal (encompassing the extent of communion, its intensity, and also its faithfulness) whereby the spiritual society might more perfectly come to know, resemble and proclaim the revelation of God in Scripture.

The interplay of this dynamic highlights the 'negotiated sovereignty' which is as much a reality to be faced in the church as in the relations among nation-states. At its essence it acknowledges that autonomy is not absolute. The catch-cry of 'interdependence' within Anglican relations has come to represent the same reality. Self-giving to the 'other' necessitates some concessionary compromise which will require not all elements of sovereignty to be apparent at all times. This is perhaps an inevitable truth of any life, whether corporate or individual, that is conceived and lived in relationship. As Hegel would have it, to know one's self one must negate that self to be found in the other. This process of recognition causes a crisis of legitimacy which has both internal and external dimensions: what are the internal organs and processes which guarantee legitimacy, and how does the requirement that they be recognized from 'beyond' serve to legitimate, or undermine, their sovereignty? For the churches of the Anglican Communion the questions might be, how might the discernment of the local church gain legitimacy, both for itself and as part of their catholic witness? How are norms of Scripture and orthodoxy settled? What of synods, bishops and 'Instruments of Communion'?

It is not immediately apparent how these nuances which have allowed the nation-state to retain its relevance in international relations might equally serve the polity of international Anglicanism, with its traditional emphasis on the self-sufficiency and autonomy of the national-church with its peculiarly 'national' characteristics. However, it is evident at least that the 'national church' does not exist entirely of its own generation, but precisely through the recognition and legitimacy which comes through being in 'communion'.

A 'contained catholicity' can no longer serve Anglicans if they continue to have any pretensions to be more than the church of one particular nation or national character. The tide of Anglican ecclesial expression has seemed, at least throughout the twentieth century, to have moved toward its internationalisation, manifest through the increased profile of international organs such as the 'Instruments' and the secretariat, the Anglican Communion Office, which serves them. Yet, the residual assumptions which lie behind the 'national church' polity are unable to respond to the challenges of global communion. This might be specifically illustrated with reference to the element of recognition, as already discussed, and which former Archbishop of Canterbury, Rowan Williams, did so much to urge the Communion to consider. Two questions, then, present themselves.

Firstly, by whom ought recognition be mediated, in order to legitimate the claim to authentic Anglican identity, doctrine, or praxis? The Archbishop of Canterbury? Some kind of global tribunal? A consensus among the 'Instruments', or piecemeal among the churches themselves? Secondly, what constitute the necessary elements for recognition as authentically 'Anglican'?

A 'national church' polity is unable to answer these questions. However, a provincial polity, lying latent in Anglican ecclesiology with its assumption of relational ecclesial identity, may prove well placed to resolve this tension between the local and the global.

Notes

1 The commitment to a 'pan-Protestant' Europe united both conservative as well as more radical Reformation players, see Gehring 2015, 7.
2 Gehring 2015, 8.

3 Chapman, Clarke, and Percy 2015, 4; a distinction is made between what Gehring describes as this 'multinational' political approach and the 'international Calvinism' which emphasized 'a transnational ideology superseding political boundaries.' See Gehring 2015, 8.

4 Chapman 2013a, 115.

5 'The 'Anglican Communion' evolved into a collection of national churches; it is a fragile theological structure. Our present unease reflects this ecclesiological reality; conflict brings this reality to the surface. This commitment to local independence shows how deeply Protestant is our ecclesiology . . . 'No Popery' has forced us into a Protestant International ecclesiology, even for those who do not value their Protestant heritage. And the inherent fissiparous tendency of Protestantism is now so self evident in international Anglicanism.' See Adam 2012, 66.

6 Creighton and Creighton 1901, 210.

7 Creighton and Creighton 1901, 212.

8 Creighton and Creighton 1901, 214.

9 Temple 1915, 54.

10 Lambeth Conference 1920, Resolutions 34, 35.

11 Lambeth Conference 1920, Resolution 43.

12 Lambeth Conference 1920, Resolution 43.

13 Montgomery 1920.

14 Montgomery 1920, 2.

15 Lambeth Conference 1930, Resolution 52.

16 E. J. Palmer 1930, 1.

17 E. J. Palmer 1930, 3.

18 E. J. Palmer 1930, 3.

19 E. J. Palmer 1930, 3.

20 E. J. Palmer 1930, 10.

21 E. J. Palmer 1930, 5–8.

22 Lambeth Conference 1948.

23 Ohmae 2008.

24 Habermas 1998, 410.

25 Habermas 1998, 398.

26 Ring 2008, 165–66.

27 Ring 2008, 160.

28 Fowler and Bunck 1995, 36.

29 Thiry 1981, 19.

30 Thomson 1995, 219.

31 Ring 2008, 162.

32 Beetham and Lord 1998, 15.

33 Ring 2008, 162.

34 Thomson 1995, 215.

35 Laughlin 2004, 70; for further articulation and development of Laughlin's conceptualisation of sovereignty as relational see Tierney 2005, 162ff.

36 Fowler and Bunck 1995, 37.

37 Pabst 2010, 573.

38 Maritain 1951.

39 Maritain 1951, 2. Maritain is careful to acknowledge, in what surely must refer to the atrocities of Nazism's racial and political philosophies, that such a

distinction 'has been misused in the most grievous manner by the theorists of the superiority of 'life' over reason.'

40 Maritain 1951, 5.

41 Maritain 1951, 12.

42 Maritain 1951, 11. Maritain further distinguishes the 'body politic' or 'political society' as the whole in which the State is only a functional part, and describes it as '. . . a really human and freely achieved communion. It lives on the devotion of the human persons and their gift of themselves,' 10.

43 Hegel 1977.

44 Krasnoff 2008, 97.

45 Hegel 1977, para. 177.

46 Krasnoff 2008, 101. Numbers in parenthesis refer to the relevant paragraphs in Phenomenology of Spirit.

47 Bubbio 2014, 139–40.

48 Bubbio 2014, 138.

49 Bubbio 2014, 142.

50 A very good initial exploration and evaluation of this may be found in Moses 2015. Moses does not, however, explicitly acknowledge the influence of Hegel which clearly lies behind much of Williams' approach.

51 Williams 1997, 29–30.

52 Williams 1997, 32.

53 Moses 2015, 149.

54 Moses 2015, 149.

55 Williams 1999, 306; 1997, 48; Moses 2015, 149.

56 Williams 1997, 38.

57 Hegel's own phrase, for discussion of its significance see Krasnoff 2008, 97

58 Williams 1999, 303; Moses 2015, 151.

59 Williams 2005.

60 Williams 2008b.

61 Williams 2008a. The particular ministry of 'primacy' is the Archbishop's focus here, but perhaps his remarks would be more fundamentally applicable to metropolitical and provincial polity. This will be discussed further in chapters 6 and 7. However, the current dominance of the 'national church' model in Anglican polity largely conflates the primatial and archiepiscopal ministries which further obscures the importance of the Archbishop's point.

62 Lambeth Commission on Communion 2004, paras 50–53.

63 Lambeth Commission on Communion 2004, para. 49. Italics mine.

64 Williams 2007.

65 Williams 2007.

66 Williams 2007.

67 Williams 2007.

68 This conceptualisation of the church as 'society' within Roman Catholic ecclesiology has its high point at the First Vatican Conference. For further discussion see Granfield 1979.

5

Independence or Interdependence: A Close Reading of Communion Constitutions

The historical exploration of the development of metropolitical authority throughout the Anglican Communion in the first three chapters has demonstrated that provincial polity has a distinct and distinctive pedigree in the Anglican tradition, albeit coming repeatedly into conflict with the pervasive acceptance of the 'national church' as an ecclesial priority. It remains to be tested to what extent this latent provincial polity might persist within Anglican ecclesiology, that it might offer some answers to the questions posed by the problem of recognition. A close analysis of current provincial constitutions provides ones means of determining the potential of provincial polity as it is already expressed and enculturated in the member-churches of the Communion. In particular, these constitutions articulate understandings of belonging and relationality within the Communion and also the particular ministry of the Archbishop of Canterbury. This chapter is particularly informed by archival research conducted at the Anglican Communion Office in 2016, through an extensive project which involved sourcing, updating and cataloguing the collection of provincial constitutions. Through this study, it may be determined to what extent a truly provincial polity is already 'hard-wired' into some of the defining texts of Anglican ecclesial identity, and how the unhelpful isolationism of the prevailing 'national church' polity might be challenged and a vision for a more coherent Communion articulated.

The Archives of the Anglican Communion Office

The Anglican Communion Office, situated in west London, houses the offices of the Secretary-General of the Anglican Communion and his secretariat, tasked with 'facilitating and encouraging conversations, cooperation, and engagement among the Churches of the Anglican

Communion, ecumenically and with other Christian communities, with inter faith partners, and with leaders in secular society.'[1] Formally, the Secretary-General is appointed by and relates to members of the Standing-Committee of the Anglican Communion in their capacity as Trustee-Members of the Anglican Consultative Council as incorporated in UK law under the Companies Act 2006 and governed by Articles of Association commonly called its Constitution.[2] The Standing Committee, whose members are appointed from both the Anglican Consultative Council and the Primates, is responsible for furthering the objects of the Anglican Consultative Council, 'to promote the unity and purposes of the Churches of the Anglican Communion in mission, evangelism, ecumenical relations, communication, administration and finance,' but this work is effectively managed and executed through the secretariat operating as the Anglican Communion Office.[3] Given this wide remit, the Office has collected an extensive archive relating to the development of the Communion, particularly in the second half of the twentieth century, with a focus on the work of the Anglican Consultative Council, Lambeth Conferences and Primates' Meetings as well as other intra-Anglican, ecumenical and inter-faith commissions. This archive has only been partially catalogued and is not readily accessible for public consultation. However, there has been a recent move to properly catalogue and make available the archives for the benefit of research into the development and formation of recent Anglican identity and polity, as well as informing contemporary reflection on the Communion's vision and direction.[4] Added momentum was given by a resolution of the Standing Committee in April 2016 to adopt objectives for the management of the archives.[5] During the summer of 2016 I spent two days per week volunteering at the Anglican Communion Office, assisting them in this wider undertaking but particularly completing a project focused on collecting current and historical constitutions from each of the thirty-nine member-churches of the Communion and the six extra-provincial churches.

This project involved a survey of all extant constitutions of the member-churches to determine how the church defined itself in relation to the 'Anglican Communion' as well as the Archbishop of Canterbury, and whether the Archbishop of Canterbury retained any residual metropolitical authority over churches which were otherwise autonomous. The survey also studied the varying understandings of metropolitical authority ascribed to archbishops, or other bodies, in the constitutions and the definition of visitorial and appellate authority. Where a member-church comprises more than one ecclesial province (which is only the case in the Church of England, the Church in Ireland, the Anglican Church of Canada, the Anglican Church of Australia, The Episcopal Church, the

Church of Nigeria and – at least at the time of writing[6] – the Province of the Episcopal Church of Sudan and South Sudan)[7] attention has been given to determining how metropolitical authority was understood constitutionally within both 'internal' provinces and across the 'national-church'. Other documents within the Anglican Communion Office archives have also proved particularly useful in charting the constitutional development of metropolitical authority in the second half of the twentieth century, particularly those relating to the inaugural Anglican Consultative Council meeting of 1971 in Limuru, Kenya and also the 1979 meeting of the Council in Ontario where metropolitical authority was specifically addressed and a survey was sent in preparation to all member-churches, the responses to which survive.

General Observations

Some member-churches of the Anglican Communion do not have written constitutions, most notably the Church of England which has been excluded from this survey as the development of its own metropolitical authority has been explored a little already here, and more extensively elsewhere.[8] A small number of other churches' constitutions were not available.[9] The most significant observations are drawn from twelve member-churches in Africa, eight in the Asian region and five in Central and South America. The majority of these constitutions date from the period between 1969 and 1973, during Michael Ramsey's term as Archbishop of Canterbury, although many of the African churches' constitutions have antecedents in the larger provinces formed in the mid to late 1950s under the direction of Geoffrey Fisher. The inclusion, in varied forms, of some kind of declaration or affirmation 'On Human Rights and the Value and Dignity of All People' (as it is worded in the constitution of the Anglican Church in Burundi) is a particular feature common to all African member-churches (with the exception of Nigeria and Jerusalem & the Middle East) and points to some common source behind them or at least substantial consultation between them. Indeed, this consultative process is reflected in the archives of the Anglican Communion Office, which facilitated this process, and explains many of the common features evident in the constitutions' understanding of metropolitical authority. Nevertheless, there are also some interesting and notable outliers which bring into focus the 'metropolitical muddle' in which the Communion has found itself.

Most constitutions of the member-churches contain some reference to their place within the Anglican Communion. Constitutions which make no mention of the Anglican Communion include the Church of Pakistan, the Nippon Sei Ko Kai and the Church in Wales. The Anglican Church of Australia commits itself to remaining 'in communion with the Church of England in England and with churches in communion therewith' while the Church of Ireland similarly looks first to maintaining communion with 'the sister Church of England' and thereafter 'all other Christian Churches agreeing in the principles of this Declaration . . . [the parameters of which give wide scope for intercommunion].'[10] Among the other member-churches, references to the Anglican Communion tend to be statements of fact rather than reflective of the relationship between a 'national church' and a wider whole, common expressions include the participle construction 'being in full communion with the Anglican Communion' or the declarative '. . . is a constitutive member of the Anglican Communion.' These declaratory statements of fact are problematic, as they do not address the basis of their communion with other Anglican churches or the means by which that communion might be negotiated or altered.

The Archbishop of Canterbury in Provincial Constitutions

References to the Archbishop of Canterbury are fewer, although those constitutions that do make some explicit mention of either a personal ministry of the Archbishop of Canterbury or attribute some significance to the see reflect the process of transfer of metropolitical authority from Canterbury to an independent provincial polity. In many cases this involved the act of a formal relinquishment of metropolitical authority which coincided with the assumption of such authority in various forms through the ratification of constitutional provisions. For example, the reorganization of the Archbishopric of Jerusalem in the 1970s saw the relinquishment of metropolitical authority from the Archbishop of Canterbury to a 'Central Synod' following a recommendation by the Anglican Consultative Council (although the Council used the language of 'delegation' rather than 'relinquishment').[11] The 1970 Constitution of the Province of Tanzania contains a Deed of Relinquishment transferring metropolitical authority from the Archbishop of its parent province, Leonard Beecher of East Africa (who himself had received authority through a Deed of Relinquishment of the Archbishop of Canterbury, Geoffrey Fisher, in 1960) to the inaugural metropolitan of the new province of Tanzania.[12]

In some instances the role of the Archbishop of Canterbury is deliberately and explicitly rejected. The Church of Nigeria has an article headed the 'See of Canterbury' which, curiously, makes no mention of

Canterbury but rather affirms the Church of Nigeria's place within the Communion and reiterates that its own tribunals have final authority in all matters of faith, doctrine and discipline. It might fairly be assumed, then, that the article is more concerned with explicitly repudiating the role of Canterbury than affirming it.[13]

Significantly, as it reflects a greater consciousness of the lines of metropolitical authority as well as the history of its development, the Church of the Province of Myanmar (Burma) contains no reference to the Archbishop of Canterbury but instead, and in similar declarative style to those constitutions that do, asserts itself to be

> . . . in full communion with the See of Calcutta and with all dioceses, provinces and regional Churches which are in full communion with the See of Calcutta [and] holds and maintains the Faith, Doctrine, Sacraments and Discipline of the Church of Christ as the Lord hath commanded in His Holy Word, and as the same are received and taught by the Church of India, Pakistan, Burma and Ceylon in the Book of Common Prayer and the Ordinal of the year 1960.[14]

However, where the Archbishop of Canterbury is referenced in other provincial constitutions, it is generally as an affirmation of some kind of Anglican identity, as well as participation in a worldwide fellowship, shaped by the acknowledgement of a particular historical inheritance.[15]

The strongest attachment to the See of Canterbury is contained within the constitutions of the Province of Central Africa and the Province of the Episcopal Church of South Sudan and Sudan, where actual appellate jurisdiction is attributed to the personal ministry of the Archbishop of Canterbury. Central Africa, which has the earlier of the two constitutions, holds metropolitical ministry to be core to the polity of the international Communion among whom it 'accepts the Archbishop of Canterbury as holding the first place.'[16] The church explicitly disclaims 'any right to depart from the standards of Faith and Order or the Principles of Worship set forth in the said formularies of the Church of England' and further provides that disputes within the church over 'its adherence to the standards of Faith and Order or the Principles of Worship herein set forth' may be referred to the Archbishop of Canterbury and Anglican Consultative Council.[17] The process for this is further articulated in Article 5 of the Constitution:

> The Episcopal Synod has always final authority in matters concerning the preservation of the truth of the Church's doctrine, the purity of its life, and the worthiness of its worship. Provided that in a question of Faith or Order if there is not unanimity, any Bishop may require that it

be submitted, to the Archbishop of Canterbury and two other Bishops (one of whom shall be nominated by the Bishop making the submission and the other by a majority vote of the Episcopal Synod), [effectively giving the Archbishop of Canterbury a casting vote], who shall determine the matter in accordance with the formularies and doctrinal teaching of the Church of England, and their decision shall be final.[18]

The Province of the Episcopal Church of South Sudan and Sudan contains a similar allowance for reference to be made at the request of the General Synod to the Archbishop of Canterbury whose determination shall be 'final and binding.'[19]

Furthermore, within the Church of the Province of Central Africa, any alteration to the Fundamental Declarations that preface the Constitution may only be made after endorsement by the Archbishop of Canterbury that such changes do not affect 'the terms of Communion between the Church of this Province, the Church of England and the rest of the Anglican Communion.' Willingly or not, the Archbishop of Canterbury has thrust upon him not only the guardianship of the inheritance of faith, order and worship within the Church of the Province of Central Africa, but is also the ultimate mediator of its membership within the Communion.

The Constitution of the Church of the Province of Uganda contains such an endorsement by Archbishop Michael Ramsey, dated 1972, although the current amended constitution of 1994 no longer requires such an endorsement, and provides for an entirely internal procedure for the interpretation of the constitution, including the application of faith, order and worship within the province (although advice may be sought from the Anglican Consultative Council).[20] The Anglican Church of Papua New Guinea contains a similar provision in its constitution that all proposed changes must be submitted to the Anglican Consultative Council for 'confirmation that the proposed changes will not put the Province outside the Anglican Communion.'[21]

This similarity between the constitutions of Uganda, Sudan and Central Africa does not come from any common predecessor in their formation. The Church of the Province of Uganda has its origins in the Diocese of Eastern Equatorial Africa established in 1884 from which the Anglican churches in Rwanda, Burundi, the Congo, Kenya and Tanzania are also descended. The Church of the Province of Central Africa, formed in 1955, has its origin in the missionary dioceses established in the second half of the nineteenth century out of the existing Province of South Africa in what is now Zimbabwe, Zambia and Malawi and organized according to the boundaries of the Central African Federation, even after its breakup in 1963. The Province of South Sudan and Sudan had its initial origins in the 1920 Diocese of Egypt and the Sudan under the Jerusalem Archbishopric, which divided to form the Diocese of the Sudan in 1945 and an independent province in 1974, changing its name in 2013 to reflect the creation of the new sovereign state of South Sudan.[22] Instead, the reason for this similarity across these diverse churches is rooted in a common process of transition from dependence to independence among those dioceses which had come to look toward the Archbishop of Canterbury for metropolitical oversight having been established through various missionary efforts and agencies.

One of the first of these independent provinces to be established was that of West Africa in 1950, following a conference in 1944 of the bishops of Accra, Lagos, Niger, Sierra Leone and Gambia & Rio Pongas to discuss provincial organization. From this meeting a draft constitution was prepared which went through two further revisions until it was proposed with an explanatory memorandum by the Archbishop of Canterbury in 1951. This early constitution contains two articles relating to interim provisions for transition to independence upon which the relevant provisions in the constitutions of Central Africa and Sudan have been modelled. Critically, the proposed constitution for West Africa envisages these to be only interim provisions, until such time as full provincial government through a provincial synod can be established:

Article XIV – Interim Provision Faith & Order:
(b) Until the Constitution and Canons referred to in Article XIII have come into effect, if the Episcopal Synod find itself in doubt or dispute concerning a matter of Faith or Order, it may and if two members of the Synod so require it shall refer the question to the Archbishop of Canterbury who shall determine the matter in accordance with the formularies and doctrinal teaching of the Church of England and his decision shall be final.[23]

This reserved and residual authority of the Archbishop of Canterbury within the province is also evident in provisions for the election of diocesan bishops, where the Archbishop of Canterbury must confirm each nomination and may send recommendations back for further consideration (Article VIII), as well as power to directly appoint the Archbishop of West Africa when the Episcopal Synod fails to give a two-thirds majority to any one candidate as required in the constitution (Article VI). These are strictly considered, however, to be interim measures and as a gesture to show, as Geoffrey Fisher explains in his memorandum, 'the continuing concern and interest of the Archbishop of Canterbury in dioceses which have grown up under his care and jurisdiction, and as providing some support and guidance to the Province as it feels its way forward and grows to maturity.'[24] This reserved jurisdiction of the Archbishop of Canterbury was also a feature of the constitution of the Province of East Africa, which further stipulated that determinations be made 'in conjunction with the Archbishop of York and the Bishops of London, Durham, and Winchester.'[25] This was discussed at the 1963 and 1964 meetings of the Lambeth Consultative Body which determined that 'this provision was rightly felt to be inacceptable, if only because of colonial overtones,' and that the offending clause be replaced with 'after consultation with the Consultative Body of the Lambeth Conference.'[26] Despite this widening of consultative scope, the Archbishop of Canterbury retained for the time being determinative jurisdiction under the provisions of the constitutions concerned.[27]

The Legacy of 'Mutual Responsibility and Interdependence'

The process of this drive toward the establishment of independent and autonomous churches along a largely 'national church' model was centrally organized through the predecessor to the Anglican Communion Office, the office of the Anglican Executive Officer of the Consultative Body of the Lambeth Conference (established through Resolutions 60 & 61 of the 1958 Lambeth Conference), and was given particular momentum following the 1963 Anglican Congress in Toronto which produced the key manifesto for provincial independence along 'national church' lines, *Mutual Responsibility and Interdependence*.[28]

The principal author of *Mutual Responsibility and Interdependence*, inaugural Anglican Executive Officer Bishop Stephen Bayne, describes the winds of change blowing through the Communion in the post-war climate as 'eager to move toward a fuller and more vigorous expression of Anglican interdependence.'[29] The document is largely a call to mission, partnership and – crucially – increased fundraising, set in a rallying tone of hopefulness for the future:

> In our time the Anglican Communion has come of age. Our professed nature as a world-wide fellowship of national and regional Churches has suddenly become a reality . . . The full communion in Christ which has been our traditional tie has suddenly taken on a totally new dimension . . . The keynotes of our time are equality, interdependence, mutual responsibility.[30]

The outcome and embodiment of these keynote chords was the implementation of a centralised system for coordinating funding and grant-making throughout the Communion, whereby directories of projects were compiled following submissions from local churches gathered together into regions. The scope of projects was extensive and take-up was not always as hoped. In his introduction to the 1967 Directories, the then Executive Officer, Bishop Ralph Dean, explains that, of the 1,148 projects listed in the previous year's Directories, the funding for only 111 had been met in full with 390 partially funded and 758 'unadopted.'[31] Despite the language of 'interdependence' a clear dynamic of dependence is set up between what are officially designated as 'requesting provinces' and 'responding provinces.'

In preparation for the first meeting of the Anglican Consultative Council, a Preparatory Committee on M.R.I. was established to reassess the effectiveness of the project and particularly to consult with member-churches. A questionnaire was sent to all member-churches and responses gathered and summarized.[32] The questions asked are relatively open and reveal the anxieties felt: 'Is there a greater sense of 'family' and interdependence? Has your feeling of dependence given way to interdependence? Has your sense of parental oversight given way to interdependence?'[33] The replies from member-churches indicate a substantial feeling that attitudes of paternalism and dependence still persisted, and a cynicism that the scheme 'is too complicated. It is no longer Mutual Responsibility and Interdependence, but something called 'Em-arr-igh'.'[34] There is still a note of optimism, however, in the Memorandum in summary of the responses prepared by Bishop Howe for the Consultative Council:

> Old attitudes die hard and countries which for many years have regarded themselves as the parent churches to infant 'missions' do not easily or quickly adapt themselves to the idea of equal partnership in a Communion of autonomous Provinces. However the general opinion seems to be that a greater family sense has been generated and a more realistic recognition of the nature of the Anglican Communion is developing . . . If a generalisation can be made it is that the older, larger and more established Provinces have been slower to adjust themselves to the changing character of the Anglican Communion but that otherwise there has been a real growth in the sense of fellowship and mutuality.[35]

Toward the Common Codification of Metropolitical Authority and Provincial Polity

One outcome of this fellowship and mutuality is that broad similarities may be discerned in how metropolitical authority is understood internally within member churches of the Anglican Communion, articulated through their constitutions. The ecclesiastical lawyer and academic, Norman Doe, has done much to draw together themes and legal principles common to the churches of the Communion.[36] This project has been given wider prominence since the establishment of the Anglican Communion Legal Advisors' Network mandated by the March 2001 meeting of Primates to 'give follow up to Professor Norman Doe's paper, looking at the parameters of an identifiable Anglican common law and how an understanding of such common law can enhance our global Communion.'[37] With regard to metropolitical authority and provincial polity, Doe provides a helpfully descriptive summary of constitutional provisions for the appointment and election of archbishops, as well as their common functions:

> The functions of the archbishop, who typically has 'authority, leadership and visitatorial power over the whole province', commonly include: convening and chairing the provincial assembly, its executive council or committee and the house of bishops; the administration and entertainment (with others) of appeals from the decisions of diocesan tribunals; representing the province in its dealings with other churches; and other duties assigned from time to time by the provincial assembly.[38]

The pursuit of common principles, however, necessarily results in a somewhat flat descriptive whitewash of the variations within and between constitutions. This was recognized at the time of the first Anglican Consultative Council in 1971 which, at best, could only offer a 'lowest common denominator' definition of provincial polity as 'a group of dioceses which for some purposes act in association under a common constitution.'[39] The Council eschewed any kind of theological reflection and determination of the nature of provincial polity within Anglican ecclesiology, 'both for the reason that the word 'province' had so wide a range of meanings, and also because a province is not a theoretical notion but a grouping of certain people in one particular part of the world,' instead settling for mere description 'of the factors to be considered when planning a new province, or diocese, or the division of an old one.'[40]

Nevertheless, this work of the Anglican Consultative Council at least represents some attempt to give some prominence to the place of provincial polity within the Communion. It also marks a shift away from the early twentieth-century trend of casting international Anglican polity purely in terms of national churches. However, provincial polity is still not understood theologically or ecclesiologically but at best as a fairly neutral happenstance of circumstance bringing dioceses together in a common purpose and, presumably, identity. This thinking was to develop by the time the Anglican Consultative Council met for a fourth time in Ontario, Canada in 1979.

In preparation for the 1979 Anglican Consultative Council meeting, a request was made through the office of the Anglican Executive Officer (then John Howe) to the Primates of the Anglican Communion for their feedback on the formulation of a common definition of metropolitical authority which might serve the Communion as new provinces were created and constitutions drawn up.[41] This marks a significant and conscious effort to not only reflect ecclesiologically on the nature of metropolitical authority and provincial polity within Anglicanism, but also to come to some common mind as to its articulation and future implementation. This request was prompted by the third meeting of the Anglican Consultative Council in 1976 following the recommendation of its Constitutions Committee which had produced a draft definition of metropolitical authority. The Council recommended:

> . . . that the officers of the ACC appoint a small committee to consider and revise a draft definition of Metropolitical authority, outlined by the Constitutions Committee, and to report if possible to the Standing Committee meeting in 1977.[42]

Such a committee, however, was felt by the Standing Committee to be 'inadequate as well as expensive' and the alternative procedure was proposed whereby 'the draft definition on Metropolitical authority produced by the Constitutions Committee in Trinidad in 1976 be sent to all Primates, Presiding Bishops, and Metropolitans for their own views, and also that they seek the views of their legal or some such appropriate body, and that these replies be collated in the ACC office.'[43] The draft definition circulated for comment read as follows:

Metropolitical Authority
Metropolitical Authority is one of the basic concepts of Anglican Church structure. This is usually exercised within the Provincial structure of the Anglican Communion but is also exercised in extra-provincial dioceses which are related to a particular Archbishop, or through relationship of Dioceses to a Council to which Metropolitical authority has been delegated e.g. CASA. This concept affirms the conviction that no Diocese should exist in isolation but should receive pastoral support and should develop within the general Anglican ethos which it should continually help to form.

This concept relates to the general welfare of the whole Church in which metropolitical authority is exercised, but is expressed primarily through the canonical responsibilities relating to Bishops. The authority is usually exercised by an Archbishop who is recognised as Metropolitan. In the view of the Constitutions Committee the exercise of this authority should include the following:

1 The provision of pastoral oversight over the area concerned, assuring both that its constitution and canonical development is in accordance with general Anglican tradition and practice, and that the provisions of its Constitution and canons are adhered to.
2 The giving of authority for the division of dioceses and the creation of new dioceses.
3 The giving of authority for the election, and/or translation, of Bishops within the diocese or dioceses concerned, and the confirming of the same.
4 The provision of adequate episcopal oversight in the case of vacancies.
5 Consecrating or issuing the mandate for the consecration of bishops in the diocese or dioceses concerned.
6 Provision for the necessary approval of all changes in the Constitution and canons of the diocese or dioceses in so far as they pertain to faith and order and the relations with other parts of the Anglican Communion.
7 Fullest consultation about the calling of meetings of Synods and Standing Committees.
8 Receiving appeals allowed by the appropriate Constitution and Canons.[44]

Responses which survive in the Anglican Communion Office archives represent a broad geographical cross-section of the Communion and a reasonable return rate from member churches.[45] Responses from South America, Tanzania and Jerusalem indicated broad agreement with the draft statement, while others were both more critical and more substantial. A particular point of contention which comes out of various responses is that metropolitical authority within those provinces is exercised corporately and synodically rather than personally. This point is made in the response from New Zealand, which ascribes to the General Synod rather than the Metropolitan many of the functions outlined in the draft definition.[46] This is reiterated in comments received by the Provincial Secretary of the Church of Melanesia, Central Africa, Canada and The Episcopal Church.[47] Comments made on behalf of the Church of England look toward the possibility of establishing supranational regional councils with metropolitical authority, 'to ensure that their constitutions and canonical developments are in accordance with general Anglican traditions and practice.'[48] These regional councils would field appeals and disputes coming from provinces which otherwise would be dealt with by the Archbishop of Canterbury or the Anglican Consultative Council. It is proposed that reserved powers may be vested in the Anglican Consultative Council, although expressly not the Archbishop of Canterbury, 'on matters of Faith and Order or the principles of Worship, insofar as these may affect the terms of communion between the provinces concerned and the rest of the Anglican Communion.'[49] These comments reveal a consistent shift in understanding metropoltical authority as moving away from the personal ministry of archbishops toward its corporate and synodical expression. The remarks on behalf of the Church of England take this further to envisage within the international Communion a diminished role for the Archbishop of Canterbury and an enhanced role for global and regional synodical structures as a check on the 'naked autonomy' of the 'national church'.

This chapter, through its close reading of provincial constitutions and by charting the movement from the 1970s onward to more accurately define the nature of metropolitical authority as new provinces were created, highlights the distinction within Anglicanism between an authentically provincial polity, predicated on relationship and mediated through the personal ministry of an archbishop yet balanced through synodical governance, conciliar and collegial ministry, and a 'national church' polity which preferences independence, self-sufficiency and self-determinism as its *raison d'être*.

The impetus for this drive toward independence rather than interdependence came largely from the anxiety for a transformation of relationships across the Communion between 'requesting' and 'responding' provinces toward genuine partnership in response to *Mutual Responsibility and Interdependence*. In the establishment of new provinces a particular concern was given to breaking any vestiges of colonial dependence and establishing them as strictly autonomous and independent. Attention is given, therefore, to establishing internal consistency with regards to metropolitical authority in the constitutions of new provinces; however, this is not matched by a similar effort to imagine how the Communion might embody a provincial polity at a supra-provincial level.

Therefore, while there is a relatively stable understanding of metropolitical authority within provinces (albeit with some significant problems, such as an unclear and ill-defined articulation of the nature of a metropolitan's visitorial ministry and authority) there is little accounting for how metropolitans might relate inter-provincially, what role the Archbishop of Canterbury ought to have in this relating, and an absence of what might be termed a metropolitical ecclesiology for the Communion as a whole. Instead, Anglican polity has proved unable to lift itself above the bare affirmation of the autonomous 'national church' with the Primates singularly standing in as tokens of this reductionist ecclesiology rather than the personification of a provincial polity through which mutual recognition and relationality is negotiated.

Notes

1 *The Anglican Communion Office: A Brief Guide* 2017.

2 *Constitution of the Anglican Consultative Council* 2010.

3 *Constitution of the Anglican Consultative Council* 2010.

4 'Anglican 'hidden Treasure' Archives to Be Restored' 2016.

5 *Report from the Meeting of the Standing Committee of 6–7 April, 2016 to the 16th Meeting of the Anglican Consultative Council* 2016.

6 The Church of the Province of Sudan and South Sudan was divided in July 2017 according to its internal provincial boundaries to establish an independent Episcopal Church of Sudan alongside the Episcopal Church of South Sudan. This chapter, however, continues to refer to the combined predecessor church as at the time of writing clear details about the constitutional and provincial arrangements for the new churches has not been available.

7 The Anglican Church in Aotearoa, New Zealand and Polynesia has three 'cultural strands' or 'tikanga' which might also be thought analogous to ecclesial provinces; albeit not in any traditional sense. The Episcopal Church, similarly, has relatively recently created provincial units but these do not clearly correspond with a conventional metropolitical authority. For a comprehensive analysis of this development within The Episcopal Church see, E. A. White and Dykman 1997, 322ff.

8 The incomparably authoritative account is given in Kemp 1961.

9 These were the Anglican Church of Southern Africa, the Church of Bangladesh (United), and the Church of South India (United).

10 Constitution, Anglican Church of Australia, 2014, Chapter 2, Section 6 [RG XIII: C(A2)CCN1]; Constitution, Church of Ireland, 2003, Preamble & Declaration, Article 3 [RG XIII: C(I2)C1].

11 Constitution, Episcopal Church of Jerusalem & the Middle East, 1980, Preamble [RG XIII: C(J2)C1].

12 Constitution, Church of the Province of Tanzania, 1970, Deed of Relinquishment [RG XIII: X-C(T)C1]. The Church of the Province of Tanzania officially changed its name to the Anglican Church of Tanzania on 11th June 1998, in order to more easily clarify its identity as 'Anglican'. See correspondence from the Reverend Canon Mkunga Mtingele, General Secretary of the Anglican Church of Tanzania, to the Anglican Communion Office, 24 June 1998 contained within [RG II: ACC/CH/CONST/4(t)].

13 This Article is not part of the original 1979 Constitution, and is part of significant constitutional changes made in 2005 reflecting controversies within the

Communion over sexuality as well as international allegiances. For further detailed discussion see, Kuehn 2008.

14 Constitution, Church of the Province of Myanmar, 1970, Preface [RGII: ACC/CH/CONST/3(m3)].

15 This is reflected, among others, in the constitutions of The Episcopal Church in the USA [RG XIII: C(U2)CCN1], the Anglican Church in Aotearoa, New Zealand and Polynesia [RG XIII: C(A1)C1], the Anglican Church of South America [RG XIII: C(S5)CCN1], and the Episcopal Church in Jerusalem and the Middle East [RG XIII: C(J2)C1].

16 Constitution, Church of the Province of Central Africa, 1969, Fundamental Declarations [RG II: ACC/CH/CONST/2(c2)].

17 The Anglican Consultative Council was substituted for the 'Lambeth Consultative Body' in 1969 [RG II: ACC/CH/CONST/2(c2)].

18 Constitution, Church of the Province of Central Africa, 1969, Article 5. Reference to the teaching of the 'Church of England' was changed to 'Anglican' in 1995. See [RG II: ACC/CH/CONST/2(c2)].

19 Constitution, Province of the Episcopal Church of South Sudan and Sudan, 2011, Article 3, para 8 [RG XIII: C(S6)C1].

20 Constitution, Church of the Province of Uganda, 1972 (Amended 1994), Articles 2 & 20 [RG II: ACC/CH/CONST/5(u1)].

21 Constitution, Anglican Church of Papua New Guinea, 1977, Article 20 [RG XIII: X-C(P1)C1].

22 Sudan and South Sudan have since divided again to become independent member-churches of the Anglican Communion. See 'Celebrations as Sudan Becomes Anglican Communion's 39th Province' 2017 as well as the explanatory note at Footnote 344.

23 Proposed Constitution, The Church of the Province of West Africa, Explanatory Memorandum by the Archbishop of Canterbury [RG II: ACC/CH/CONST/5(w2)]. This reference to the Archbishop of Canterbury was removed from the eventual 1963 Constitution and later revisions.

24 Proposed Constitution, The Church of the Province of West Africa, Explanatory Memorandum by the Archbishop of Canterbury, 4 [RG II: ACC/CH/CONST/5(w2)].

25 Constitution, Province of East Africa, 1960, Article 19:3 [RG II: ACC/CH/CONST/3(k1)].

26 Lambeth Consultative Body and Advisory Council on Missionary Strategy 1964.

27 The Archbishop of Uganda expressed a similar concern at the meeting.

28 Advisory Council on Missionary Strategy 1963; there is a significant growing literature relating to both Stephen Bayne and the influence of Mutual Responsibility and Interdependence, not least as it has become something of an aspirational 'catchphrase' in imagining the polity of the Anglican Communion. It is not necessary to enter or recall this discussion here, but may be followed up in, Cox 1987; Zink 2011; Danaher 2011; Groves 2010, 22–36.

29 Bayne 1964, 6.

30 Advisory Council on Missionary Strategy 1963, 1–2.

31 General Introduction to the New 1967 Directories by Ralph Dean, Executive Officer, in ACO Archives ACC/MRI/3/1(c).

32 Fortunately all responses received and preparatory material is extant in the ACO Archives ACC/C/1/1(e).

33 'Questionnaire on M.R.I' in 'Review of Mutual Responsibility and Interdependence' prepared by John Howe for the Anglican Consultative Council 1971, 3 in ACO Archives ACC/C/1/1(e).

34 'General Comments from Parish Clergy' in the response of the New Zealand Anglican Board of Missions to the Questionnaire on M.R.I. in ACO Archives ACC/C/1/1(e).

35 'Memorandum on Questionnaire on M.R.I.' by John Howe, Executive Officer, in ACO Archives ACC/C/1/1(e). The draft contained in the archives, however, shows a grudging acceptance that the picture is not quite so rosy: one sentence which in the typed original reads 'There is evidence that there has been some mutually helpful exchange of information on liturgical and educational matters' has by hand been annotated first to '. . . some but very little mutually helpful, &c' and then again finally redacted to '. . . very little mutually helpful, &c.'.

36 See particularly, Doe 2013; 2008; 1998.

37 *Anglican Communion Legal Advisors' Consultation Report* 2016, 1.

38 Doe 1998, 107.

39 *The Time Is Now: Anglican Consultative Council First Meeting. Limuru, Kenya.* 1971, 32.

40 *The Time Is Now: Anglican Consultative Council First Meeting. Limuru, Kenya.* 1971, 32. The resulting guidelines are found as Resolutions 21 and 22 of the 1971 Limuru meeting of the ACC.

41 Letter from Bishop John Howe, Secretary General to the Anglican Consultative Council, to the Primates of the Anglican Communion, 28th June 1977 in *Collected Provincial Responses to Request of Anglican Executive Officer for Comment on Metropolitical Authority in Preparation for ACC-4* 1977, ACC/C/4/2(e).

42 ACC-3 1976, Resolution 31: Comparative Study of Constitutions.

43 Letter from John Howe to Primates, 28 June 1977, *Collected Provincial Responses to Request of Anglican Executive Officer for Comment on Metropolitical Authority in Preparation for ACC-4* 1977, ACC/C/4/2(e).

44 Draft Definition on Metropolitical Authority produced by the ACC Constitutions Committee in Trinidad, 1976, *Collected Provincial Responses to Request of Anglican Executive Officer for Comment on Metropolitical Authority in Preparation for ACC-4* 1977, ACC/C/4/2(e).

45 Responses were received from Australia, Canada, Central Africa, Ceylon, England, The Episcopal Church, Japan, Jerusalem and the Middle East, Melanesia, New Zealand, South Africa, South America, and Tanzania.

46 Letter from H.M.S. Dawson to Archbishop A.H. Johnston providing comments on the draft definition of metropolitical authority, 1 August 1977, ACC/C/4/2(e).

47 This correspondence may all be found in ACC/C/4/2(e).

48 Letter from Chantry House, Canterbury, Kent to Bishop J. Howe, Secretary General of the Anglican Consultative Council, 28 July 1977, ACC/C/4/2(e).

49 Chantry House to J. Howe, ACC/C/4/2(e).

Part Three

The Rise of the Primates

If we go on in the fifth century, we shall find its conclusion distinguished by an endeavour in the Western Church, among the greater metropolitans, to become primates. There surely never was a more vague authority than that which this much coveted office bestowed; and the absolute titularity into which it sank before long, would almost seem absurd if we were not so used to it.[1]

There has been a proliferation of Primates within the Anglican Communion since J.M. Neale, almost a decade before the first Lambeth Conference, noted the preference for primatial preferment among metropolitans prevalent in the Western Church since the fifth century. Neale's assessment of the 'vague authority' which accompanies the gift of primacy remains as true for the forty-one Primates of the contemporary Communion, as it did for the four Anglican Primates one hundred and fifty years ago.[2] Indeed, the tenfold multiplication of Primates within Anglicanism has redefined the nature of primacy itself with a peculiarly Anglican distinctiveness and has necessitated a reappraisal of its proper place within the polity of the church, as well as prompting a rediscovery of metropolitical jurisdiction as an instrument serving the unity of the international Communion.

Due at least in part to the rapidly evolving landscape of Anglican ecclesiology in response to contemporary controversies, the task of ecclesiological and theological reflection on the role of primacy within Anglicanism remains very much a current and pressing concern. The distinction between primatial and metropolitical jurisdiction has largely been lost in contemporary Anglicanism as a by-product of the dominance of the 'national church' ideal in our international polity.

The concern throughout the 1970s to establish independent national-churches, each one self-governing and autonomous, made sense in the context of deconstructing colonial attitudes and frameworks which perpetuated unequal, dependent and unjust relationships but left neglected and unanswered the ecclesiological questions of how these reformed relationships ought to be negotiated, encouraged and protected. The developing status of the Primates within the Communion has matched this development, as the concept of primacy has become blurred with metropolitical authority and the office of Primate has come to stand in as a personification of the absolute autonomy and sovereignty of the 'national church'. The rise of the Primates is not an antidote to the autonomy of the 'national church', as might be supposed given the respective priorities played out through the controversy concerning human sexuality. Instead, these two phenomena within Anglican polity are deeply related and exist within the same ecclesial paradigm, threatening to eclipse a more primitive understanding of metropolitical authority and provincial polity.

The nature of metropolitical authority within Anglicanism is, then, inextricably tied up with the highly fluid and rapidly developing understanding of the primatial office. Through some reflection on this dynamic, the following two chapters will seek not only to untangle and bring into sharper focus the distinctiveness of these two ecclesial concepts, in order to enable greater critical insight into their purpose and operation, but also to establish in what direction the currents of Anglican polity are moving to determine the potential for an authentically Anglican awakening of provincial polity and metropolitical authority in the Age of the Primates.

Notes

1   Neale 1863, 288; originally published anonymously as, 'Article VIII: Φιλολογικὴ Καὶ Κριτικὴ Ἱστορία, &c.' 1859.

2   To the Archbishops of Canterbury and York, as Primates of All England and England respectively, and the Archbishops of Armagh and Dublin, as Primates of All Ireland and Ireland respectively, have been added primates in every member-church of the Anglican Communion, most commonly corresponding with the archbishop of single-province churches but in some churches having more general responsibilities of leadership and representation. See Doe 1998, 103ff. Two of the modern primacies have, at least until recently, affected the style 'Primate of All . . . X': the Primate of All Nigeria, and the Primate of All Canada. In the latter case it seems the reasoning was because of the confusion otherwise occasioned by having an internal ecclesial province of 'Canada' which preceded Canadian Confederation, although the style has at least since the 1970s fallen out of use. Within the Church of Nigeria the usage began haphazardly in the late 1990s: letterhead of Archbishop Joseph Abiodun Detiloye from June 1998 styles him as 'Metropolitan Primate of all Nigeria' whereas in 1999 he is styled 'Archbishop of the Church of Nigeria' and John Peterson, Anglican Executive Officer, addresses him as 'Primate of the Church of Nigeria'. Nevertheless, the style 'Primate of all Nigeria' was particularly taken up from 2000 by Archbishop Peter Akinola. It is not, however, a term used in any version of the Nigerian Anglican constitutions: the original 1978 Constitution does not mention the ministry of a Primate at all, only an Archbishop, and the most recent 2005 constitutional revision refers to the 'Primate, Archbishop and Metropolitan of the Church of Nigeria'.

6

Primus Inter Pares: All Bishops are Equal, but Some are More Equal than Others

With characteristic Anglican polarity, discussions of the historical development of primacy from the perspectives of both ecclesiastical history and ecclesiological reflection have tended to one of two extremes. For, as on the one side, there persists a penchant for rather excessive and exorbitant detail in the matter of particulars, such that any obvious application is crowded out by the foibles and factoids of the enthusiast for ecclesiastical antiquities, so, on the other side, brevity breeds paucity.

The former approach was, perhaps, particularly popular in the heady days of the 'Catholic Revival' in England as nineteenth-century scholars searched the sources of Early Church history seeking to securely graft themselves in as a faithful branch 'of that true and divine church.'[1] Liturgiologist and hymnist, J.M. Neale, provides a characteristically typical example, although uncommonly refreshing in its whimsical tone:

> It is difficult to say whether Rome gave or received most in the fifth and sixth centuries by the institution of primacies and the donation of the pallium. Now of course every metropolitan calls himself a primate of something or other. If York cannot be Primate of All England, he will at all events be Primate of England; as so Dublin of Ireland. In France they managed in a different way. Thus the Archbishop of Rouen is Primate of Normandy; the Archbishop of Auch, of Novempopulania; the Archbishop of Lyons calls himself Primate of all Gaul; while he of Vienne, to be a step above the others, calls himself Primate of the Primates of Gaul. But these titles are infinitely less unmeaning than those of the East. Thus the Bishop of Caesarea calls himself Most Excellent of the Most Excellent; while the metropolitan of Heraclea contents himself with that of the First of the Most Excellent. The name of Primate is not in use, but every little prelate is Exarch of something or other. The Archbishop of Mesembria, having nothing better by way of a title, is Exarch of the Black Sea; and the petty bishoprics of Lemnos and Embros strive together for the title of Exarch of the

Aegean Sea; of the sea itself, that is, for the exarchy of the islands in it is already occupied.[2]

Despite Neale's droll scepticism, there is still an effort to engage with the nature of the office and the implications of its jurisdiction in his own context. At the other extreme, and perhaps a symptom of more contemporary sensitivities, is the tendency to downplay and dismiss the ecclesiological significance and even theological depth to which the ministry of primacy may attest and instead write it off as no more than benign organizational jargon for a senior functionary or, worse, tainted by the trappings of hierarchical grandiosity. The outworking of this is to relegate primacy to little more than a generic synonym for episcopal leadership with special responsibilities.

A study document prepared for the 2001 Primates' Meeting setting itself out as a 'reflection piece on the ministry of Primates in the Anglican Communion' focuses, in its historical introduction, almost entirely on early discernible patterns of episcopal ministry in the New Testament leading to a brief acknowledgement of the organization of the Early Church into provinces with metropolitans by the Council of Nicea in 325.[3] Discussion of primacy as it relates to the 'Anglican experience' is limited to a descriptive account of the *status quo*:

> With the growth of the Communion and the establishment of new Provinces, 'metropolitans' have come into being as Primates or Presiding Bishops. Not all of these primacies are attached to fixed sees (e.g. Wales and Scotland) and it is not everywhere that the Primate has a see as his own (cf. United States and Canada).[4]

It is perhaps somewhat unfair to criticise this paper too harshly for its brevity, it being prepared only as a discussion paper for the 2001 Primates' meeting intended no doubt to prompt further reflection by the Primates themselves. However, it does tend to conflate the concepts of metropolitical authority and primacy both in their historical development and in their present Anglican incarnation. For example, the paper explains that the 'title of 'primate' (prima sedes) was used originally of the metropolitans of a province.'[5] Not only is this statement factually incorrect, but it also confuses a number of different – albeit related – juridical questions.

Prima Sedes: Papal or Primatial?

The term *prima sedes* ('first see') is one which is overwhelmingly employed in the promotion of papal supremacy and, to this end, is found within the Roman Catholic Code of Canon Law. Canon 1404, heading the section of canons setting out the competent authorities for trials, contains the maxim *prima sedes a nemine iudicatur* – 'The First See is judged by no one.'[6] Even where *prima sedes* does not necessarily imply acceptance of papal primacy it is almost invariably used as a synonym for Rome, whether alongside the second and third sees of Alexandria and Antioch[7] or in defining the properly conciliar dynamic of the sees which constitute the Orthodox Pentarchy.[8] Where the term was employed in the Western Church, such as in rivalry between the primacies between Canterbury and York, it seems to have been an interpolation from the forged Pseudo-Isidorian texts.[9] Apart from this rather spurious precedent, along with some other isolated examples, the term is almost never used to refer to primacy as it developed in the Western Church.[10] The Agreed Statement of the tenth plenary session of the Joint International Commission for the Theological Dialogue between the Roman Catholic and the Orthodox Church, known as the 'Ravenna Document', articulates the commonalities between those two Communions in the development of ministerial seniority according to the language of *protos*, which operates in a conciliar context and across different jurisdictional boundaries:

> In the history of the East and of the West, at least until the ninth century, a series of prerogatives was recognised, always in the context of conciliarity, according to the conditions of the times, for the *protos* or *kephale* at each of the established ecclesiastical levels: locally, for the bishop as *protos* of his diocese with regard to his presbyters and people; regionally, for the *protos* of each metropolis with regard to the bishops of his province, and for the *protos* of each of the five patriarchates, with regard to the metropolitans of each circumscription; and universally, for the bishop of Rome as *protos* among the patriarchs. This distinction of levels does not diminish the sacramental equality of every bishop or the catholicity of each local Church.[11]

The most recent meeting of the Commission has produced a further text exploring the relationship between primacy and conciliarity which is principally concerned with the kind of primacy claimed by Rome for that see, the primacy of the *prima sedes*.[12] Apart from this sense, primacy as understood and employed within Anglicanism ought also to be distinguished from metropolitical jurisdiction and, unlike metropolitical authority and even patriarchal polity, it is a peculiarity of the Western Church only.[13] The medieval development of primacy exhibits a multifarious exercise of authority which, in some places, meant real powers of jurisdiction and, in others, only privileges of precedence and honour.

If we are to believe J.M. Neale's somewhat sceptical assessment as to its value, it was used chiefly as an instrument of papal control serving 'as one of the many steppingstones by which Rome attained to her present exaltation' presumably through the exchange of pre-eminence in dignity for fealty and loyalty.[14]

Primacy of Honour

The language of primacy from which we inherit contemporary ecclesiological assumptions and structures has its origins in the early codification during the fourth century of metropolitical and patriarchal prerogatives and precedence. The third canon of the first Council of Constantinople in 381 introduces the phrase πρεσβεῖα τῆς τιμῆς, commonly translated as 'primacy of honour', to describe the growing status of Constantinople in relation to Rome.[15] The subsequent interpretation and application of this 'terse sentence, tantalizing both in what it implies and in what it leaves unexplained,' has been a key sticking point in Roman Catholic and Orthodox relations.[16] However it has also infiltrated into Anglican ecclesial terminology, particularly in describing the ministry of the Archbishop of Canterbury, and in no small way continues to perpetuate the somewhat exalted but persistent myth of a Canterburian patriarchate.[17] This usage can be traced to the 1968 Lambeth Conference which, somewhat ironically, attempted to define the more limited parameters of the Archbishop of Canterbury's jurisdiction and thus lower the expectations of those that might look to him to be both Patriarch and Prophet:

> Within the college of bishops it is evident that there must be a president. In the Anglican Communion this position is at present held by the occupant of the historic See of Canterbury, who enjoys a primacy of honour, not of jurisdiction. This primacy is found to involve, in a particular way, that care of all the churches which is shared by all the bishops.[18]

Of course, whether a 'primacy of honour' stands as antithetical to one of jurisdiction is precisely the million-dollar ecumenical question which has caused such controversy between the East and West since the fourth century and its application within Anglicanism is no more settled. The Jesuit theologian and Patristics scholar, Brian Daley, has presented a careful and compelling study of the language of the canons of Constantinople and contemporary understandings of the nature of authority and power to argue that a 'primacy of honour' implies much more than a hollow dignity, and his concluding reflection – insofar as it might also speak to Anglicanism – is worth reproducing at length:

> Our difficulty, as modern Westerners, in grasping the full implications of the phrase 'primacy of honour' is mainly due, no doubt, to the fact that we live in societies in which honour and patronage are carefully distinguished – at least in theory – from the judicial and executive power that are defined by constitutions and realised in the impersonal func-tioning of bureaucracies . . . [However] these early councils, bishops and emperors were struggling to define a structure of Church authority that would *not* simply rest on the personal charisms of individuals, or exhaust itself in ceremony alone . . . they were attempting, in a rather daring way, to assure and confirm for both of them a position of emi-nent and coordinated power within the rapidly evolving institutional structures of the Christian Church. Whatever use the Churches make of this hoary phrase today, in their delicate ecumenical discussions and in their own internal theological and structural renewal, they must also take into account the very concrete ecclesiological implications of its original meaning. If either 'primacy' or 'honour' are to be genuine, they must still imply the ability to make a practical difference.[19]

This pivotal question of whether primacy involves more than merely elevated dignity and honour also underlies the development in the West during the eleventh and twelfth centuries of the distinct office of 'Primate'.

Primacy, the Pseudo-Isidorian Forgeries and the Rivalry between Canterbury and York

Recent work has been done to identify significant diversity in this devel-opment, which emerged out of both local claims to authority and power as well as from papal preferment which legitimized the 'confirmation of new and contested prerogatives, which were perceived none the less as immemorial.'[20] Not only did papal approval help secure the claims of these new 'Primates', but so too did their deference to Rome further strengthen the place of the papacy within the polity of the West. A signif-icant instrument in the validation of this mutually beneficial arrangement was the appropriation of supposed ancient precedent, particularly the Pseudo-Isidorian 'False Decretals', by which were employed:

> . . . strategies which mobilised the distant past as a source of legitimacy for a superior power . . . Certain forgeries of Pseudo-Isidore, ascribed

to the earliest popes, conceived of the existence of primates ('primates', 'primae sedis episcopli') equated with patriarchs and holders of a hierarchical grade interposed between the metropolitans and the supreme pontiff.[21]

That these authorities have long since been discredited has not dampened the enthusiasm, at least within Anglicanism, to not only set up primacy as a keystone of ecclesial polity but also to presume that it possesses an unquestionable pedigree that stretches back to the definitive and almost mythical norms of the Early Church. From the study of the development of primacies in England, the Iberian Peninsula, Ireland and Gaul, Fabrice Delivré has charted a 'typology of supra-metropolitan primacies' which all rely on the weight of cherished, and often embellished, tradition to establish a kind of 'soft power' whereby authority is both claimed and exercised in delicate negotiation with the cultural and historical associations which give them legitimacy.[22]

Some exploration of the development of primacy in England, including the typically Anglican 'fudge' in resolving the rivalry between the primacies of Canterbury and York that they be styled Primates of 'All England' and 'England' respectively, is sufficient here to illustrate the exercise of this kind of negotiated 'soft power'. Pope Gregory the Great's original design for the Augustinian mission to Britain was that there would be two provinces in England with the primatial sees to eventually be centred on London and York. Augustine was to exercise metropolitical authority over both provinces from Canterbury until his death; after which Gregory intended to send the pallium to both York and London respectively, thus establishing their independence from each other.[23] Gregory and Augustine died in 604 and Paulinus was not consecrated Bishop of York until 625. Following the collapse of political support for Christianity after King Edwin's death, Paulinus escaped southwards where he was made bishop of Rochester. The pallium which was sent to him, therefore, arrived too late and northern England came under the influence of Celtic Christianity centred at Lindisfarne.[24]

The bishopric at York was re-established after some interval; however the pallium was not again bestowed until Egbert became bishop of that see in 734.[25] Meanwhile, the southern province was experiencing a time of prosperous growth and Canterbury continued to maintain a primacy in practice, if not strictly legitimate, over both provinces.[26]

In this way were sown the seeds of a rivalry and struggle for primacy which was not finally settled until the fourteenth century. The question came to a head following the Norman Conquest when the newly appointed Archbishop of York, Thomas, approached his fellow Norman counterpart at Canterbury, Lanfranc, requesting consecration at his hands. Lanfranc agreed but stipulated that first Thomas must swear obedience to Canterbury, claiming this to be well established custom, but which Thomas disputed:

> This demand – unheard of, according to contemporaries – provoked a lively polemic before Pope Alexander II and in assemblies of English bishops and abbots. The result, favourable to Canterbury, coincided with the first instances of the use of the title of primate of Britain.[27]

Lanfranc, taking advantage of the weakened northern province which Thomas had inherited, had strong political motivations for asserting his claim; establishing a unified national platform for civil and religious reform in the post-Conquest kingdom.[28] It was not surprising then that William I backed Canterbury's claim against York, and Thomas reluctantly (and even, it is suggested, tearfully) agreed to make a verbal, though not written, oath of obedience to Lanfranc with the only concession that it did not extend to his successors.[29]

Attempts to have the matter settled by Rome were referred back to the English bishops to be settled internally, whereupon a council was called at Winchester in 1076 with Thomas relying entirely on Gregory's initial mandate given to Augustine, and those supporting the Canterbury cause placing their trust in the *Collectio Lanfranci*, excerpts from the Pseudo-Isidorian 'False Decretals', to substantiate Lanfranc's claim.[30] William of Malmesbury records Lanfranc's evidence to the council and gives an account of the judgement, which sides in eventual favour of a Canterbury supremacy:

> . . . Lanfranc put an end to the discussion, meeting him with this most wary answer: 'The view on which you rely needs substantiation in asserting that to Augustine alone was granted the submission of all the bishops of Britain, and even of those who had been consecrated by the Bishop of York. That would have been a very poor and trifling gift bestowed by the pope on his old friend, this new Englishman; especially when the Archbishop of York consecrated none who should be subject to Augustine in his lifetime, as there was no bishop there at all . . . Knowing this, the supreme pontiffs have confirmed to the successors of Augustine the submission of all the bishops of England . . . Now they hold that all the Churches of the English should borrow the discipline of life from that place from whose fire they caught the flame of faith . . . The result is, that as Canterbury is subject to Rome, because it received the faith thence, so York is subject to Canterbury which sent preachers thither.'[31]

The decision at Winchester seemed to settle the question; although successive Archbishops at York continued to resist making an oath of obedience, some more successfully than others, with frequent papal appeals being made but with little definitive clarity emerging until the mid-fourteenth century.[32] By this time the sticking points of the dispute centred not so much on archiepiscopal jurisdiction but rather on the honours associated with primacy: namely, the privilege of conducting coronations; negotiating places of honour in the presence of the monarch; and the seemingly trivial, yet vehemently contested, right of each Archbishop to process within each other's province with their own metropolitical cross preceding.[33]

These disputes were finally resolved in 1352 whereby the honour of the Archbishop of York was upheld in his being styled 'Primate of England', but nevertheless a deference made to Canterbury as 'Primate of All England'. Each was allowed to bear their metropolitical cross in front in each other's province; albeit when the narrowness of the path necessitated a clash or confrontation it would be the cross of York which would give way to Canterbury.[34] Where the wideness of the path allowed, however, each was to process equally abreast: the *via media* of Anglicanism exhibits itself long before either Cranmer's 'mean-between-extremes' or Hooker's 'three-legged-stool'.[35] The resolution of the dispute might well be said to represent something of a characteristic Anglican 'fudge', as the very real problems of competing jurisdictions are reduced to a squabble over privileges and precedence, and its resolution is one that panders more to the latter set of concerns than the former.[36]

Primates with Power and the Notitia Galliarum

Outside England, there were more substantial features of primatial authority which did em erge, such as the hearing of appeals and the prerogative of visitation, and these moves reflect an attempt to invest the office of Primate with more than mere honorific authority. The most influential 'proofs' for the establishment of these norms, centred particularly on the primacy of Lyon, was the 'catalogue of cities' which made up the *Notitia Galliarum*, an early fifth-century text setting out the administrative hierarchy of the Gallic provinces within the late Roman Empire and, employed during the Middle Ages to establish an ecclesiastical equivalency, was 'held to be a list of bishoprics instituted by the first popes, in continuity with the pagan *divisio provinciarum*.'[37] The influence of the *Notitia* in establishing primacies of jurisdiction as well as precedence was most notable in Lyon, Narbonne, Bourges and Vienne.[38]

What emerged were two very different expressions and understandings of primatial authority within the wider polity of the Western Church, each bearing familiar marks of dignity and honour in their appearance but behind which lay different assumptions regarding the providence of their legitimacy as well as their relationship with the local contexts from which they had evolved:

> But superficial similarities – the use of the primatial title and the privilege of cross bearing – should not be allowed to conceal the great diversity of detail . . . The primates of England, Spain and Ireland, heirs to long traditions of pre-eminence, did not succeed in going beyond honorial precedence. The obedience of the metropolitans, really considered and partially applied, was not admitted in these regions. Debate concentrated more on the crowning of sovereigns and the presidency of clerical assemblies . . . the *Notitia galliarum* offered, on the contrary, an opportunity to develop a genuine superior jurisdiction ('ius primatus, ius primatie') – summoning to council, right of visitation and reception of appeals – where the metropolitan became, in a certain sense, the primate's suffragan.[39]

The Problematic Appropriation of Primacy within Anglicanism

Whether primacy involves any kind of tangible juridical authority or whether it simply denotes an honorific precedence to the bearer of the office remains the central question in contemporary Anglican discussion of this contested concept. Even the term's etymology confuses the issues involved: while clearly related to the Latin *primus*, too much over-identification with ecclesiologically, and ecumenically, loaded phrases such as *prima sedes* and 'primacy of honour' introduce further complications in the discernment of its nature. A case for primacy as the 'first see' may well be made for the primacy of Canterbury, although casting Canterbury as the 'sower' from which the seeds of the Communion have been cast is not only historically anomalous but also incongruous with the developing appreciation, sensitive to post-colonial concerns, for how Anglicanism has been at least equally impacted by the local ground in which the seed has been planted. In any case, considered chronologically, the primatial see is not always the 'first see'.[40]

Furthermore, the Anglican appropriation of the term *prima sedes* is ecumenically problematic because of its far more widespread association with the see of Rome, which incidentally makes it much more agreeable to a grossly simplified 'branch theory' of Anglicanism coloured by a certain colonialist tint: first Rome, from which – through the missionary efforts of Augustine and the reassertion of Roman influence in the 'barbarian' territories – comes Canterbury, from which – through various missionary endeavours and the expansion of the British Empire – comes the Communion. Qualifying the primatial office, and particularly that of the Archbishop of Canterbury, as a 'primacy of honour' similarly imports a key disagreement between the Eastern and Western churches into questions of intra-Anglican polity and authority, as if they weren't complex enough: today's troubles are enough for today!

While metropolitical and primatial authority are ecclesiologically distinct, within Anglicanism they have fused to become largely synonymous through the influence of a 'national church' polity which has seen each province provided with a Primate. Furthermore, the Anglican axiom of 'provincial autonomy' has meant that the primatial office has come to personify the sovereignty of the national church, regardless of the dynamics of each province's internal polity. While there remain multi-province national-churches where the office of Primate and Metropolitan are discrete and can be distinguished, for the majority of member-churches of the Communion the two terms are better understood to denote two aspects of traditional metropolitical authority and jurisdiction: metropolitan referring to the role of the pre-eminent bishop within the polity of that church, a role which is largely well defined by constitutional documents and canon law, whereas primacy representing its less well defined international, relational and inter-provincial dimension. The limits and character of this latter dimension are still being worked out, principally through the semi-regular 'Primates' Meeting' which was instigated in 1979 but traces its conception back to the reconstitution of the Lambeth Consultative Body at the 1958 Lambeth Conference.

This role of the Primates' Meetings in defining the relational and international nature of metropolitical authority within the Communion shall be further explored with some brief notes relating to the nature of the meetings themselves and their origins in the Lambeth Consultative Body. This is followed by an account of the first meetings of the late 1970s and early 1980s and their purposeful discernment of what the role of primacy might be in the increasingly globalized Communion. Attention will be given to how this developing understanding was brought sharply into focus and articulated during a period of tension at the turn of the twenty-first century between 2000 and 2004 and, finally, how this has been given renewed expression at the 2016 meeting of Primates in Canterbury. Examination of the place of primacy within the Communion is critical for adequately understanding and reimagining metropolitical authority within Anglicanism as it particularly embodies its relational and inter-provincial aspects and offers a way through the roadblock of provincial autonomy within a multi-provincial polity which purports to be a global 'Communion'

Notes

1 W. Palmer 1838, 2:365. Palmer's two volume 'Treatise on the Church of Christ', setting out the 'Branch Theory' which would preoccupy Anglo-Catholic ecclesiology, is itself an example.

2 Neale 1863, 289–90.

3 Dyer 2001, 2.

4 Dyer 2001, 3.

5 Dyer 2001, 3.

6 Canon 1404, 'Roman Catholic Code of Canon Law' 2016. Official Latin and English translation given.

7 'Chapter 3: Roman Primacy and the Legal Vindication of Reform' in Cushing 1998, n. 36.

8 Phidas 2006, 75–76.

9 Delivré 2008, 387.

10 Such examples include the styling of the Archbishop of Lyon's primacy as prima sedes Galliarium, 'Chief See of Gaul', see Benson 1968, 335; the term was also used in 1900 by the Archbishop of Sydney at the third General Synod of the Church of England in Australia and Tasmania in reference to the location of the primacy at the prima sedes of the Diocese of Sydney, see S. Smith 1900, 5.

11 Joint International Commission for the Theological Dialogue between the Roman Catholic Church and the Orthodox Church 2007, para. 44.

12 Joint International Commission for the Theological Dialogue between the Roman Catholic Church and the Orthodox Church 2016.

13 Although, as J.M. Neale notes, it has its parallel in the equally elaborate honorifics of the Eastern Church.

14 Neale 1863, 288.

15 Tanner 1990, 32. The English translation given in Tanner's volume prefers the perhaps more literal 'privileges of honour'; however, 'primacy of honour' is employed far more frequently; a common translation of the full canon reads 'The Bishop of Constantinople shall have the primacy of honour after the Bishop of Rome, because Constantinople is new Rome.' See Stevenson and Frend 1989, 117.

16 Daley 1993, 529.

17 Fabrice Delivré explains that the origins of this can be traced to William of Malmesbury's *Gesta pontificum* which depends upon the spurious claim of the forged Pseudo-Isidorian second decretal of Anacletus that *'patriarchas vel primates qui unam formam tenent, licet diversa sint nomina* – [elevating] thereby the bishop of the 'first see' of Canterbury to the rank of primate and patriarch of all England.' See Delivré 2008, 387.

18 Lambeth Conference 1968, 137; this styling has been echoed repeatedly since, most influentially in the 1998 Virginia Report (Para 3:13), the 2004 Windsor Report (Footnote 55 - where extraordinarily it attributes its genesis to Thomas

Cranmer), the Anglican Communion Covenant (Section 3.1.4), and was used recently by Lambeth Palace to describe the role of Justin Welby upon his confirmation as Archbishop, see Lambeth Palace: Press Release 2013.

19 Daley 1993, 552–53.

20 Delivré 2008, 383.

21 Delivré 2008, 384.

22 Delivré 2008, 384.

23 Delivré 2008, 393.

24 R. Shaw 2016, 484.

25 Reynolds 1995, 597.

26 The increase in Canterbury's profile may well have been attributed to the particular understanding of metropolitical authority which Theodore brought with him, 'as a Greek, brought up at Tarsus in the patriarchate of Antioch, he was from an ecclesiastical culture which had a maximal view of the role of metropolitans and from the start he was keen to enhance Canterbury's position.' See Thacker 2008, 56.

27 Delivré 2008, 385.

28 Cowdrey 2003, 88.

29 Tindal Hart 1986, 17.

30 Delivré 2008, 385.

31 Gee and Hardy 1896, 55.

32 For an account of York's victory over Canterbury in the dispute of the 1120s between William of Corbeil and Thurstan, Archbishop of York, see Bethell 1968.

33 Makower 1895, 289.

34 Tindal Hart 1986, 24.

35 It is perhaps telling that neither of these Anglican maxims originated directly from the writings of Cranmer or Hooker, but were instead attributed to them by later reflection on Anglican identity, as the myth of the *via media* was born. The nature of the settlement of the primacy between Canterbury and York demonstrates something of this myth-making in the Anglican psyche.

36 The dispute between Canterbury and York has been colourfully likened to 'when two children cry for the same apple, the indulgent father divides it betwixt them; yet so that he giveth the bigger and better part to the child that is his darling." See, Fuller 1837, 321.

37 Delivré 2008, 400.

38 Delivré 2008, 401.

39 Delivré 2008, 405–6.

40 Inter-Anglican Standing Commission on Unity, Faith and Order 2012, para. 4.1.4.

7

'Leisurely thought, prayer and deep consultation': The Primates' Meetings

I do not think there is a quick or easy answer to the question, 'Where is Authority to be found?' Nor do I think it is of the genius of Anglicanism to define too rigidly, though there is always on the part of some of us, a craving for rigid neatness. But I am coming to believe that the way forward in the coming years – and it may be a slow process – will be along two lines: first, to have meetings of the Primates of the Communion reasonably often, for leisurely thought, prayer and deep consultation . . . The second line, I think, on which we might make progress would be to see that the body of Primates, as they meet, should be in the very closest and most intimate contact with the ACC.

Archbishop Donald Coggan on
'Authority in the Anglican Communion'.[1]

Donald Coggan's conception of regular Primates' Meetings as a forum for 'leisurely thought, prayer and deep consultation' was nothing new, nor did it mark out a particularly radical path in the development of Anglican polity. Nevertheless, his threefold aspiration for the tone of those meetings has now become not only somewhat axiomatic but also representative of the contested nature of the Primates' Meetings as they have been pressed into service by those who would imagine them as little more than convivial fellowship.[2] Coggan's remarks also suggest something of a tension with the Anglican Consultative Council in that he should make so explicit his desire that they work productively and equally with the Primates. This tension has characterized the somewhat uneasy relationship between the two up to the present day.

The Primates' Meetings and the Anglican Consultative Council: an Uneasy Relationship

In 1986 a small working group convened by the Archbishop of Armagh, Robin Eames, was commissioned by the Standing Committee of the ACC to explore structures of intra-Anglican co-operation, with a particular focus on assessing the viability of drawing up and adopting a constitutional document for the Anglican Communion; a process which, in the questions it asked around authority in the Communion, prefigures the attempts of the Lambeth Commission on Communion two decades later, of which Eames was also Chair, to propose an Anglican Communion Covenant.[3] A paper presented to that group, written by the then Vice-Chair of the ACC Standing Committee Canon Colin Craston, notes the widely held perception that the Primates' Meeting was intended, at least in part, as a check on the growing influence of the Anglican Consultative Council:

> Two further and similar matters demand scrutiny. They are the relationship of the ACC with the Primates' Meeting and with the Lambeth conference. John Howe admits that the purpose of the Primates' Meeting, recommended by Lambeth '78, was not wholly clear, but "basically it was advisory to the Archbishop of Canterbury". The perception remains, however, that *it was a response by Lambeth to the threat of a too powerful ACC* — a meeting of bishops every ten years did not sufficiently balance a synodical gathering every two or three. A gathering of all the Primates for mutual support and to advise the Archbishop of Canterbury – as recommended by the 1978 survey done for Archbishop Coggan – is one thing, a meeting of Primates to provide a sort of episcopal House for the Communion relating to and balancing the ACC is something different.[4]

This tension between the Primates and the Anglican Consultative Council has its roots in the two antecedent bodies, the Advisory Council on Missionary Strategy and the Lambeth Consultative Body, which existed until 1968 when they were abolished to make way for the current Anglican Consultative Council.[5] While the Advisory Council on Missionary Strategy allowed for some limited non-episcopal representation, foreshadowing the inclusion of laity, clergy and bishops at the Anglican Consultative Council, the Lambeth Consultative Body was in many ways a direct predecessor to the current Primates' Meetings.

Although established at the end of the nineteenth century as a kind of 'standing committee' for the continuation of business between Lambeth

Conferences, the Lambeth Consultative Body was reconstituted in 1958 during that year's Lambeth Conference. On the second day of that Conference, on the 4th July, a 'Meeting of Primates' was held in the Small Dining Room of Lambeth Palace, with the Archbishop of Canterbury presiding. Among a number of other items of business, the constitution of both the Advisory Council and Consultative Body was discussed and it was noted that 'both of which bodies as at present constituted could not work with efficiency.'[6] A month later a 'Meeting of Metropolitans' was held, the Archbishop of Canterbury again in the chair, at which it was proposed and decided (with the support of the Advisory Council) to replace Resolution 50 of the 1930 Lambeth Conference, which set forth the nature and functions of the Consultative Body, with a revised resolution.[7]

The new resolution largely follows the wording of the original. However, the most significant change is that an additional mandate is given to the Consultative Body to 'take such action in the discharge of the above duties, as may be appropriate, subject to the condition that with regard to churches, provinces and dioceses of the Anglican Communion its functions are advisory only and without executive or administrative power.'[8] The age-old Anglican aversion to centralisation as opposed to autonomy is evident in the proviso, but there is still an effort to invest the Body with authority, or at least transfer a delegated authority, from the Lambeth Conference itself.

The other significant change was that, whereas previously the Consultative Body comprised eighteen members chosen by the Archbishop of Canterbury, 'with due regard to regional requirements, after consultation with the metropolitans and presiding bishops,' its membership was fixed to the 'Primates or Presiding Bishops' themselves. It was further proposed that each member be given the right to nominate an alternate, 'clerical or lay,' at meetings but this was changed in the eventual resolution to allow only bishops to be nominated as alternates.[9] The Advisory Council on Missionary Strategy was also similarly restructured to include all those on the Lambeth Consultative Body as well as all other metropolitans, which at the time included the Archbishops of Algoma, Montreal, British Columbia, Brisbane, Perth and Melbourne as well as the eight Presidents of the PECUSA 'provinces'. Alternates needed not be bishops.[10]

The Legacy of the Lambeth Consultative Body Reconsidered

A reflection paper on the nature of the Primates' Meetings and their genesis in the Lambeth Consultative Body was prepared for the Secretary General of the Anglican Consultative Council, Sam Van Culin, by the Primus of the Scottish Episcopal Church, Alastair Haggart, and itself reflects what has become a prevailing sentiment that not only was the link between the Consultative Body and Primates' Meetings fairly tenuous, but that their business was also incomparable, the former being restricted largely to a planning and continuation committee of the Lambeth Conference while the latter has much greater remit and scope:

> I suppose the origin of the Primates' Meetings lies in the Lambeth Consultative Body, which was a vaguely defined body that met infrequently, the last occasion being in Jerusalem in 1966 when a meeting of about eighteen senior bishops from various parts of the Anglican world met to prepare for the 1968 Lambeth Conference. This body no longer existed at the lead up to the 1978 Lambeth Conference. Instead the question of whether there should be a Conference or not was discussed at the ACC Meeting in Trinidad in 1976, and the then Archbishop of Canterbury, on the advice of the Council, took the decision to have a Residential Conference in 1978, and it was at the 1978 Lambeth Conference that what was then called the Primates' Committee came into existence. The name, not through any deliberate decision, but by use and wont, has been changed to Primates' Meetings. Perhaps "Meetings" reflects the more personal, less formal style than "Committee" would suggest.[11]

However, while its momentum might have slowed toward the end of the 1960s, from its early inception the Lambeth Consultative Body met relatively frequently. In fact it met four times in six years – in 1963, 1964, 1966 and 1968 – which is a frequency not matched by the Primates' Meetings until their unprecedented regularity between 2000 and 2011. The business of the meetings of Primates and metropolitans through the Lambeth Consultative Body was also not merely confined to planning for Lambeth Conferences, or implementing previous Conference resolutions. The meeting of 1963, for example, spanned three days and covered topics as diverse as the constitution of bishops and ecumenical engagement at the Lambeth Conferences, growing moves toward full communion with other Reformation churches in the 'Wider Episcopal Fellowship', Church Union in Nigeria, constitutional amendments in Central Africa, the establishment of regional councils, and the future of St Augustine's College, Canterbury and the Jerusalem Archbishopric.[12] The establishment in 1968 of the Anglican Consultative Council eclipsed this emphasis on structures of formal primatial and metropolitical fellowship until it was reintroduced a decade later in the now familiar Primates' Meetings. Nevertheless, the Primates' Meetings were nothing new and far from codifying and formalising irregular and ad hoc attempts to draw the Primates and Metropolitans together, this had been happening in a structured and systematic way for the past twenty years. In fact, as the Primus of Scotland's comments reveal, there is a tension as to whether the Primates' Meetings were an attempt to escalate or deescalate the formal authority which the meetings themselves might have, and this is evident through the contrast between Coggan's call for 'leisurely thought, prayer and deep consultation,' or at least that phrase's common interpretation, and the mandate given to the Primates at the 1978 Lambeth Conference.

The Early Primates' Meetings

The first of the Primates' Meetings is commonly taken to have been held in Ely, England in 1979, following its formal recommendation at the 1978 Lambeth Conference.[13] The resolutions of that Conference also demonstrate a significant weight of authority being shifted to the Primates for collegiate determination or at least consultation, particularly in matters of ecumenical or inter-Anglican significance. For example, Resolution 11 of that Conference offers a broad-brush recommendation to member churches not to:

> . . . take action regarding issues which are of concern to the whole Anglican Communion without consultation with a Lambeth Conference or with the episcopate through the Primates Committee, and requests the Primates to initiate a study of the nature of authority within the Anglican Communion.[14]

Following this, further resolutions recommend the Primates have a direct role in consultation with the Archbishop of Canterbury concerning the calling of the Lambeth Conference, with a particular emphasis on ensuring 'the guardianship of the faith may be exercised as a collegial responsibility of the whole episcopate' (Res. 13), as well as promoting the fuller expression of communion among the 'Wider Episcopal Fellowship' (Res. 14). Decisions within member churches regarding the consecration of women to the episcopate are to be referred to the Primates for consultation (Res. 22), and – in the only example of partnership with the Anglican Consultative Council – the Primates are also to advise in the establishment of an inter-Anglican doctrinal commission (Res. 25).

Between this Lambeth Conference and the last meeting of the Lambeth Consultative Body, there had also been two other meetings of Primates:

one in 1975 and another in 1978. The meeting in 1975 was initiated particularly with the encouragement of the Presiding Bishop of the Episcopal Church of the United States of America, John Allin, and intended to coincide with the meeting of the World Council of Churches in Nairobi in November.[15] Since the 1968 Lambeth Conference there had been a significant turnover in the composition of the Primates, with all except one being new, and much of the impetus for the meeting was the 'widespread feeling that few of them have the chance to know one another as people and personal friends.'[16] The nature of the gathering as an informal meeting is repeatedly stressed in both the preparatory materials and also the concluding statement:

> The gathering had no agenda. Its purpose was to enable leaders of the Churches to know one another better, to pray together, and to share thoughts, experiences and problems. They decided to meet sometimes together and sometimes individually as they wished.[17]

Despite its informality and apparent lack of agenda, there were two items of business proposed by John Howe which particularly engaged the Primates: '1. The shape of the Anglican Communion with special reference to the co-ordination and communication within it, and, 2. Its structure, the Lambeth Conference and the Anglican Consultative Council.'[18] Although no minutes of the meeting were kept, a valuable record survives in the report of the Australian Primate, Frank Woods, to his compatriot bishops. Along with valuable insights on the personal contribution each of the Primates made to the discussion, in which he highlights particularly the input of Ted Scott of Canada and John Allin of The Episcopal Church, he summarizes the consensus reached on the two topics of discussion proposed by John Howe:

> We ranged far and wide over these subjects and reached eventually a consensus of opinion:
> a) That we don't want anything in the nature of a central bureaucracy, such as either the Vatican or as the World Baptist Alliance, but that we do want better co-ordination and communication and are beginning to get it through the Anglican Consultative Council.
> b) The very existence of the Anglican Consultative Council put a question mark against the value of Lambeth Conferences. Furthermore, the great increase in the participation by the laity in all aspects of church life since the last Lambeth Conference is bound to bring criticism of a Conference of Bishops only. If the said Bishops are to make decision for the Anglican Communion, then the priests and laity ought

to be associated with them. If they are not to make such decisions, is the enormous cost in time and money of such a Conference justified? Eventually a consensus was reached that a Lambeth Conference should be held of not more than about 250 Bishops, that the preparation of documents beforehand which would be discussed in Provinces and would enable the Bishops to come to the Conference with the backing of their people behind them, and with proposals from those same people. It was agreed that the Conference should be held in 1978, that it should be wholly residential, and that the Anglican Consultative Council should hold its meeting either just before or just afterwards.[19]

This meeting of Primates was followed by a further meeting in January 1978, over four days, of a small group personally selected by the Archbishop of Canterbury: Ted Scott of Canada, Allen Johnston of New Zealand, Festo Olang' of Kenya and, on the nomination of and representing Arthur Kratz of Brazil who was unable to be present, Bill Flagg the former president of the Anglican Council of South America.[20] The purpose of the meeting was essentially to be a sounding-board for the Archbishop of Canterbury in his own preparations for the upcoming Lambeth Conference, and the minutes of the meeting record this somewhat hazy dual purpose 'to take a steady look at the Lambeth Conference,' and 'to consider the direction and development of the whole Anglican Communion.'[21] At that meeting it was proposed that a 'steering committee' of Primates meet throughout the Lambeth Conference to 'provide a means of keeping the pulse of the conference with each Primate being asked to keep in touch with the Bishops from his Province and report on their concerns.'[22] This committee did indeed meet during the 1978 Conference and provides another precursor to the 1979 meeting at Ely.[23]

During what is taken to be the inaugural meeting of the Primates' proper at Ely in 1979, the question of what the nature and character of the gatherings might be was again raised with some reflection on how a ministry of primacy might be expressed within Anglicanism. Although the meeting again reaffirmed its intention that it 'could not be, and was not desired as, a higher synod' nevertheless it had evidently abandoned the pretence of informality, with an agenda of seventeen items ranging from the *filioque* to women priests.[24] Nevertheless, the minutes do reflect an apparent range of opinion regarding the nature of authority itself and particularly how it might be expressed through primacy:

There was an apparent diversity of ideas about authority, and a beginning of consideration of that subject was made later in the Meeting . . .

It was agreed that generally Primates were expected to exercise some leadership, but that was not of an identical kind everywhere; the expectation tended to be for something more positive in the Third World, and more diplomatic in the West.

The personal and charismatic roles characterizing Anglican primacy were seen to be important, and intrinsic. On the one hand a primate had a personal relationship with his Church and people's problems such as a synod could not have; on the other hand the relationship between the heads of Churches and the Archbishop of Canterbury was what held the Anglican Communion together.[25]

The Primates certainly don't overreach themselves in accepting that they might be 'expected to exercise some leadership,' but do at least acknowledge that this involves a mediating role both within their provinces as well as amongst themselves and with Canterbury as a personal expression of corporate communion. The minutes relating to discussion of authority, while not reflecting a consensus, do record a frustration at the lack of clarity concerning Anglican articulations of authority, a resistance to any kind of centralisation or 'individual headship' with explicit allusions to the Vatican and Pope, as well as the presumption of a somewhat 'top down' process of discernment and reception which, in light of almost all historical and contemporary doctrinal and ecclesiological shifts and innovations, is defensible perhaps more as theory than in practice:

The theory underlying present Anglican procedure was that on major matters the whole family, through its representatives – as for example through a Lambeth Conference or an Anglican Consultative Council meeting – conferred together; and then, in the light of that conferring, and of local history and culture, each Province through its Synod enacted what Canon Law was required.[26]

This account of the beginnings of the Primates' Meetings, and their antecedent in the Lambeth Consultative Body, demonstrates that meetings of Primates, or more widely of metropolitans, is nothing particularly new or innovative in the development of Anglican polity. Furthermore, the meetings of Primates through the Lambeth Consultative Body were both frequent and formalised, with a wide-ranging agenda, contrary to their characterization as somewhat haphazard and limited in scope. After the 1968 Lambeth Conference, efforts of inter-Anglican consultation and cooperation were channelled through the newly established Anglican Consultative Council which promised a new kind of conciliarity modelled on the synodical government which had become a common feature of the internal ordering of Anglican dioceses and provinces. However, the advent of the Consultative Council and its seeming supersession of the other forums for international Anglican engagement brought tension, not least with regard to the place of the episcopate and the metropolitans and Primates in particular. Notes made by John Howe following the 1975 meeting of Primates at Nairobi reveal this tension, when he includes the telling comment 'it is necessary to realise that the ACC is a reality – it exists' and that 'the old form of the episcopal 'special place' has gone for ever.'[27] The mood had changed by the end of the 1970s when – despite its doubtful future after 1968 – the Lambeth Conference met again.[28] The begrudging acknowledgement of the place of the Consultative Council in the new order of Anglican polity marks an ecclesiological shift which, as contemporary tensions between the Primates and the Anglican Consultative Council and the enduring relevance of the Lambeth Conferences attest, has never been entirely resolved. Nevertheless, there is no doubt that throughout the deliberations of the Lambeth Consultative Body, in the first instance, and the formally constituted Primates' Meetings which succeeded it, a resistance within international Anglican polity to centralisation or coercive jurisdiction is explicitly and consistently articulated. However, despite these protestations, there is an increasing sense, for example through the mandate given to the Primates at the 1978 Lambeth Conference, that the primatial ministry within the Communion is to mean something tangible and authoritative and that their meetings ought to at least address, if not accomplish, more than the extension of personal and friendly relationships.

Collective Primacy: Conciliarity and Collegiality

The exercise of metropolitical authority, and the design of provincial polity within the Church, involves a twofold focus that is in both respects inherently relational: the place of the metropolitan within the province, governed generally but variously through written constitutions and codified in canon law, and the witness to 'communion' that the metropolitan makes in their supra-provincial relationships. This second aspect of metropolitical authority is even less defined than the first but the Anglican attempt to sketch its characteristics and boundaries may be discerned through the developing self-understanding of the Primates. At the heart of this development and discernment lies the vexed question of what is the nature of 'authority' within Anglicanism and where might it be found?

While too broad for the purposes of this study, this question has been explored valuably elsewhere.[29] Nevertheless, with regard to the particular nature of metropolitical authority as exercised by the Primates, the key question is 'whether moral authority is real authority?'[30] Whereas the more closely defined powers and privileges which together constitute the nature of authority within provinces may be relatively easily identified, the authority claimed by inter-Anglican bodies such as the Primates or, as is equally controversial, the Lambeth Conferences, depends instead on their reception by the wider church, on the one hand, and, on the other, of the appropriate regard for an acknowledged, yet often neglected, authority which is implicit in the office of the episcopate.[31]

This dual emphasis within metropolitical authority is matched more widely by a balance within an Anglican polity that is 'constructed from a combination of primacy and conciliarity.'[32] This construction is identifiable chiefly in the relationship between bishops and their synods, but also may be discerned through the tensions already discussed between the Primates and the Anglican Consultative Council. Philip Thomas argues that this partnership, and the creative tension it generates, results in a multi-faceted primacy that speaks authoritatively only through the symphony of its voices rather than in unanimity:

> Anglicans do not hear the last word from any one office or agency, but from the way in which revelation and history and prayer and leadership converge on particular issues in such a way as to gain the consent of their faith community. The function of primacy is exercised by all the sources of authority collectively.[33]

This 'collective primacy' is one expression of the 'dispersed' authority so often attributed to Anglicanism: the 'conviction that wholeness of vision is achieved through the convergence of many parts.'[34] It also counters the intensive emphasis on the personal and charismatic authority of individual office-bearers which is a prerequisite for the healthy balancing of the *auctoritas* and the *imperium*. The evolution of this convergence throughout Anglican history has tended against creating clear lines of authority or sketching any single recognizable corporate identity:

> Nearly 150 years of history makes it plain that the Anglican Communion is not to be understood in terms of strict hierarchy – Lambeth, shareholders; ACC, non-executive directors; Primates, Board of Governors; leaving the Archbishop of Canterbury hovering uncertainly between the role of Managing Director and a Colonel Sanders-like symbol of brand-loyalty.[35]

However, the exercise of a collective primacy which does not execute authority itself but rather gathers together the corporate discernment of what might be deemed authoritative within the faith community sits uneasily alongside a recent and increasing trend that the 'Primates' Meeting' is more and more coming to resemble a 'Board of Governors'.

'The Anglican Communion: Identity and Authority': The Rise of the Primates

The development of this trend escalated in the decade following the 2000 Oporto Primates' Meeting, and most recently may be seen in the January 2016 Canterbury meeting; however its early beginnings may be traced to the 1988 Lambeth Conference and subsequent meeting of the Primates together with the ACC Standing Committee in 1989. In particular, it was articulated in a document presented jointly by the 1989 Cyprus Primates' Meeting together with the Standing Committee of the Consultative Council, based upon the mandate of Resolutions 52 and 18 of the 1988 Lambeth Conference.[36] That document, 'The Anglican Communion: Identity and Authority', sets itself out as 'a basis of consultation between the two bodies [the Primates' Meeting and the ACC] from now on.'[37] Specifically, it speaks of the 'developing role' of the Primates' Meeting in terms of its exercise of collegiality, 'to be to the Church at large a sign and symbol of collegiality in both mutual care, encouragement and support in the One Body of Christ . . . in offering guidance on doctrinal, moral and pastoral matters.'[38] The document essentially describes the relationship between the Primates and the Anglican Consultative Council as that of 'executive', with the Primates exercising 'leadership in the Communion's response' to challenges, and 'secretariat', leaving 'much of the practical outworkings' to the 'work-horse' of the Anglican Consultative Council.[39]

A number of critical responses to the document were received, along with a substantial paper in response prepared by Mary Tanner of the Church of England's Board for Mission and Unity. A comprehensive response was also made by the Anglican Church of Australia.[40] The collected responses demonstrate a considerable level of discontent with the functioning of the Consultative Council, including the extraordinary claim that 'it originated when there were thoughts of introducing a legislative function into the Anglican Communion . . . Since the structures of the Anglican Communion have remained purely consultative, it has never had a definable role, and should perhaps now be disbanded.'[41] However, the response from the Anglican Church of Australia reflects what seems to be a widely held dissatisfaction with the nature of representation at the

Consultative Council. It is described in one submission from the Diocese of Perth as 'the unrepresenting Anglican Consultative Council' and separate submissions from the Archbishop of Adelaide and the Diocese of Melbourne note its 'necessarily unrepresentative' character given the size of representation allowed to each province.[42]

In defence of the continuing relevance of the Anglican Consultative Council in the life of the Communion, a significant critique of 'Identity and Authority' is offered by the then outgoing delegate from Australia, and later Archbishop of Adelaide, Ian George, in a letter to ACC Secretary General Sam Van Culin. George laments what he considers to be an ecclesiological shift toward the Primates and away from the Anglican Consultative Council, 'which I believe is in the process of signing its own death warrant.'[43] George takes issue with the Primates together being described as a 'sign and symbol of collegiality,' which he considers an overstepping of their primary purpose offering 'mutual care, encouragement and support.' Collegiality, he rightly points out, within ecclesiology 'is only relevant to the exercise of authority.'[44]

The particular association of the Primates' Meetings with the exercise of episcopal collegiality formed part of the preparatory work undertaken by the working group commissioned to lead the 'Dogmatic and Pastoral Concerns' Section at the 1988 Conference, chaired by future Australian Primate, and then Archbishop of Adelaide, Keith Rayner. This group's initial report was produced in 1987 and identifies 'three structures' into which understandings of Anglican authority might be categorized: 'personal (the bishops), collegial (the corporate episcopate and the bishop together with the presbyters) and the communal (synodical).'[45] What is evident in this schema is a clear division between the authority seemingly inherent in the episcopate, which comprise the first two 'structures', and that of laity which is confined only to the 'communal' and then only in tandem with bishops and clergy. So, a fairly facile comparison is made across the various 'levels' of ecclesial ordering that associate the diocesan bishop (at the 'local' level), the Primate (at the 'provincial' level) and the Archbishop of Canterbury (at the 'international' level) within the 'personal' sphere of authority; the bishop and clergy (local), House of Bishops (provincial) and Lambeth Conference and Primates' Meetings (international) constituting collegiality; and, diocesan synods (local), national synods (provincial) and the Anglican Consultative Council (international) being examples of 'communal' authority.[46] This ecclesiological framework goes on to inform the final report of the group which comes out of the 1988 Conference, and in particular its call for an 'enhanced role of the Primates' as a strengthening of collegiality in the international Communion to promote 'increased commitment to the interdependence of the Churches of the Communion' as they 'take special care for the universal coherence of the Communion in major questions affecting its unity.'[47] There is a clear shift here away from the 'communal' model expressed through the Consultative Council in favour of the 'collegial' authority treated as inherent in the episcopate. This finds further expression in the explanatory notes on Resolution 18 of the 1988 Conference:

> We see an enhanced role for the Primates as a key to a growth of interdependence within the Communion. We do not see any inter-Anglican jurisdiction as possible or desirable; an inter-Anglican synodical structure would be virtually unworkable and highly expensive. A collegial role for the Primates by contrast could easily be developed, and their collective judgement and advice would carry considerable weight.[48]

Ian George's critique centres on this ecclesial shift from the 'communal' outworking of synodical governance within the international Communion, through the organ of the Anglican Consultative Council, to the exercise of a 'collegial' authority by the Primates based upon the ecclesiological assumption that the episcopate bears ultimate responsibility for the unity of the church and its decision making. Accordingly, the Primates come to resemble something like a 'college of cardinals exercising a de facto authority with a capacity to impose decisions upon the rest of the Communion,' which is, ultimately, 'at great risk of upsetting the balance of power within the Communion.'[49]

The Limits of Primatial Responsibility: Intervention or Interference?

Despite misgivings such as these, and the persistently professed aversion to centralisation as a shibboleth of orthodoxy in Anglican ecclesial discourse, this movement toward a greater authority and responsibility for the Primates acting collegially in international Anglican polity continued steadily until a significant development was made at the 1998 Lambeth Conference which mandated the Primates to expand their responsibilities to include 'intervention in cases of exceptional emergency which are incapable of internal resolution within provinces, and giving of guidelines on the limits of Anglican diversity' (Resolution III.6b) and that 'the exercise of these responsibilities should carry moral authority calling for ready acceptance throughout the Communion' (Resolution III.6c). This call was enthusiastically taken up in the decade following the 2000 Oporto meeting of the Primates, and found particular expression in the Primates' close involvement with the Lambeth Commission on Communion which produced the Windsor Report in 2004 and the subsequent proposals for an Anglican Communion Covenant.[50] Of the eighteen Primates' Meetings which were called between 1979 and 2011, half occurred in the decade following 2000 with five meetings called in the first four years.

Just as Ian George predicted almost fifteen years earlier, another Australian bishop and theologian, Stephen Pickard, acting Chair of the IATDC in 2007, similarly bemoans the gradual and almost clandestine usurpation of authority by the Primates at the expense of the Anglican Consultative Council. The 'creeping' use of provincial terminology, identified by the IASCUFO report *Towards a Symphony of Instruments*, has been evidently matched by a 'creeping primacy' whereby the Primates 'ought to be the final arbiters of the ills that afflict us' which, given the need for a 'high degree of ecclesial intelligence and capability,' can only end in 'cynicism and disappointment whilst concealing deeper problems regarding right disposition, character and motives with respect to ecclesial leadership.[51]

This development in the formalisation of primatial roles and responsibilities within global Anglican polity has been largely in response to repeated calls from 'that older, more fundamental, and more universal' body, the Lambeth Conference,[52] together with the increasing conviction that the Primates bring with them not only a more representative concern for their provinces than perhaps might be the case for delegates, who may reflect particular interest groups or more narrow constituencies, but that the Primates also constitute a relatively agile and flexible instrument in tracking and responding to a quickly shifting ecclesial landscape.

The 2000 Oporto Primates' Meeting was significant for including on its agenda some discussion of the role of primacy within the Anglican experience, under the title 'Anglican Wisdom: Primacy'.[53] Experiences of primacy within provinces were shared, along with what a 'Communion wide' ministry of primacy might involve. This latter discussion was informed by input from three of the Primates whose 'provinces' extended across national boundaries: Archbishop Sinclair of the Southern Cone, Archbishop Makhulu of Central Africa, and the Archbishop of Canterbury (whose formal archiepiscopal oversight, of course, is confined to only one nation within the United Kingdom, presumably he was reflecting either on his role as a 'focus of unity' for the Communion as a whole, or else on his oversight of the extra-provincial churches). Nevertheless, this emphasis in discussion on the 'experience of Primacy in roles which cut across national boundaries,' does little to address inter-provincial relationships and wider concerns around the Primates' roles outside of their provinces. This notwithstanding, the agenda time devoted to these reflections does represent the first attempt to take up the call from previous Lambeth Conferences to exercise an 'enhanced responsibility' for the life of the Communion.[54] The Primates also resolved to meet together more frequently, in order to enable 'the practice of a collegial ministry . . . in which the challenges and opportunities of different Provinces can be discussed honestly and constructively, so that we may seek wisdom together.'[55] The Oporto meeting was also the first occasion on which the Primates issued a 'communique', which marked a subtle but not insignificant shift away from the previous custom of putting out little more than a summary statement. A 'communique' hints at something more like an official proclamation from a clearly defined body, coming close to – though of course not quite – a magisterial declaration. Memos relating to the planning of the 2001 Primates' Meeting articulate a deliberate distinction made by the planning committee in their organization between the issuing of a 'communique' and a 'pastoral letter'.[56]

One other telling development to come out of the Oporto meeting was an agreed response by the Primates to questions concerning lay presidency. Lay presidency had been raised by the Primates of Australia and the Southern Cone as an issue which, although resting ultimately with provinces, concerned the wider Communion. Archbishop Sinclair advised that action had been halted in the Southern Cone because of wider implications for the Communion, but there was renewed pressure from the Diocese of Sydney which was in the process of soliciting provincial responses on their intention to formally sanction lay and diaconal presidency within the diocese.[57] A common response was drawn up and approved by the Primates which itself betrays an insight into how they imagined a particular model of Anglican ecclesial polity which places Canterbury at the centre, through whom alone each province participates in 'communion' with each other, and who (presumably with the council of the Primates in the exercise of a collegial authority) is ultimate arbiter of Anglican authenticity:

> Given that the member churches of the Anglican Communion are all in communion with one another because of the common relationship of communion with the Archbishop and See of Canterbury, theoretical questions relating to the international impact on our Communion, if the Diocese of Sydney were eventually to choose to go ahead with lay presidency, should therefore be referred to him.[58]

The statement was originally agreed to by the Primates' Standing Committee and circulated by Primate of Australia, Archbishop Peter Carnley who, it seems likely, was its principal drafter. Carnley may have been particularly influenced by the Constitution of the Anglican Church of Australia which contains a similar implicit ecclesial model of Anglican 'communion' in its 'Ruling Principles', namely that 'this Church will remain and be in communion with the Church of England in England and churches in communion therewith,' envisaging the Communion as a kind of bicycle wheel whereby the spokes are related only insofar as they meet in a central hub.[59]

'To Mend the Net': the Primates Push for an 'Enhanced Role'

Following their resolve to meet more frequently, the Primates met again in 2001 at the Kanuga Retreat Centre in North Carolina. A key document presented to this meeting was the recently published booklet *To Mend the Net* authored by Archbishops Gomez and Sinclair, Primates of the West Indies and the Southern Cone respectively. *To Mend the Net* sets out a detailed proposal for a resolution to tensions currently facing the Communion and in particular advocates the 'patient and pastoral exercise' of an already existing 'political authority [in contradistinction to new legislative structures] at the international level,' exercised chiefly through the agency of the Archbishop of Canterbury but with the counsel of the Primates in the discretionary choosing 'to call together the Bishops of the Communion, to withhold this invitation in specific cases and in extreme circumstances to suspend communion with a given Province or diocese.'[60] The working out of their exact proposal depended on a gradated series of escalating steps which would be initiated 'when in the judgement of at least a significant minority of the Primates [any] contemplated changes exceed the limits of Anglican diversity.' The first response would be a call for restraint in not implementing any such 'unauthorized innovation' within the particular member-church concerned, followed by the creation and promulgation of guidelines 'which address the situation created and identify its remedy' and, if they are not assented to by the offending member-church, the Archbishop of Canterbury would effectively break communion with the 'non-co-operating Province(s) and diocese(s)' in offering them only 'observer status' and limited participation in the institutional manifestations of international communion (such as the Primates' Meetings, Lambeth Conferences and – although it is not mentioned by *To Mend the Net*, the Anglican Consultative Council).[61] While such an 'observer status' (which is not at all an ecclesiological term) does not in itself necessarily imply a formal break in communion, this is demonstrated by the 'parallel' measure that in such circumstances the Archbishop of Canterbury should, following recommendation from the Primates, 'authorize and support' alternative means of 'evangelization, pastoral care and episcopal oversight' with the long-term view to permanently establishing an alternate jurisdiction, or province, which would replace the 'intransigent body' as being 'recognized as a representative part of the Anglican Communion.'[62] There is much that calls for scrutiny and critique in these rather crude proposals, particularly in that such a break in communion could be initiated by only a minority of Primates, and that the Archbishop of Canterbury should exercise a ministry of jurisdiction in his personal capacity quite outside his own province of Canterbury and divorced from his legal and canonical relationship to the Church of England. Admittedly, such jurisdictions already exist in the curious examples of the 'extra-provincials' (which include a single parish, single dioceses and the Church of Ceylon which has two dioceses) but not only are these quite peculiar, born of historical circumstance, but exist also through mutual goodwill and agreement and not imposition.

Further criticism of the model of authority articulated in *To Mend the Net* is offered by Martyn Percy who finds similarities with the agreed statement of the Second Anglican-Roman Catholic International Commission, *The Gift of Authority*. Percy identifies and proposes three innovations in the ecclesiology of *To Mend the Net*, in common with *Gift of Authority*, which threaten to undermine the delicate nuance and balance by which Anglican understandings of authority might be characterized:

> First, both attempt to intensify episcopal power as an instrument of unity, and as a guarantor of authority and identity. Secondly, both attempt to re-define and clarify the nature of episcopacy in order to achieve unity. Thirdly, both exhibit a marked lack of tolerance towards cultural and theological diversity . . .[63]

To Mend the Net was not itself included on the agenda for formal discussion by the Primates at the 2001 Kanuga meeting; however it was referred by them to the Inter-Anglican Theological and Doctrinal Commission and is listed as a key resource to inform a session at the 2002 Primates' Meeting specifically to address the role of the Primates and Primates' Meetings. The 2002 Meeting in Canterbury, however, did not include this on the agenda but instead put emphasis on the theme of 'Unity of the Communion' through the lens of developing a common approach to Anglican canon law, and heard a presentation by Norman Doe and John Rees reflecting on the recently held Legal Advisors' Meeting and encouraged the establishment of a Legal Advisors' Network.[64] The meeting also commissioned papers by Archbishops Williams (Wales) and Peers (Canada) on 'non-geographic networks within our geographically structured dioceses and the appropriateness of such ministry networks transcending diocesan boundaries.'[65]

The Primates met again in May 2003 in Brazil, the first meeting with the new Archbishop of Canterbury Rowan Williams. Specific discussion of the role of the Primates, again, did not make the agenda as the presenting issue of human sexuality came to demand more particular and focused attention.[66] The 'extraordinary meeting' of the Primates in October 2003, precipitated by the consecration of Gene Robinson as Bishop of New Hampshire in The Episcopal Church, further reflected this climate of 'crisis' out of which the Lambeth Commission on Communion was established to explore the underlying questions of Anglican polity that might otherwise be lost in the charged and emotive debates on identity and sexuality prompted by the consecration. *To Mend the Net* was again commended by the Primates to be studied by the newly established Commission and this Commission produced the influential *Windsor Report* in 2004 from which followed the establishment of a 'Covenant Design Group', chaired by one of *To Mend the Net*'s authors Archbishop Gomez, to implement its proposals in the form of an Anglican Communion Covenant.[67] The Primates endorsed the Windsor Report at their 2005 meeting in Dromantine and, for the first time since 2000, issued a 'communique', which goes further than any previous statement in making the 'request that the Episcopal Church (USA) and the Anglican Church of Canada voluntarily withdraw their members from the Anglican Consultative Council for the period leading up to the next Lambeth Conference.'[68] If this were not evidence enough of the Primates 'taking authority' to themselves, the initial draft in 2007 of an Anglican Covenant produced by the Covenant Design Group gives a privileged role to the Primates as the body to which disputes are referred, the 'common mind' of the church discerned, and 'guidance and direction' offered and determined.[69] This role appointed to the Primates was removed from subsequent drafts.

Foundational to this movement is a rediscovery of the inherent authority of the episcopate and, specifically, the nature of metropolitical authority, as it is exercised in relationship between provinces, in an attempt to enunciate with more clarity this inter-provincial aspect of metropolitical jurisdiction just as the roles of metropolitan and Primate in relation to their provinces and national-churches are defined by their own constitutions and canons. Eric Kemp, in his response to 'The Anglican Communion: Identity and Authority', sets out this ecclesial deficiency:

In some respects the heart of the problem is the failure to give as much weight to the Bishop in relation to the college of bishops of the universal Church as to his relationship to the college of bishops of his national Church and his relationship to the clergy and people of his diocese.[70]

Since successive calls were made at the Lambeth Conferences of 1988 and 1998 for the Primates to take up an 'enhanced role' for fostering the unity of the Communion and mediation of disputes, the Primates' Meetings have, since Oporto, assumed a greater authority and profile which may well exceed Coggan's original vision of a forum for 'leisurely thought, prayer and deep consultation.' The Primates' Meetings of 2000, 2001 and, to a lesser extent, 2002 all attempted to reflect introspectively on the nature of primatial authority and the particular role the Primates might have within the Anglican dynamic. While the Primates continued to resist any articulation of increasing centralisation of power, and continued to affirm the three-legged stool of dispersed authority, subsidiarity and provincial autonomy, they were nevertheless increasingly influenced by a movement to codify the authority that the Primates might exercise in defining and maintaining the terms and nature of Anglican 'communion'. This was specifically articulated in documents such as *To Mend the Net*. However, after 2002 this attempt at purposeful reflection – which had never been particularly well developed – gave way to the implicit and reactive exercise of such an authority in response to the heightening tensions of the 'crisis' over human sexuality. Crucially, there was no communication of any theological or ecclesiological reflection as the Primates came to act, by default, as the pivotal body through which the Communion might discern a path through these tensions. Instead, authority was incrementally assumed: simply enough, at first, through more frequent meetings, then through referrals and mandates issued to bodies such as the Inter-Anglican Theological and Doctrinal Commission (which had originally been answerable only to the Consultative Council), then through the establishment of new bodies such as the Lambeth Commission on Communion, and finally in the making of presumptive requests through directive communiques. By the mid-2000s, the Primates had well and truly assumed an 'enhanced role' for the life of the Communion, even if it had not been particularly informed by much in the way of theological and ecclesiological reflection. This, ultimately, prevented widespread 'buy in' from the Communion and goes some way to explaining the – at best – lacklustre reception of the proposed Covenant. As events overtook the Primates, even conservative commentators noted the 'Laudian' proposals of *To Mend the Net*.[71] The influence of that document lives on and was recently lauded by the GAFCON movement as of continuing relevance in the lead up to Justin Welby's calling together of the Primates, for the first time in five years, at Canterbury in January 2016:

So, of what relevance is 'To Mend the Net' now? It serves as a reminder that a degree of separation is not necessarily church discipline. If the outcome of the Canterbury meeting is the 'not a divorce but separate bedrooms' scenario already suggested to the media by a Lambeth source, the Communion might be more manageable for a while, but if the See of Canterbury emerges as the hub to which all can still relate as Anglicans in good standing then the key question of discipline and the ecclesial integrity of Anglicanism is unresolved. The tear in the net will not be mended, but institutionalised.[72]

GAFCON, led by its 'Council of Primates', is certainly not shy of the centralisation of power and articulation of authority through the collegial assembly of a magisterial primacy. If this was the direction in which the Primates' Meetings seemed to be heading through the decade of the 2000s then the outcome of the January 2016 meeting, after a five-year hiatus, reflected this all the more forcefully.

The 2016 Primates' 'Gathering' (A meeting by any other name . . .)

Two tell-tale observations characterize the ecclesiological commitments of Justin Welby in his calling together of a 'gathering' of Primates in January 2016: first, that it was preceded by the ambitious as well as symbolic gesture of personally visiting each one of the then thirty-eight Primates in their province, or region; and, second, that the announcement of his intention and invitation to gather the Primates seems to have come from the personal initiative of the Archbishop, communicated through Lambeth Palace, thus bypassing, in the first instance, the Anglican Communion Office which traditionally would have taken the lead in the organization and preparation of Primates' Meetings.[73]

In fact, whether this was a Primates' Meeting at all was from the beginning unclear. The terminology of a 'Primates' Meeting' was deliberately avoided, in favour of the supposedly more informal 'Primates' gathering'. In part, the reasons for this may well have been political, as any pretence that this was anything other than a Primates' Meeting in continuity with those which had preceded it has since been dropped and the Anglican Communion Office lists this meeting, along with each of the others, as a perfectly regular calling together of this 'Instrument of Communion'. The reason that its formal designation as a 'Primates' Meeting' may have been initially avoided was perhaps due to the concerns and commitments of particular Primates to their provincial constituents, notably in relation to the rhetoric of boycotting participation in bodies where The Episcopal Church, or other supposed apostate provinces, were represented. For example, the Archbishop of Uganda outlined this reasoning in a letter released prior to the meeting:

> The Provincial Assembly of the Church of Uganda has resolved to not participate in any official meetings of the Anglican Communion until godly order is restored . . . Godly order has not yet been restored in the Anglican Communion and, therefore, as Archbishop of the Church of Uganda, I am constrained by the resolutions of our Provincial Assembly to not participate in a Primates' Meeting.

> At the same time, the Archbishop of Canterbury contacted me personally, along with every Primate of the Anglican Communion, and invited us to come together for a 'gathering' to consider if there was a way forward for the Anglican Communion.

> Together with the other GAFCON Primates, we have agreed to be part of a 'gathering' of Primates in Canterbury to discuss the future of the Anglican Communion . . .[74]

The gathering was thus distanced from any association with the formal 'Instruments of Communion' – increasingly being criticised as not 'fit for purpose'[75] – and instead cast as the extension of the Archbishop's own personal charism of drawing together the 'family'. This preference for the personal was brought out in an interview with the US-based think tank, the Council on Foreign Relations, shortly after the announcement of the gathering where Welby attributes the particular stresses which characterize contemporary Anglican division to the challenges of ever increasing globalization which intensifies geopolitical and 'geoecclesiastical' encounters but without 'the personal face-to-face contact which enables you in the way that, through diplomacy, through prayer, through interaction at a human level, through facing, to deal with that diversity.'[76] The Archbishop's conviction that 'diversity is held in personal relationship'[77] is at the heart of his ecclesiology but stands in marked contrast to the institutional approach hitherto pursued through such means as the proposed Anglican Communion Covenant. This emphasis on personal engagement at the expense of institutional investment in the building and manifestation of relationships is typical of Welby's style but, as will be shown, ultimately shortcuts ecclesiology and reduces theological reflection on ecclesial polity to little more than 'structural reorganization'.

Despite this there was clearly an expectation surrounding the announce-ment of the gathering of Primates that their business would chiefly con-cern questions of Anglican ecclesial polity with radical reforms being mooted in the media. An article in the Guardian, which was to break the news, quoted a 'Lambeth Palace source' expressing Welby's dissatisfac-tion with the Archbishop of Canterbury's role within the Communion as one of 'spending vast amounts of time trying to keep people in the boat and never actually rowing it anywhere.'[78] Hinting that Welby had a concrete proposal for reforming the Communion's structures, the source described Welby's plan for international Anglican polity as like 'sleeping in separate bedrooms.'[79] The Archbishop's own press release too indi-cated that 'a review of the structures of the Anglican Communion' and a 'look afresh at our ways of working as a Communion and especially as Primates' would be central to the meeting's agenda, and much subse-quent commentary focused on this clear emphasis on the ecclesiological questions of how the Communion might be ordered.[80] In particular, the restoration of 'godly order' was the express purpose and hope of the GAFCON Primates, including the Anglican Church in North America's Archbishop Foley Beach, in their acceptance of Justin Welby's invitation.[81]

My own part in the preparations for this gathering involved working with Bishop Graham Kings who had been asked by the Archbishop of Canterbury to put together resources and discussion papers to aid the Primates in their reflections and conversations. I worked to draft the ecclesiology paper, taking into particular account the expectation that the Primates would review the nature of international Anglicanism's ecclesial structure. Central to my own concerns in this was the place of provincial polity and metropolitical authority, not to mention its par-ticular manifestation through the ministry of the Primates which would become the most significant ecclesiological outcome of the meeting.

The basic brief for the project was to draft a discussion paper for the Primates structured around the axiomatic Anglican triad of Scripture, Reason and Tradition, to provoke and inform their ecclesiological reflec-tions and imaginings for the shape and nature of Anglican polity into the future. Conscious of Justin Welby's preliminary comments that this reflection should pay 'proper attention to developments in the past,' the paper drew heavily on the previously received work of the Inter-Anglican Theological and Doctrinal Commission, the Inter-Anglican Standing Committee on Unity, Faith and Order, the Bible in the Life of the Church project, and the ecclesiological reflections of former Archbishop of Canterbury, Rowan Williams. The discussion paper also contained mod-els and metaphors for the Primates' imagining of structures and polity, the drafting of which was largely the contribution of Bishop Graham

Kings.[82] Of these models, the only one to make much of metropolitical and archiepiscopal jurisdiction was in relation to Eastern Orthodox polity, but its simplified characterization is marked by a perhaps too eager effort to find parallels with Anglicanism.[83] Nevertheless, questions for the Primates in their reflection included:

> Are nationalistic based churches helpful for interdependence? Is divisiveness a natural result of this model? Could the See of Canterbury serve in a similar way to the Patriarchate of Constantinople? Do the 38 Provinces of the Anglican Communion group together under any historic patriarchates? Could 6 'Metropolitan Primates' represent 6 continents? Could they be supported by 6 continental regional offices of the Anglican Communion, which would coordinate Regional Conferences, eg like Council of Anglican Provinces in Africa (CAPA)?[84]

The contemporary commentary and observations of the gathering itself, which met over the five days between the 11th and 15th of January 2016, was characterized by frustrated speculation, internal leaking, and 'an Anglican version of Kremlinology – divining meaning by who stands next to whom on the podium as the primates take the salute for the May Day Parade.'[85] The Archbishop of Canterbury's opening address, which was leaked early on to an online Nigerian news site, was carefully constructed to contain not only a sweeping survey of the scandal of disunity throughout Christianity's history, and a reminder that the first Lambeth Conference was boycotted by the Archbishop of York and a number of other English bishops, but also a defence of the Church of England's orthodox and evangelistic credentials, pointing toward the Church's influence in defeating assisted suicide in parliament and gaining exemptions from same-sex marriage, as well as church planting and the Archbishop of York's 'evangelistic pilgrimage' which is hailed as a first for 'perhaps over 1,000 years.'[86] Welby's emphasis on the Primates' ministry as one of personal encounter with each other is also apparent: 'now we are in the same room,' he tells them, '[we] can speak truth to each other, but truth that is spoken with a deep sense of love for the other, not as a thing, a Primate, but as a person, loved by God whatever their faults.'[87]

There was intense speculation surrounding the meeting as to whether there would be a 'walk out' by conservative, and particularly GAFCON-aligned, Primates partway through the gathering.[88] That such an exodus was avoided, with the exception of the Archbishop of Uganda who quietly left the meeting after the second day, could alone be considered a significant accomplishment and vindication of Welby's authority. In fact, it was acknowledged in conservative circles that there was 'some disquiet about the continued presence of the conservative Primates,'[89] while the GAFCON leadership excluded from the proceedings, including their General Secretary and former Archbishop of Sydney, Peter Jensen, waited in the wings poised to take over in a coup that never came to pass.[90] The reception of the meeting's resolution was, then, somewhat mixed as neither 'camp' came away feeling either fully endorsed or entirely repudiated, The Episcopal Church and the Anglican Church of Canada had not been expelled or anathematised and the GAFCON-minded Primates had not formally and finally switched their allegiance away from the leadership of the Archbishop of Canterbury but instead committed to 'walk together' through the existing Instruments of Communion.[91] While the ecclesiological reflection on the nature of Anglican organization did not result in any 'restructuring' of the institutional shape of the Communion, which had been the most prevalent expectation prior to the meeting, there was a subtle and yet important development in the articulation of the Primates' authority which came out through the language used in their final communique.[92]

The communique issued by the Primates following their meeting was most significant, at least in its ecclesiological implications, for the inclusion of two *hapax legomena*: 'requiring', and 'consequences'. The former tested the limits of the Primates' authority and sharply brought into focus the question of what was the nature of their ministry within international Anglican polity and how was it to be exercised. The latter, a dogged insistence to use the term 'consequences' over and against the media-favoured 'discipline' or 'sanctions', speaks to how the Primates imagined they might balance the competing demands of 'Godly Order' and 'Provincial Autonomy'.

The Primates as a whole did not of their own initiative introduce the language of 'requirement' in imagining the 'consequences' that might flow for The Episcopal Church in the wake of its recent change to the doctrine of marriage.[93] Instead they quote from, in receiving and adopting by majority vote, the report and recommendations from a smaller working group of their members:

It is our unanimous desire to walk together. However given the seriousness of these matters we formally acknowledge this distance by requiring that for a period of three years The Episcopal Church no longer represent us on ecumenical and interfaith bodies, should not be appointed or elected to an internal standing committee and that while participating in the internal bodies of the Anglican Communion, they will not take part in decision making on any issues pertaining to doctrine or polity.[94]

The protestation was widely and almost immediately made that, of course, the Primates possess no formal mechanism by which they could enforce this requirement, and it was unclear what was intended or envisaged within the scope of 'decision making on any issues pertaining to doctrine or polity,' within the 'internal bodies of the Anglican Communion.'[95] However, while some decried the move as a novel and audacious primatial grab for power, it does reflect the clear direction toward which the Primates had been moving since their encouragement by the 1988 Lambeth Conference to take up an 'enhanced role' for the life and unity of the Communion. In fact, it looks even further back to the resolutions of the 1978 Lambeth Conference which gave to the Primates, under the leadership of the Archbishop of Canterbury, the task of discerning 'the way to relate together the international conferences, councils, and meetings within the Anglican Communion' (Res. 12) as well as a mandate to review, 'by whatever means they feel best,' the ongoing work of the IATDC (Res. 25).

How influential this latest extension of the Primates' particular responsibility and concern for the ecclesiology of the Communion will be depends largely on how their communique is received. They have exercised not a juridical but rather a moral authority which is tested by 'a process of negotiating among various possibilities, in and through an array of ventures.'[96] This exercise of 'moral authority', and the nature of its reception, is a key element of the metropolitical jurisdiction embodied by the Primates. Metropolitical authority within the Anglican Communion lays emphasis on the 'relational, the personal, and the concrete and contextual' in a way which consistently has resisted being flattened into a codified or clear-cut universal constitution.[97] While this codification has rightly taken place in relation to the exercise of metropolitical authority within provincial jurisdictions through constitutions and the conventions of synodical governance, the external and relational element of metropolitical authority, exercised personally through the Primates, properly relies on the more complex negotiation of moral authority. Rather than obliterating dissent, moral authority has the capacity to contain disagreement in matters of contention while preserving 'in relatively coherent and continuous ways the common values and beliefs that are essential to the church's identity and its thriving.'[98]

How this moral authority is received is equally as important. The formal doctrine of 'reception' has become rather confused in Anglican circles, seemingly misunderstanding and misappropriating its development out of the Roman Catholic theological reflection which followed the Second Vatican Council.[99] According to this Roman Catholic conciliar reflection, the terms *sensus Ecclesiae*, as used in the Decree of the Apostolate of the Laity, and *mens Ecclesiae*, in the Dogmatic Constitution on Divine Revelation (*Dei Verbum*), both equally translated into English as 'Mind of the Church', refer to the authoritative teaching of the Church's magisterium which must take root in ordering and shaping the lives and world of the faithful.[100] The process by which this is actualised, itself considered something of a foregone conclusion, is the *sensu fidei* which is explored in the Dogmatic Constitution on the Church (*Lumen Gentium*).[101] Within Anglicanism this distinction between the source of authority and its *telos* has been collapsed into what the Windsor Report describes as the *consensus fidelium*, or the authority of the ecclesial opinion poll:

> The *consensus fidelium* ('common mind of the believers') constituted the ultimate check that a new declaration was in harmony with the faith as it had been received. More recently, the doctrine has been used in Anglicanism as a way of testing whether a controversial development, not yet approved by a universal Council of the Church but nevertheless arising within a province by legitimate processes, might gradually, over time, come to be accepted as an authentic development of the faith.[102]

The reception then of teaching, or any other declarative articulation of authority, is understood within Anglicanism to be a shared endeavour among the whole people of God. However, holding the distinction between the authority of the teaching itself and the authoritative testing of its veracity through the lived experience of faithfulness to the Gospel is essential for avoiding the 'democratisation of doctrine' and maintaining the integrity of reception in the absence of any definitive magisterium. A developed understanding of the nature of metropolitical authority offers the potential to achieve this distinction, as it harnesses the personal and relational possibilities of moral authority set within the context of the unfolding and still contested discernment of Anglican international polity. Sensitivity to how the Primates' communique might be received, then, is one likely explanation for the insistence of the language of 'consequences' rather than 'discipline' or 'sanctions' to describe their determination that The Episcopal Church be excluded from ecumenical and interfaith dialogues, standing committees and other intra-Anglican doctrinal and polity discussions. However, the conceptual nuance inherent in 'consequences', as opposed to any other term, was not appreciated either by those who welcomed the imposition of 'sanctions' or by those who deplored them. The Anglican Church of North America's Archbishop Foley Beach, whose invitation to and participation in the gathering was controversial, used the language of 'sanctions' in his pastoral letter following the meeting noting that 'the sanctions are strong, but they are not strong enough . . .'[103] A joint statement from GAFCON chairman, Kenyan Archbishop Eliud Wabukala, and General Secretary, Peter Jensen, also emphasized the punitive character of the 'sanctions' while yet calling into question their likely effectiveness 'to guard biblical truth and restore godly order.'[104] At the other end of the spectrum Changing Attitude Scotland released a statement commenting that:

It appears that the Anglican Communion has applied sanctions to itself rather than to the US based Episcopal Church . . . Rather than seeing the 'sanctions' being applied to the US based Episcopal Church as that church being sent to the naughty step for three years, Changing Attitude Scotland believes that it is possible that in time this may be seen as the emergence of a group of provinces in which the full inclusion of LGBT people will be an unquestioned badge of honour.[105]

The Archbishop of Canterbury was keen to distance the Primates' communique from the language of 'sanctions' and to stress the more impersonal 'consequences' as an inevitable outworking of the effect to relationships precipitated by the exercise of, albeit perfectly legitimate, autonomous innovation.[106] In fact, the language of 'consequences' is reminiscent of and closely aligned to the proposed 'relational consequences' envisaged by the Anglican Communion Covenant.[107] While Welby seems to have quietly dropped the question of the Covenant's ongoing promotion, and abandoned its more institutional approach to envisaging Anglican ecclesial polity in favour of a commitment to personally invested and intensified relationality, the outcome of the 2016 Primates' Meeting looks – to all intents and purposes – like the Covenant by the back door.[108]

Notes

1 Lambeth Conference 1978, 123.
2 For further discussion of this quote in context, see Podmore 2009, sec. 4.17.
3 Goddard 2013, 121.
4 Craston 1986. Emphasis added.
5 Podmore 2010, 26; note particularly Ramsey's later unease at this move, saying 'I think Lambeth 1968 erred in giving power to the ACC ... I quickly came to think that it was not the right way to run the Anglican Communion and that it was a poor substitute for a meeting of archbishops,' see Chadwick 1991, 277–78.
6 Minutes of Meeting of Primates during 1958 Lambeth Conference, Friday 4 July at 5.30pm, in *Lambeth Consultative Body & Executive Officer, Papers Relating to Formation of 'Consultative Body' and Appointment of Executive Officer, 1958 to 1960.*
7 The notion that a resolution of a previous Lambeth Conference could be 'replaced' is itself intriguing and says something about how the authority of Lambeth Conferences has been perceived and negotiated.

8 Original text of proposal to replace Resolution 50 of the Lambeth Conference of 1930, in *Lambeth Consultative Body & Executive Officer, Papers Relating to Formation of 'Consultative Body' and Appointment of Executive Officer, 1958 to 1960*.

9 Compare the proposed resolution, located in Anglican Communion Office Archives ACC/LCB/1(a), with Resolution 61 of the 1958 Lambeth Conference, 'Progress in the Anglican Communion Missionary Appeal.'

10. Stephen Bayne, Executive Officer, 'Notes for Primates and Metropolitans,' *Lambeth Consultative Body & Executive Officer, Papers Relating to Formation of 'Consultative Body' and Appointment of Executive Officer, 1958 to 1960*.

11 Haggart 1983.

12 Lambeth Consultative Body 1963.

13 Lambeth Conference 1978, 103.

14 Lambeth Conference 1978, 41.

15 Letter from Bishop John Howe to the Primates of the Anglican Communion, 27th January 1975, in *Primates' Meetings: Informal Meeting of Primates - Nairobi 1975*.

16 *Primates' Meetings: Informal Meeting of Primates - Nairobi 1975*.

17 Statement: Informal Gathering of Anglican Archbishops, Trinity College, Nairobi 20th November 1975, in *Primates' Meetings: Informal Meeting of Primates – Nairobi 1975*.

18 Frank Woods, 'Report to the Australian Bishops on the Anglican Primates" Conference," Nairobi, November 17–21, 1975 in *'Primates' Meetings: Informal Meeting of Primates - Nairobi 1975*.

19 Frank Woods, 'Report to the Australian Bishops on the Anglican Primates" Conference," Nairobi, November 17–21, 1975 in *'Primates' Meetings: Informal Meeting of Primates - Nairobi 1975, 3*.

20 Papers relating to this meeting may be found in, *Primates' Meetings: Small Group of Primates Meeting 1978*.

21 'Minutes of Meeting in Tunbridge Wells with Archbishop of Canterbury, 10th–13th January, 1978' in *Primates' Meetings: Small Group of Primates Meeting 1978*.

22 Document prepared by E.W. Scott outlining his 'Understanding of the consensus reached at the meeting held at Allen Gardner House January 10-13, 1978' in *Primates' Meetings: Small Group of Primates Meeting 1978*.

23 The minutes of the meeting of a Committee of Primates during the 1978 Lambeth Conference may be found in *Primates' Meetings: Selected Documents 1978*.

24 *Primates' Meetings: Primates' Meeting, Ely - Agenda and Minutes 1979, 4.*

25 *Primates' Meetings: Primates' Meeting, Ely - Agenda and Minutes 1979, 4–5.*

26 'Appendix E: Authority,' page 2 in *Primates' Meetings: Primates' Meeting, Ely - Agenda and Minutes 1979*.

27 John Howe, 'Lambeth 1968: A turning point and the end of an era', notes first made at Trinity College, Nairobi, 19 November 1975, in *Primates' Meetings: Small Group of Primates Meeting 1978*.

28 'In 1968 it was quite likely that Lambeth Conferences were coming to an end: in 1978 it was certain they are not,' see John Howe, 'Memorandum for the Archbishop of Canterbury, and the Primates of the Anglican Communion, relating the international conferences, councils and meetings of the Anglican Communion,' April, 1979 in *Primates' Meetings: Selected Documents 1978*.

29 Sykes 1978; 1981; E. Norman 1999; Avis 2006; 2014; Driver 2014.

30 Thomas 2002, 89.

31 F. Chaplin, 'Metropolitical Authority,' revised definition produced for the ACC Constitutions Committee, 1977 in *Collected Provincial Responses to Request of Anglican Executive Officer for Comment on Metropolitical Authority in Preparation for ACC-4 1977.* The language of 'auctoritas' as 'the weight of opinion which must be respected' and 'imperium' as 'the right to be obeyed' was influentially introduced into Anglican understandings of authority through a paper prepared by Bishop James Schuster on 'Metropolitical Authority in South Africa' in which he values personal charisma in the office of metropolitan above all else 'since he is generally expected to make himself responsible for the welfare of the Church but must depend upon auctoritas rather than imperium to fulfil this responsibility,' 7.

32 Thomas 2002, 86.

33 Thomas 2002, 89.

34 Thomas 2002, 94.

35 Thomas 2002, 93.

36 'The Anglican Communion: Identity and Authority' in *ACC-8 Wales, 22 July to 3 August 1990: Preparatory Files 1989.*

37 *ACC-8 Wales, 22 July to 3 August 1990: Preparatory Files 1989,* 1.

38 *ACC-8 Wales, 22 July to 3 August 1990: Preparatory Files 1989,* 2.

39 *ACC-8 Wales, 22 July to 3 August 1990: Preparatory Files 1989,* 3.

40 These collated responses are contained in *ACC-8 Wales, 22 July to 3 August 1990: Preparatory Files 1989.*

41 Response by Roger Beckwith, Latimer House Oxford, in *ACC-8 Wales, 22 July to 3 August 1990: Preparatory Files 1989.*

42 The Anglican Communion: Identity and Authority - Response from the Anglican Church of Australia, page 8, in *ACC-8 Wales, 22 July to 3 August 1990: Preparatory Files 1989.*

43 George 1989.

44 George 1989, 2.

45 'Dogmatic and Pastoral Concerns,' page 32 in *Working Papers for the Lambeth Conference 1988: Prepared at the Saint Augustine's Seminar Held at Blackheath, London, England. 29 July - 7 August 1987.*

46 *Working Papers for the Lambeth Conference 1988: Prepared at the Saint Augustine's Seminar Held at Blackheath, London, England. 29 July - 7 August 1987.*

47 *The Truth Shall Make You Free: The Lambeth Conference 1988, the Reports, Resolutions, Pastoral Letters from the Bishops 1988,* 112.

48 *The Truth Shall Make You Free: The Lambeth Conference 1988, the Reports, Resolutions, Pastoral Letters from the Bishops 1988,* 217 This also puts a not so subtle stop to any suggestion that the ACC might increase its sphere of influence. The explanatory notes go on to curtly comment, 'we value the present work of the ACC. We do not see, however, that it ought to move beyond its present advisory role.'

49 George 1989, 3.

50 A clear and concise account of the precursors to, and development of, the Anglican Communion Covenant and its later reception is given in Goddard 2013.

51 Pickard 2013, 251. Stephen Pickard was also chiefly influential in the drafting of Symphony of Instruments.

52 McGowan 2016, 3.

53   Minutes, Primates' Meeting, Oporto 2000 [RG XIII: P(2000)M].

54   The minutes reflect, for example, that the Archbishop of Canterbury describes a twofold responsibility of the Primates, to 'represent their Provinces and [that] they had an international commitment to each other as Primates.'

55   Communique, Primates' Meeting, Oporto 2000 [RG XIII: P(2000)C].

56   *Facsimile Message from Archbishop of Canterbury to Members of the Drafting Group* 2001.

57   For more discussion and background to this issue see *Appellate Tribunal Opinion: Reference Concerning Diaconal and Lay Presidency* 1997.

·   58   *Statement Concerning Lay Presidency, Agreed by Primates and Distributed by John Peterson, 30 March* 2000.

59   Constitution, Anglican Church of Australia, 2014, Section 6 [RG XIII: C(A2)CCN1]. An unsuccessful attempt was made to revise this section through the Constitution Amendment (Relations with other Churches) Canon 2004. This canon set out a clear procedure by which General Synod could determine by canon the nature and extent of its communion with other churches. This would mark a clear change to how communion with other churches is currently constitutionally governed in the Anglican Church of Australia, allowing General Synod a much more active role in specifying its relationships, rather than simply looking to the Church of England 'and those in communion therewith.' This constitutional amendment has not taken effect, however, as it was rejected by the synod of the metropolitical diocese of Adelaide. In Australia, constitutional amendments made by General Synod require assent by ordinance of three quarters of all diocesan synods and all metropolitical sees. Dr Sarah Black, Archivist at the Anglican Diocese of Adelaide, points toward concern expressed by the diocese's Ecumenical Affairs Commission of 'a possible narrowing effect on the Church,' as well as the overwhelming imperative faced by the 2006 diocesan synod to respond to recently revealed scandals of child abuse within the diocese, as factors contributing to its defeat. The utility of the unamended Section 6 was recently tested at the 2017 General Synod, where a motion was presented declaring that 'by virtue of Section 6 of the Constitution of the Anglican Church of Australia . . . the Scottish Episcopal Church has put itself out of communion with the Anglican Church of Australia.' The motion was subsequently revised on the floor of synod, however, to avoid the constitutional question of communion.

60   Gomez and Sinclair 2001, 13–14.

61   Gomez and Sinclair 2001, 22.

62   Gomez and Sinclair 2001, 22.

63   Percy 2001, 328.

64   *Anglican Communion Legal Advisors' Consultation Report* 2002.

65   *Primates' Meeting 2002: Action Plan. For Internal Use* 2002.

66   The Pastoral Letter issued by the Primates following the Meeting draws particular attention in its discussion of human sexuality to the publication 'True Union in the Body' written by Andrew Goddard and commissioned by Archbishop Gomez of the West Indies. This document was the subject of a session at the Meeting led by Archbishop Gomez with a response by the Archbishop of Canterbury. See Goddard 2003.

67   This description is necessarily brief. In charting the process by which the Primates as a group came to exercise their 'enhanced responsibility' during this important period it is beyond the scope of the discussion to enter into the detail

of both the 'Windsor Process' let alone the presenting questions of human sexuality. However, reliable and accessible summaries of the former may be found in: Sadgrove et al. 2010, 195; Goddard 2013; Wilkins 2005; Wondra 2005.

68 Communique, Primates' Meeting, Dromantine 2005 [RG V: ACC/PM/6].

69 Covenant Design Group 2007, sec. 6.5.

70 Eric Kemp, in *ACC-8 Wales, 22 July to 3 August 1990: Preparatory Files* 1989.

71 Paul Zahl, quoted in conversation with Ian Douglas, in Douglas and Zahl 2005, 10.

72 Raven 2015.

73 The Secretary General, Josiah Idowu-Fearon, made his response via the Anglican Communion News Service, which runs out of his Anglican Communion Office. The announcement, however, is not quite on message as it refers to a 'Primates' Meeting' rather than Welby's preferred 'gathering', and while he pledges the support of the Anglican Communion Office as 'positioned to assist in fostering a desirable outcome,' it is apparent that the ACO was caught somewhat unawares in that the planning and initiative for the gathering had not come through them – as would usually be the case - but from Welby directly. See 'Response from the Secretary General of the Anglican Communion to the Archbishop of Canterbury's Call for a Special Primates' Meeting in January 2016' 2016.

74 Ntagali 2016.

75 Chapman, Clarke, and Percy 2015, 9.

76 'A Conversation with the Archbishop of Canterbury' 2015.

77 'A Conversation with the Archbishop of Canterbury' 2015.

78 A. Brown 2015.

79 A. Brown 2015.

80 'Archbishop of Canterbury Calls for Primates' Gathering' 2015; see also, for early commentary: Guardian Editorial 2015; Percy 2015; Langham 2015; Living Church Editorial 2015; Goddard 2015; Brittain 2016.

81 Beach 2015; Ntagali 2016; Ould 2015.

82 Of the original ten models and metaphors proposed for discussion – a 'Loose Federation Model', 'Confessional Model', 'Covenant Model', 'Roman Catholic Model', 'Eastern Orthodox Model', 'Lutheran Model', 'Hub and Spokes Metaphor', 'Planetary System Metaphor', 'Hour Glass Metaphor', 'Weaving Metaphor' – it was the models rather than the metaphors which found their way into the final report.

83 For example, fourteen 'independent churches' are described as constitutive of Eastern Orthodoxy and in communion with the Ecumenical Patriarch, with a '15th independent church (of America) recognized by only 5 churches (Russian, Bulgarian, Georgian, Polish, Czech and Slovak).' There is clearly an intended parallel here with the Anglican Church in North America, currently not in communion with the Archbishop of Canterbury nor recognized as a member church of the Anglican Communion but still having established communion with a number of individual Anglican member-churches which similarly recognize it as the legitimate Anglican presence in North America. This was all the more pertinent at the time as the House of Bishops of the Episcopal Church of Sudan and South Sudan had, at the end of November 2015, recommended to its Provincial Synod to 'sever relationship with TEC and any other Provinces or Dioceses that approves liturgy for blessing same sex relationship' and, in their own capacity apart from the authority of

the Provincial Synod, 'to formally recognise the Anglican Church of North America (ACNA) . . .' See Deng et al. 2015.

84 *Papers for Primates' Meeting - Canterbury 2016* 2015, 14.

85 Conger 2016. The reference relates to leaked photographs of Evensong held in Canterbury Cathedral and the surrounding outside speculation, in the absence of any official reporting, around who was attending, who was standing next to whom, and what this might mean for the internal dynamic of the meeting. It should be noted that the veracity and virtue of commentary offered through the largely polemic 'blogosphere' is questionable. For some insightful exposition of this, including some exegesis of George Conger's own reporting, see Brittain 2015b.

86 'Primates 2016: Archbishop of Canterbury's Address' 2016.

87 'Primates 2016: Archbishop of Canterbury's Address' 2016.

88 Ould 2016.

89 Ould 2016.

90 'Peter Jensen Speaks to GAFCON Supporters - End of Day 1' 2016.

91 'Communique from the 2016 Primates' Meeting' 2016.

92 'Statement from Primates' 2016. This document had been leaked prior to the release of the final communique, prompting the Primates to release it separately in a preliminary statement.

93 For an outline of these changes see Meyers 2015.

94 'Statement from Primates' 2016.

95 See particularly the comments by Norman Doe, hardly a radical voice in questions of Anglican polity: Davies 2016.

96 Wondra 2016, 537.

97 Wondra 2016, 538.

98 Wondra 2016, 539.

99 The importance of 'reception' for Anglicans may be traced back at least to the 'Grindrod Report', see: *Report of the Working Party Appointed by the Primates of the Anglican Communion on Women and the Episcopate 1987.*

100 Vatican Council and Tavard 1966. Notably, the work of Biblical scholarship is particularly reminded to heed this teaching authority (*Dei Verbum*, para 23).

101 Vatican Council, Peters, and Baum 1966, para. 12.

102 Lambeth Commission on Communion 2004, para. 68. This discussion of differences between Anglican and Roman Catholic understandings of 'reception' is based on a paper I prepared for the 2014 Jessie Nicholson Memorial Lecture, exploring the notion of the 'Mind of the Church' within Anglicanism. In that lecture I acknowledge that the term consensus fidelium does have a legitimate place within reception doctrine in describing the resulting agreement and judgement manifest in the sensus fidelium. This was explored by John Henry Newman a century and a half earlier in his article 'Consulting the Faithful on Matters of Doctrine' (1859).

103 Beach 2016.

104 P. Jensen and Wabukala 2016.

105 'Statement on the Primates' Meeting' 2016.

106 Welby 2016.

107 *The Anglican Communion Covenant* 2009, secs 4.2.4; 4.2.5; 4.2.7.

108 In particular, the final text of the Covenant had envisaged that the Standing Committee of the 'Anglican Communion' (although, more formally, it is the Standing Committee of the Anglican Consultative Council as stipulated in its Constitution, para. 7.3, which according to a recent revision has included

five Primates chosen by the Primates' Meeting) would be the coordinating body through which 'relational consequences' would be determined (Covenant, 4.2.4) and referred back to the Instruments of Communion (4.2.5, 4.2.7). In the 2016 communique, however, the Primates have unilaterally taken over this role and responsibility, without the consultative checks and balances outlined in the formal process offered by the Covenant and, importantly, without the concurrence of the Anglican Consultative Council.

Part Four

Paradigm for Provincial Revival

Throughout this exploration of international Anglicanism, and the place within it of metropolitical authority and provincial polity, there has emerged a clear tension between the largely centralist and self-contained structures of autonomous national churches and the loose and often ill-defined polity of the international Communion. Historical analysis of the development and emergence of the contemporary Communion, with particular attention to how metropolitical authority and provincial polity have been understood and applied within the Anglican context, has revealed a varied and colourful ecclesial landscape which makes it impossible to speak of a single or normative application of provincial polity or metropolitical authority. Nevertheless, this plurality has been embraced within the Communion and even encouraged through the drive toward autonomous self-government in the ecclesial equivalent of the post-colonial era. The gradual emergence throughout the second half of the twentieth century of an Anglican awareness of itself as an international 'Communion' has challenged this plurality and threatened to flatten the contours of this diversity with retrofitted norms, maxims and mantras which privilege the autonomy and self-sufficiency of the 'national church' as well as the assumption of a growing magisterial authority invested in the supposedly representative Primates.

Some prominence has been given throughout this study to the Australian context in illustrating this development. As has already been detailed, Anglicans in Australia played a key role in the mid-nineteenth-century discussions about the nature of authority within the church and its relationship with the state at the new frontiers created by colonial expansion and the abandonment of the old assumptions of 'establishment'. It was in Australia that the authority of Letters Patent to create and empower bishoprics was first tested, and where – along with New Zealand – early moves were made to break the 'English nexus' and secure and settle an independent but recognizably 'Anglican' ecclesial polity which was both 'episcopally led and synodically governed.'[1] Although the distinction of the first Anglican metropolitical see to be established since the middle ages belongs to Calcutta, it was only with the promotion of Australia as the second see to such a status that there is evidence of conscious ecclesial reflection on how a provincial polity might be the vehicle of Anglican colonial expansion and settlement and how this might change not only the relationship between the church 'at home' with the church 'abroad', but also the nature of the Archbishop of Canterbury's role: would his presidency of a new Anglican patriarchate be papal, on the one hand, or, on the other, as *primus inter pares*?

The Australian context has been described as a 'microcosm' of the Anglican Communion, intimating that the experience of Australian Anglicanism may have something to offer the international Communion particularly in questions of polity.[2] This language of a 'microcosm' was coined by former Primate Keith Rayner, drawing principally on the observation that both polities display 'limited power and resources of [their] central organs of governance.'[3] A comparison may also be made between the Australian and international Anglican contexts by means of the diversity of theological commitments and expressions of ecclesial identity, or 'churchmanship', which characterize diocesan and regional identities.[4] The limited nature of centralised power and governance has its corresponding antithesis in the robust assertion of diocesan auton-omy, not unlike the autonomy claimed for national churches within the Communion. This 'diocesanism' has long been a feature of Australian Anglican polity and is evident not only in the 1962 national constitu-tion, but in much earlier provincial constitutions.[5] This is a somewhat surprising result, as it tends to go against a trend that would suggest greater centralisation among those member-churches which developed through the subdivision of larger ecclesial units (as the twenty-three dio-ceses and five provinces of the Anglican Church of Australia emerged from a single 'Diocese of Australia').[6] The influence of constitutional fed-eration in Australia's own political history, as well as a strong sense of regionalism across expansive distances, gives some explanation to this peculiar feature of the Australian church.[7] The formation of a province in Western Australia in 1914, significantly isolated from the eastern states and with a political history of separatism and state independence, typ-ifies the importance of regionalism.[8] The burdens of economic as well as geographic viability, archiepiscopal ambitions, and the strength of local identity all played their part in the establishment of the Province of Western Australia.[9] Perhaps the most pronounced difference between the Australian church and the Communion is that the former is founded and organized upon the basis of a written constitution, one which also makes provision for a system of tribunals with both original and appel-late jurisdiction.[10]

Beyond superficial similarities, the veracity of the claim that the Australian context contains within it a 'microcosm' of the Communion deserves further exploration in order to establish the basis upon which any kind of instructive analogy or parallel might be drawn.[11] Indeed, whether the nature of comparison is to be by way of analogy, on the one hand, or parallel, on the other, itself requires some clarification. For example, an analogy might accord some equivalence to the autonomous Australian dioceses and autonomous member-churches of the Communion, suggesting that the Australian provincial structures (existing as they do within the national church) might equally accord with a kind of supra-provincial regional polity within the Communion.

Alternatively, if the Australian ecclesial context can make some claim to offering itself as a representative 'microcosm' of the Communion then it might also serve as a more direct parallel in understanding the contribution that a provincial polity (ie. the experience of Australia's five 'internal' provinces) might make to the ecclesiology of international Anglicanism. As the focus of this research has been on the province itself as a unit of polity within Anglicanism, with the thesis being that the flexibility and dynamism of provincial polity is threatened by the flattened and colourless ecclesial landscape dominated by the 'façadism' of the 'national church' governed by a magisterial council of Primates, this naturally leads to a greater weight being given to the latter concern: namely, the example of the Australian provinces themselves in demonstrating what a rediscovery of a provincial polity might have to commend itself to the Communion.

However, as so many of the Communion's member-churches are themselves single provinces, so that their provincial identity has become intertwined with their identity as a national, or even multi-national, autonomous ecclesial unit, it would be reasonable to extrapolate how supra-provincial networks might themselves prompt a rediscovery of an authentic provincial ecclesiology over and against the narrow isolationism of the autonomous 'national church'

Notes

1 Sharwood 2004, September 2005:3.

2 This is a central claim made by former Adelaide Archbishop Jeffrey Driver, drawing on similar observations by former Primate Keith Rayner and the Australian church historian and commentator Bruce Kaye. See Driver 2014, 90.

3 Rayner 2006a, 50.

4 Archbishop of Canterbury Geoffrey Fisher observed this in 1950 in a confidential address to the Australian Bishops' Conference in which he lamented the lack

of that 'happy admixture of Anglicanism' in Australian dioceses, see Hilliard 2006, 57; see also Frame 2002, 108.

5   For example, the 1866 Provincial Constitution for New South Wales. See Frame 2007, 75; it was also enshrined in Clause 8 of the 1872 Constitution of the General Synod, see McPherson 1994, 85; Rayner 2006b, 42; for a comparison with the more centralised 1890 constitution of the Canadian Church, see Hilliard 2006, 60.

6   This point is made by Philip Thomas in a paper prepared for the 1981 Primates' Meeting entitled 'Some Principles of Anglican Authority', quoted in Rayner 2006b, 32.

7   For discussion of regionalism and the relationship between national, provincial and diocesan polities as they emerged in the decades after Australian Federation see Kaye 2002, 162.

8   Population increases, the gold rush, and missionary zeal all contributed to the multiplication of dioceses in Western Australia. See Holden 1997, 183, 238.

9   Holden 1997, 253–54.

10   Driver 2014, 94.

11   Comparisons have also been drawn between the nature of moral authority exercised by the Lambeth Conference and the Australian General Synod. See Davis 1993, 181.

8

The Anglican Church of Australia: 'Microcosm' or 'Ecclesiastical Monstrosity'?

Perhaps the most obvious feature of Australian Anglican polity, by which parallels with international Anglicanism might be drawn, is in its loose federated national structure and notoriously autonomous dioceses. This assertion of diocesan autonomy has given rise to the term 'diocesanism', which it seems is particularly associated with the experience of Australian Anglicanism.[1] One of its earliest uses was recorded in 1883 in a sermon given at the parish of Christ Church South Yarra in the Diocese of Melbourne by the newly arrived Bishop of Tasmania, Daniel Fox Sandford:

> The remembrance of their [the neighbouring dioceses of Melbourne and Tasmania] corporate fellowship and unity was apt to be least present to them just when it was most necessary. Individualism and congregationalism might go farther than narrow and abridge their sympathies and keep them exclusively intent only on their own immediate interests. They might foster in their spirit and efforts a new diocesanism, which would stunt and mar their church organisation and life quite as effectually, and lead them to think that they were mere accidental congeries of individuals, or of parishes, and not a living branch of the church of Christ . . .[2]

This identification of a 'new diocesanism' as a potentially pernicious characteristic of the colonial church predates the federation of the Australian colonies into a single Commonwealth, and reveals the extent to which the holding of strong diocesan identities within the Anglican church was felt to threaten not only the move toward a national expression of Anglicanism, but also the church's claim in Australia to represent a 'living branch' of the One, Holy, Catholic and Apostolic Church.

This anxiety was perhaps most keenly felt in the 1930s as the difficulties of 'diocesanism' were more frequently discussed.[3] The employment of the term in all its early uses is pejorative, and the concept itself has more recently been criticised as antithetical to a right understanding of Anglican polity, representing 'at diocesan level the parochialism which is more characteristic of sectarian rather than Anglican ecclesiology.'[4] Despite the optimism of the Bishop of Newcastle at the turn of the century, with the accomplishment of Australian Federation in 1901, that ecclesial polity might similarly follow and 'diocesanism and provincialism will be secondary to things Australian,'[5] there continues to be not only division between dioceses but the fierce assertion of diocesan autonomy and a resistance to any actions which might compromise this independence. That it remains such an enduring and distinctive marker of Australian Anglican polity, then, is somewhat surprising and prompts the question of whether it is simply an ecclesiological inadequacy which has yet to be rectified or whether it has some ecclesial merit which commends itself for continuation?[6]

The Origins of Australian 'Diocesanism'

The entrenched 'diocesanism' of the Anglican Church of Australia has been widely attributed to the theological diversity which has grown up between dioceses and particularly incarnated in the churchmanship of individual bishops.[7] However, recent scholarship has highlighted the impact of regionalism and geography in shaping this diversity, as well as the prominent influence of the laity.[8] Keith Rayner locates some of the earliest beginnings of this division in the unlikely context of the Bishops' Conference of October 1850, the first gathering together of the Australasian bishops and the first concrete expression of collaboration between the bishops in order to address the challenges faced by the church in the colonies.[9] This division was expressed in the varying approaches taken to the questions of settling authority and governance, particularly synodical, whether by 'consensual compact' or through acts of the local legislature.[10] Whatever the motivations of each diocese, or bishop, in pursuing one course of action over another, the fact remains that each diocese acted independently in establishing its own constitution, synod, and, crucially, definition of its continued communion with Canterbury and the Church in England.[11]

While 'diocesanism' may have persisted in defining the Australian ecclesial landscape, it is not necessarily a given or immutable axiom of Anglican identity in Australia. In fact there have at times been efforts at ecclesial organization which have pushed back against this 'diocesanism'; albeit not always so successfully. There was, for example, an early push for 'provincialism' as a means of uniting dioceses and standing in as an interim measure toward establishing a 'national church' in Australia.[12] Similarly, there were moves in the late twentieth century, coinciding with the 'Bicentenary of Australia' in 1988, to reimagine the primacy within Australia as fixed in the nation's capital, Canberra, and the establishment there of a 'National Anglican Centre' as a 'place of national identity.'[13] Even within the Diocese of Sydney (which has a reputation for being a somewhat isolationist Evangelical island within Australian Anglicanism)[14] there has been a concern for the impact of unilateral diocesan action on catholic order, evidenced by the restraint shown in not implementing a controversial decision to authorize and regularize the celebration of Holy Communion by deacons and lay persons.[15] Nevertheless, even in these examples, the failure of the Australian church to take action as a national unit, and the subsequent retreat to 'diocesanism', is evident.

Provincial Polity in Australia

Of these efforts, however, it is the potential of a movement toward 'provincialism' which has found fresh momentum in the face of an ineffective national church, and an account of the development of provincial organization in Australia offers some insight into the wider need for a renewed appreciation and application of provincial polity within global Anglican ecclesiology.

Provincial organization in Australia was first established by Letters Patent in 1847 as Bishop Broughton's continental see was divided to form the dioceses of Sydney, Newcastle, Melbourne and Adelaide which, together with the existing sees of Tasmania and New Zealand, were brought under his metropolitical authority.[16] In 1866 the Province of New South Wales was created, comprising the dioceses of Sydney, Grafton and Armidale, Newcastle, and Goulburn then in existence in that colony. This earliest provincial constitution itself enshrined 'diocesanism' since 'any Diocesan synod could stop Provincial action by holding aloof.'[17] Theological tensions certainly played a part in this protectionism. Bishop Tyrell of Newcastle, a diocese which 'was edging towards Tractarianism as its prevailing ethos,'[18] was opposed to any such concessions to diocesan autonomy but 'was willing to submit in the hope (which proved a vain one) that these provisions were only temporary.'[19] Resistance to the establishment of a province came predominantly from Evangelical dioceses, Sydney and Goulburn in particular, which, negatively, feared the encroachments of ritualism as well as, positively, held a stronger commitment to ecclesial identity in the local church gathered in a particular context rather than as part of a visible universal whole.[20] While the

Province of New South Wales may have been established in 1866, those existing dioceses which were not part of its establishment, and those new dioceses since established outside New South Wales, were left without any provincial organization for another forty years. While the 1866 constitution for the Province of New South Wales was appended as a schedule to the *Church Properties Act (NSW)* of the colonial legislature, the new political reality of a federal Commonwealth of Australia after 1901 meant that subsequent provincial development would not simply reflect the fossilization of old colonial boundaries but a push toward the greater imagination of a national ecclesial identity.

The five Victorian dioceses (Melbourne, Ballarat, Bendigo, Gippsland and Wangaratta) came together to form a province in 1905, following a meeting of the Victorian bishops and other diocesan representatives held the previous year.[21] However, the establishment of a Provincial Assembly had been anticipated as early as 1853 in the *Victorian Church Constitution Act (Vic)*:

> 17. So soon as a province shall have been constituted in Victoria it shall be lawful for the Metropolitan thereof from time to time to convene the Bishops thereof and to require them to convene the members of the several Diocesan Assemblies or such Representatives of the same as shall hereafter by any such Provincial Assemblies be determined at such time and place as he may deem fit to consider of and determine upon all such matters and things as may concern the affairs of the said Church in Victoria . . .[22]

The fifty-year delay from the passing of the 1853 Act to the final establishment of a province in Victoria in 1905 was necessitated by the want of a sufficient and requisite number of dioceses; a minimum of three as set out in the 1872 Constitution of the General Synod.[23] The diocese of Ballarat was formed out of Melbourne in 1875, but it was not until 1902 that Bendigo, Wangaratta and Gippsland were established. The Bishop of Melbourne, Henry Lowther Clarke, warned against a provincial structure which kowtowed to 'diocesanism', quoting the opinion of former Primate and Bishop of Sydney, Alfred Barry, who described 'the existence of a Provincial Synod which is obliged to report humbly to the Diocesan Synods, as an ecclesiastical monstrosity.'[24] Nevertheless, Clarke's ambitions for any provincial arrangement were modest, envisaging 'constitutional unity and an outlook as wide as the State itself [as] the sole object which the Diocese of Melbourne has in view.'[25] There was, nevertheless, opposition to such provincial organization, led by the Bishop of Ballarat, Arthur Green, who among other things feared the hijacking of the provincial agenda and synod because of a lack of proportional representation as set out in the 1853 Act, allowing 'three smaller dioceses out of five the power to paralyse all legislation within the walls of the Provincial Synod itself.'[26] The three newly created dioceses of Bendigo, Wangaratta and Gippsland had been carved out of Ballarat only two years earlier. The final provisions of the provincial constitution accepted and adopted on the 14th November 1905 followed the precedent of the 1872 General Synod constitution in providing that 'Ordinances or Determinations as are passed without reference from any Diocesan Synod shall not be binding upon the Church in any Diocese, unless and until such Ordinance or Determination shall be accepted by the Church in such Diocese.'[27] Once again, 'diocesanism' had prevailed.

The Province of Queensland: an Exception

The one place where a strong and meaningful provincial polity was established was in Queensland, and its 1905 provincial constitution stands in stark contrast to that of Victoria. The required number of dioceses within the colony was achieved in 1892 with the establishment of the see of Rockhampton, numbering alongside the dioceses of Brisbane (1859) and North Queensland (1878). Bishop William Webber of Brisbane had raised the subject with his diocesan synod as early as 1887 and has been credited as the principal architect of the scheme.[28] Momentum throughout the 1890s was slow and resistance came largely from North Queensland, a diocese which had not been formed out of Brisbane but instead had a historical lineage linking back to the Diocese of Sydney. Concerns in North Queensland that they might be overwhelmed by the dominance of Brisbane in any provincial structure were assuaged with the creation of the Diocese of Carpentaria in 1900, an ally in the north.[29]

The 1905 provincial constitution is exceptional among Australian ecclesial jurisdictions. It sets out in relative detail the areas of determinative competency of the provincial synod, including the 'mode of election of a Metropolitan, the prerogatives of a Bishop, the definition of the spiritualities of a Diocese . . . [and] the taking of measures for promoting intercommunion with other branches of the Holy Catholic Church in the Province, so far as is consistent with the doctrine and laws of the Church of England.'[30] Furthermore, determinations and canons coming down from General Synod were reserved to the province for adoption on a provincial basis rather than piecemeal by dioceses (Section 21) and the comprovincial bishops were afforded a formal role in the election of the metropolitan whenever the see of Brisbane should become vacant (Section 17). Unlike

Victoria, representation at the Provincial Synod was not proportional to the size of each diocese concerned, which protected the concerns of the smaller dioceses. Most significantly, the constitution explicitly states:

> 15. All Canons shall be promulgated by the President of Synod, and shall, when so promulgated, be binding thereafter upon all the Dioceses of the Province. Provided always that nothing therein contained shall be or be construed in any manner contrary to or inconsistent with the ancient Canons whereby the Diocesan Synods have the free adminis- tration of their own internal affairs . . .[31]

Nevertheless, despite this strongest of efforts toward provincial orga- nization within the Anglican Church of Australia, the province itself would never attain the kind of profile perhaps imagined and indicated by the constitution. Keith Rayner offers an assessment of the reasons for this:

> The tradition of diocesanism was deeply rooted, and the dioceses (or sometimes the parishes) continued to hold the purse-strings. At the same time, the growing national spirit within Australia, which looked towards a national constitution for the church as for the nation, was already threatening to render the province obsolescent as the major form of wider ecclesiastical organisation.[32]

Whether provincial organization was a boon or bane to the cause to establish a 'national church' was contested. In Queensland, it was hoped that efforts to organize provincially might give a foretaste of what a 'national church' could achieve.[33] During the negotiations toward a con- stitution for a 'national church' in the 1930s, Bishop George Frodsham of North Queensland saw the potential of the province to pioneer the adoption of the draft constitution even without the cooperation of the other Australian dioceses, whereas Archbishop of Brisbane, William Wand, cautioned that such independent action 'would serve to empha- sise the differences that already exist between us.'[34] The most significant difference between provincial organization in Queensland and the rest of Australia, perhaps, was in the relatively unified Anglo-Catholic identity of the Queensland dioceses and their strong support for surpassing the pitfalls of 'diocesanism', as evidenced in their provincial constitution.[35] This has been the distinctive contribution of the Province of Queensland, its witness to an ecclesiology which peers beyond diocesan interests and insularity and understands its own provincial polity to be a type and model of what ought to be achievable nationally:

That has been one of the continuing contributions of the church in Queensland: an opposition to any understanding of the national church and of the General Synod as just a federation of dioceses, but that it ought to be a real national entity, both for the sake of the church itself and for the sake of the influence of the church in the life of the nation; and that as long as the church was just a collection of individual dioceses each doing our own thing we cannot be the spiritual force in the life of this nation, which has had a steadily developing sense of its national identity, that we ought to be.[36]

As well as the relative uniformity within dioceses, and even provinces as in the example of Queensland, of various expressions of theological identity along the churchmanship continuum, regionalism and the immediate affinity felt between dioceses within colonial and, later, state borders also promoted the push toward provincial organization. Bruce Kaye has done much work to emphasize the impact of this regionalism, and the potential which provincial polity may have had for breaking the impasse between 'diocesanism' and an ineffective federated 'national church':

These two examples [Victoria and Queensland] reveal a considerable support for a greater provincial or state grouping in the church organisation. That grouping remains in both Victoria and Queensland in institutions such as university colleges (St John's in Brisbane) and theological colleges (Trinity in Melbourne). Given the developing demographics of Australia, a move to provincial structures might well have led to more powerful provincial organisations and the polarity between extremely powerful local diocese and relatively weak national synod might not have eventuated.[37]

This potential did not come to pass and by the time of the eventual ratification of a national constitution for the Church of England in Australia in 1962 (it would take a further twenty years before the name was changed to the Anglican Church of Australia) 'diocesanism' had well and truly won out and become formally entrenched in Australian ecclesial polity.

Diocese, Province and National Church in Australia

The definitive dominance of the diocese over the province in Australian polity was highlighted by the Australian General Synod's response to the document 'The Anglican Communion: Identity and Authority', presented to the 1990 Anglican Consultative Council meeting in Wales, which staunchly defended the peculiarity of 'diocesanism' within Australian Anglican polity:

> The reality of diocesan autonomy is a characteristic note of our Anglican Church of Australia, and a principle fundamental to the Constitution of this Church. In Constitutional terms the ultimate powers are reserved to the Dioceses. This means that in matters of canonical change to our order, and in such matters as financial provision for objectives beyond the Dioceses, the ultimate decisions lie with the Dioceses. This does, of course, create our own internal difficulties at the national level, but we would not wish to see the external structural relationship within the Communion as a whole inimical to this, or applying through its own operations any covert pressure for us to change, to move into alignment with the international model, or the structural models of other Provinces.[38]

A more recent assessment made by the 2014 Report of the Viability and Structures Task Force, commissioned by the Standing Committee of the General Synod, articulates both the relatively weak position of the Australian provinces within the polity of the Anglican Church of Australia, as well as their latent potential to address the challenges faced by the contemporary Australian church:

> Provincial structures vary from province to province, but are generally about establishing meetings at a provincial level, which are opportunities to share and learn rather than establishing policy or passing legislation. They can be a very helpful forum for seeking to establish common policy across dioceses such as in professional standards or identifying ways of collaboration. The strength, potential and effectiveness of provinces are very much dependent upon the commitment of the individual dioceses and the Metropolitan as to what they see the Province for. Potentially provinces could be a very effective means by which dioceses work together and share resources, but history so far shows that they have not been greatly utilised, with Provincial Councils and Synods meeting often only once a year.[39]

Without the potential of provincial polity being realized in Australia, the ecclesial landscape is most defined by the tension between hard 'diocesanism' and the pretentions of an ineffective 'national church' structure. This tension is exemplified in the complex provisions of the Anglican Church of Australia's Constitution. It is notable that the influence of

Archbishop of Canterbury, Geoffrey Fisher, was crucial in motivating the Australian bishops to persist in the movement toward establishing a national church, after a series of failed attempts to pass a constitution, and he himself provided the first draft of what would eventually become the 1962 Constitution.[40]

The Constitution of the Anglican Church of Australia provides that the 'diocese shall in accordance with the historic custom of the One Holy Catholic and Apostolic Church continue to be the unit of organization of this Church.'[41] Nevertheless, the Constitution attributes to General Synod a mandate to:

> make canons rules and resolutions relating to the order and good government of this Church including canons in respect of ritual, ceremonial and discipline and make statements as to the faith of this Church and declare its view on any matter affecting this Church or affecting spiritual, moral or social welfare, and may take such steps as may be necessary or expedient in furtherance of union with other Christian communions.[42]

Despite this seemingly wide remit, a significant authority is reserved to dioceses concerning any canons concerning 'ritual, ceremonial and discipline' in that they do not come into effect within any diocese until and unless that diocese adopts such a canon by means of ordinance through its own diocesan synod.[43] Thus dioceses ultimately retain an effective veto insofar as they are affected by any proposal that may impact them under the almost all-encompassing purview of 'ritual, ceremonial and discipline.'[44]

These constitutional provisions reflect a long-standing preference in Australian Anglican polity for maintaining diocesan autonomy at the expense of a national, and even provincial, ecclesiology. Diocesan autonomy was enshrined in the original 1872 Constitution of the General Synod, which contained the proviso that 'no Determination of the General Synod shall be binding upon the Church in any Diocese unless and until such Determination shall be accepted by the Church in such Diocese.'[45] It is this proviso which persists in the procedure set out for Canons concerning 'ritual, ceremonial and discipline' in Section 28 of the current 1962 Constitution.[46] The story of constitutional revision between 1872 and 1962 has been competently told elsewhere,[47] clearly highlighting the long-standing impediments to national church organization and the resulting compromise which 'is not able to meet the needs and pressures' of the contemporary church and 'remains as a nettle for Anglicans in Australia to grasp.'[48]

Australia as a 'Microcosm' of the Communion

The unique and persistent place of 'diocesanism' within Australian Anglicanism bears out the claim that it represents something of a 'microcosm' of international Anglican polity, at least insofar as the analogy may be drawn between powerful dioceses in Australia and the autonomous member-churches of the Communion. There are, of course, some important differences: the Anglican Church of Australia has a formal system of national tribunals which is unmatched in the Communion; the depth of moral and spiritual authority associated with the role of Archbishop of Canterbury is not nearly as evident in the influence of the Australian Primate; similarly, the historic and symbolic associations with place, such as Canterbury and Lambeth, have not been realized in Australia, at least in the national context, with its 'roaming' primacy and lack of national centre or cathedral; furthermore, there have not developed in the Australian church scene quite the same conciliar, consultative and representative forums as are embodied in the 'Instruments of Communion'.

The extent to which 'diocesanism' in Australia, and the complete autonomy of member-churches within the Communion, is a perversion of polity (as Archbishop Barry decried it, an 'ecclesiastical monstrosity') has equally been contested. In Australia it would be fair to make a broad characterization according to familiar theological 'camps', whereby those dioceses at the more 'Anglo-Catholic' end of the churchmanship continuum have been more open to stronger provincial and national structures (as is evident in the constitutional organization of the Province of Queensland) than more 'Evangelical' dioceses. Archbishop of Sydney, Howard Mowll, for example, exclaimed to his diocesan synod (immediately following his failure to secure the primacy, which for the first time since 1872 had gone to an archbishop other than that of Sydney):

> If I judge the spirit of Sydney Churchmanship aright, it has its roots in a deep conviction that Sydney has its own specific contribution to make to the life of the whole Australian Church, and believes that she can make that contribution best only if she is entirely free to make her own way. She has held to the belief that neither in her own interest nor in the interest of the Church as a whole can she lightly surrender that freedom.[49]

Thus the persistence of 'diocesanism' in Australia, as well as the assertion of autonomy within the Communion, reflects the principle of 'competency' but not 'catholicity'. The diocese, as a discrete Christian community gathered around the apostolic leadership and guardianship of the bishop, is perfectly competent to govern itself according to its own synodical structures and norms, but this in and of itself is not enough to express its catholicity. So too with regard to the competency of the 'national church' within international Anglican polity.

This competency is by no means a detrimental quality of ecclesial organization, and so 'diocesanism' as well as other expressions of autonomy can quite rightly be defended. However, there still remains the real potential for the hyper-assertion of this competency to morph into the 'monstrosity' of a perverted polity which compromises catholicity for the sake of self-sufficiency. It is this lesson which the Australian context offers international Anglicanism, as a 'microcosm' of the Communion with particular reference to the analogous relationship between 'diocesanism' and the autonomy and dominance of the 'national church'.

The confluence of theological diversity, geographical particularity and remoteness, varying socio-political circumstances, and the independent development of constitutions and synods within each Australian diocese meant each 'was a self-contained legal entity which over time created a jealously guarded tradition, ethos and identity, protective of its own interests.'[50] These distinctive diocesan identities have become even more guarded in the past thirty years as controversies over the ordination of women and, more recently, human sexuality mean 'the goodwill required within individual dioceses to maintain a genuinely national Church is being slowly dissipated as notions of authority become more divergent.'[51]

The notable exception to the somewhat 'monochrome' nature of the Australian diocesan scene has been the Diocese of Melbourne, which has never seen one particular party or churchmanship dominate.[52] While the divided nature of the Diocese of Melbourne has given rise to its own fair share of acrimony in diocesan politics, it is also uniquely positioned to become a driving influence in offering a provincial response to the need for a coordinated approach to the increasingly prominent issue of Professional Standards and Safeguarding across the Anglican Church of Australia.

Notes

1 A cursory glance through the 223 Google results for 'diocesanism' will bear this out.

2 *Australian Town and Country Journal* 1883, 38. Sandford had been appointed to Tasmania from the Scottish Episcopal Church. See also the exhortation of one correspondent from the Diocese of Newcastle in the Province of New South Wales regarding the importance of payments to the controversial 'Centennial Fund', that 'the selfish sectarian spirit of Diocesanism, Parochialism, Congregationalism

(a growing evil), may be abated, if not abolished, by the corporate union in a common work and for a common end of all the members of the Church throughout the province,' Bode 1888, 3.

3 See for example Wyatt 1937, 14.

4 McPherson 1994, 86.

5 Fletcher 2002, 305.

6 For example, Bruce Kaye posits that 'The regional dynamic has meant that Australian Anglicanism has emerged in a highly subsidiarist form and that Australian Anglican synods are distinctively democratic in character, a quality which has antecedents in the longer tradition of conciliarism in Anglicanism.' See Kaye 2002, 175.

7 Macneil 2006, 206.

8 In particular the contribution of Bruce Kaye. See Hilliard 2006, 59.

9 Rayner 2006b, 39.

10 See page 73.

11 Rayner 2006b, 39.

12 Keith Rayner recognizes the sentiment commonly held in Queensland that 'the natural way to proceed toward national autonomy was from diocese to province to national church,' but considers provincialism itself to be ultimately 'a threat to a national structure' halted only because of the 'providential outcome' of war with Japan in 1941. See Rayner 2006b, 44.

13 The strapline 'a place of national identity' comes from *National Anglican Centre - a Brochure Prepared for General Synod* 1985; Hilliard 2002, 127; more detailed discussion of how the expression of a 'national church' might take more visible form, whether in a devoted Primatial See or the building of a 'National Church Centre', is given in Frame 2007, 88–99.

14 For an example of the polemical case against 'Sydney Anglicanism' see Porter 2011. A reply is given in M. P. Jensen 2012.

15 Tom Frame provides a detailed account from an Evangelical perspective, concluding that 'although efforts to protect those who encourage or engage in lay presidency from legal action are contrary to Anglican custom, the diocese has shown genuine regard for prevailing sentiment within the Anglican Communion by recognising and respecting the limits of diversity that the Communion would appear ready to tolerate.' See Frame 2007, 182–88.

16 'Letters Patent appointing Bishop Broughton Metropolitan of Australia, 25 June 1847' in Giles 1929, 231–37.

17 Giles 1929, 110.

18 Frame 2007, 75.

19 Giles 1929, 110.

20 Dickey 2002, 57–58.

21 Giles 1929, 91; a report of the conference is given in, *The Argus* 1904, 5.

22 The Victoria Church Constitution Act (Vic), 18 Vic 45, reproduced as originally enacted in Giles 1929, 250–51.

23 This number is also peculiar to Australian Anglicanism. The 1867 and 1878 Lambeth Conferences recommended 'that all those Dioceses which are not as yet gathered into Provinces should, as soon as possible, form part of some Provincial organisation.' See Davidson 1920, 101. Resolution 43 of the 1920 Lambeth Conference suggested a minimum of four, and this was reiterated in advice issued by the Anglican Consultative Council in 1971 which commented that 'a college

requires to be more than a mere trio of bishops and is severely limited if it consists of less than four diocesan bishops.' See *Guidelines for the Creation of New Provinces and Dioceses: Resolutions Passed by the Anglican Consultative Council*. The most recent province to be established in Australia, South Australia, was formed from three dioceses in 1970.

24   Giles 1929, 91. Note that the date, 1844, given by Giles is incorrect. The address by Barry was given on 7 October 1884, in his Presidential Address to the Fifth Session of the Provincial Synod of New South Wales. See, Sydney Morning Herald, 8 October 1884, 7.

25   Giles 1929, 91.

26   Giles 1929, 92.

27   Section 8 of the Constitution of the Province of Victoria, reproduced in Giles 1929, 253.

28   Rayner 1962, 128.

29   Rayner 1962, 128.

30   Queensland Provincial Constitution, Section 2, reproduced in *Provincial Constitutions of New South Wales, Victoria, Queensland and Western Australia* 1967.

31   *Provincial Constitutions of New South Wales, Victoria, Queensland and Western Australia* 1967.

32   Rayner 1962, 130.

33   J. Norman 1953, 167.

34   General Synod Proceedings, 1937, 23, quoted in Rayner 1962, 236.

35   The dysfunction of the 'national church' and division along churchmanship lines was comically exemplified at the opening service of the 1937 General Synod at St Andrew's Cathedral, Sydney, when the Primate, the then Archbishop of Perth Henry Le Fanu, was almost prevented by an 'arch-evangelical archdeacon' from processing with the Primatial Cross. See Davis 1993, 94.

36   Keith Rayner in his 1987 lectures to the Brisbane Clergy Summer School quoted in Aspinall 2009, 8.

37   Kaye 2002, 162–63.

38   'The Anglican Communion: Identity and Authority - Response from the Anglican Church of Australia,' 3, in *ACC-8 Wales, 22 July to 3 August 1990: Preparatory Files* 1989.

39   *Report of the Viability & Structures Task Force, and Other Materials Impinging on the Small Groups Discussion Program* 2014, 8–020.

40   Frame 2007, 85; Brian Fletcher contends that, more important than even Fisher's contribution, 'was a deep-rooted tradition that lay at the core of Anglicanism - namely its insistence on the need to maintain unity as well as diversity.' See Fletcher 2006, 20.

41   Constitution, Anglican Church of Australia, 2014, Section 7 [RG XIII: C(A2)CCN1].

42   Constitution, Anglican Church of Australia, 2014, Section 26 [RG XIII: C(A2)CCN1].

43   The procedure to be followed for such 'special bills' is set out in Section 28 of the Constitution.

44   Importantly, 'Discipline' is defined in Section 74(9) as:

    (a)   in Chapters II to VII and X to XII the obligation to adhere to, to observe and to carry out (as appropriate):

(i)   the faith, ritual and ceremonial of this Church; and
(ii) the other rules of this Church which impose on the members of the clergy obligations regarding the religious and moral life of this Church; and

(b) in Chapter IX, as regards a person in Holy Orders licensed by the bishop of a diocese or resident in a diocese both:
(i)   the obligations in the ordinal undertaken by that person; and
(ii) the ordinances in force in that diocese.

45 'Document T - The Original Constitution of General Synod, adopted by General Conference, October 23, 1872,' in Giles 1929, 273.

46 The limits on General Synod to make canons which 'affect the order and good government of the Church within a diocese,' as set out under Section 30 of the Constitution, has recently been tested by determination of the Appellate Tribunal in April 2007 with respect to the Special Tribunal Canon 2004 and the National Register Canon 2004, where the force of the verb 'affect' was construed according to a 'narrow' rather than 'wide' interpretation. See Blake 2008.

47 The definitive account remains Davis 1993; a short summary is provided in Frappell 2002, 89–91.

48 Davis 1993, 188.

49 Davis 1993, 86.

50 Hilliard 2006, 59.

51 Frame 2006, 141.

52 Hilliard 2006, 62.

9

Provincial Possibilities: a Theological Reflection on the Potential of Provincial Polity

If the Anglican Church of Australia, as a microcosm of the Communion, does offer a relevant and instructive context for addressing questions of Anglican international polity, it would seem that its strong preference for 'diocesanism' at the expense of both a provincial or national-church ecclesiology ought to mitigate against whatever contribution it might make in rediscovering and reimagining provincial polity within the wider Communion. Provincial structures within the Australian church have long been inhibited by diocesan interests, on the one hand, and national-church ambitions, on the other. Archbishop of Brisbane, Philip Aspinall, has articulated this weakness with reference even to the Province of Queensland which constitutionally, at least historically as has been shown, was the most advanced in its adopted powers and prerogatives:

> The powers and obligations of an Archbishop in a diocese not his own, but in his Province, are limited and somewhat uncertain . . . The Queensland Provincial Synod I think has met only once in my 12 years as Archbishop . . . If there is a Provincial Tribunal it has never met in my time. In practise, provincial structures are weak, rarely used and do not play a big role.[1]

However, in the last decade there has been a resurgence of provincial action and activity particularly in the field of Professional Standards and in responding to the concerns and recommendations of the Royal Commission into Institutional Responses to Child Sexual Abuse established by the Australian Federal Government in 2013. The Royal Commission has recognized particularly that the 'Anglican Church of Australia has assumed a role of leadership within the international Anglican community in relation to child sexual abuse.'[2] Much of this leadership has been provincial, as noted by the General Synod's Viability and Structures Task Force, which also identified the potential for other aspects of the church's mission to be tackled provincially:

At the recent annual Australian Bishops' Meeting held in Ballarat in early April, over 40 bishops of our Church had the opportunity to read a draft of this Report and there was strong endorsement for the strategy that a way forward to act on many of the issues raised in this report was to work provincially.

Although it was recognised that provincial structures vary, it was also strongly affirmed that already the provincial structure is being used to good effect with the administration of professional standards and other matters. In Victoria the move towards incorporation of dioceses is being managed through the Provincial Council structure and this shows an effective means by which we can work as dioceses in future: not alone, but together! Another example from Victoria is the move towards Anglicare Victoria being a welfare agency for the whole state. This already happens in Western Australia with the three dioceses in that province.

The bishops felt that there was more capacity and energy to work together provincially than trying to get the National Church to work as an organic entity in addressing issues. The complexity of our Church's Constitution and with General Synod meeting only every three to four years, it was felt provincial structures offered a more immediate way forward. Provincial Councils and Synods have the capacity to meet annually and more if required. The bishops were largely of the opinion that provincial co-operation was a more achievable goal than trying to work as a National Church.[3]

Rather than being a merely pragmatic or practical structural solution to challenges of ecclesial polity, both within the Australian context and the international Communion, this revival of a provincial polity within the Anglican Church of Australia demonstrates an ecclesiology which is able to negotiate the competing demands between autonomy and interdependence and to model a holistic vision of the Church's life – encompassing questions of authority, mission, communion, reciprocity and recognition – which has both ecclesial authenticity and integrity. With reference to the work of the Royal Commission, as well as provincial responses to Professional Standards across Australia but most particularly in Victoria, this authenticity and integrity will be explored according to the four creedal 'marks' of the Church: that it is One, Holy, Catholic and Apostolic. One, in its unity of purpose over and against fractured 'diocesanism' and ineffective national structures. Holy, in its commitment to a practical response to holiness in the church. Catholic, in a response which is recognizable across dioceses, while still protecting their integrity as autonomous but still interdependent. Apostolic, in modelling a response that centres authority and responsibility on personal, rather than merely institutional, agents of ecclesial identity.[4] These marks are identifiable in the provincial polity which is demonstrated by the example of work being done around Professional Standards in the Australian church and reflection on this work is able to point toward what such a polity might have to offer the Communion.

Royal Commission into Institutional Responses to Child Sexual Abuse

The Royal Commission into Institutional Responses to Child Sexual Abuse was established by Letters Patent on 11 January 2013, naming New South Wales Judge of Appeal Justice Peter McClellan as its Chair. Its Terms of Reference mandate it to investigate and recommend on preventative measures to be adopted by government and institutions to protect children against sexual abuse in institutional settings, best practice with regards to reporting and responding to reports of such abuse, addressing structural and institutional impediments to effective reporting and responses, and the provision of redress by institutions to victims of sexual abuse as well as other forms of support and accessibility to avenues of criminal investigation and prosecution.[5] In addition, much of the work of the Royal Commission has been to hear the stories of those directly and indirectly affected by abuse: not only to inform their own understanding of the scope of abuse within institutions, but also to offer a safe and supportive space where those who have been abused will be listened to, their credibility not interrogated, and be offered appropriate referrals. As of November 2017 the Royal Commission has received over forty thousand calls, around twenty five thousand written submissions, held almost eight thousand private sessions and made almost two and a half thousand referrals to police.[6] The wide scope of the Commission's investigations are grouped into Case Studies, of which the most relevant here is Case Study 52 which was heard in March 2017 at a public hearing 'to inquire into the current policies and procedures of Anglican Church authorities in Australia in relation to child-protection and child-safety standards, including responding to allegations of child sexual abuse.'[7]

The extent of abuse within Australian Anglican institutions uncovered by the Commission and the details which have been made public through submissions, exhibits and the final report make for harrowing reading. However, the scope of this study – without mitigating the importance of that testimony – is concerned more with the perhaps belated but still energetic response to addressing these institutional and ecclesial failures which is being driven through provincial structures, and then to reflect theologically on what this demonstrates more broadly about the nature of provincial polity not only for the Anglican Church of Australia but for the Communion as a whole.

Provincial Response to Professional Standards and Safeguarding in Victoria

One gauge of the effectiveness and relevance of provincial polity within Australia is discernible through the industriousness, or not, of its primary organ of governance and representation: the Provincial Synod. Provision is made under Section 40 of the Constitution of the Anglican Church of Australia for a 'Provincial Synod or Provincial Council' in each of the five Australian provinces.[8] In Western Australia and South Australia the Provincial Council ordinarily meets every two and three years respectively. In New South Wales it is every five years.[9] In Queensland the Provincial Synod has only met three times in the past twenty-two years. An exception is the Victorian Provincial Council which in the seven-year period between 2010 and 2017 has met ten times – annually in the first three years, biannually in 2014 and 2015, and annually again in 2016 and 2017. As well as having an active Provincial Council, Victoria is also the only province to have a Provincial Legal Committee which was recently described as 'a lively group, a rich resource for the province and a mutual support,' as well as, 'believed to be the most active and high order group in the national church.'[10] The minutes of the Provincial Council over this period reveal not only the persistence and eventual dominance of Professional Standards and the Royal Commission on its agenda, but also a commitment to provincial action across these and other wider interests.

Draft model legislation was prepared by the national Church Law Commission in 2003 which became the General Synod's 2004 *Model Professional Standards Ordinance*. This was intended to provide uniformity in regulating and enforcing Professional Standards across all dioceses of the Anglican Church of Australia. However that legislation, which in order to take effect in a diocese must have been accepted into the law of that diocese through an act or ordinance of its own synod, came under considerable criticism by the Victorian Provincial Legal Committee and was not adopted in any of the Victorian dioceses.[11] The concerns of the

Provincial Legal Committee were partly constitutional, but other aspects of the proposed legislation were described as 'ambiguous . . . confusing and in any event impracticable and potentially unfair,' as well as, 'puzzling and disturbing . . . [it being] questionable whether the fair operation of principles of natural justice [are] accommodated.'[12]

The synod of the metropolitical see of the Province of Victoria, the Diocese of Melbourne, introduced and enacted its own legislation in 2009 in the form of the *Professional Standards Act*. A distinctive, although not entirely unique, feature of synodical legislation passed by dioceses within the Province of Victoria is that they are given legal force through the 1854 *Church of England Constitution Act* of the Victorian State Parliament and become binding on the bishop, clergy and laity resident in the respective diocese.[13] It was partly because of this legal nexus between diocesan and state law that the proposed 2004 ordinance was deemed so problematic. The 2009 legislation, however, was drafted after extensive provincial consultation with 'complainants, respondents, the Director of Professional Standards, the members of the Professional Standards Committee and the Provincial Legal Committee' within Victoria and was able to avoid the pitfalls which characterized the 2004 ordinance of the National Church, and offer a 'clear legislative 'complaint based' framework for dealing with complaints against clergy and certain lay people based on the question of fitness of the Church worker.'[14] Virtually identical legislation was subsequently adopted in the dioceses of Ballarat and Wangaratta. This work was largely driven by the incoming Chancellor of the Diocese of Melbourne, Michael Warner Shand QC, who was also Chancellor of the Diocese of Ballarat between 2002 and 2010: the impact of personal influence on achieving provincial action should not be underestimated.

The minutes of the 2010 Provincial Council note this development, although do not go much further than describing the situation in the dioceses of Melbourne, Ballarat and Wangaratta (which had adopted uniform legislation) and Gippsland and Bendigo (which had retained the non-legislative 2003 *Power and Trust Protocol*).[15] Minutes of the 2011 Provincial Council again simply report the situation in individual dioceses, although they do reflect a little on the cooperation between dioceses, such as Gippsland and Melbourne, in improving the old protocols and acknowledging, as in the case of Bendigo, the limitations of that regime in favour of the legislative basis adopted in Melbourne, Ballarat and Wangaratta. Even where a uniform approach has been adopted, however, local adaptations are evident. For example, in Wangaratta changes to the legislation allow for the right of a defendant to cross-examine a complainant.[16] These early indicators of some dissatisfaction with such a variety of approaches within the Province are discussed more fully the following year when Provincial Council explicitly acknowledges the need for a coordinated provincial approach and establishes a subcommittee to investigate this more fully:

> Discussion focused on the differences among the dioceses and whether there should be a single approach. It was noted that: the wider community does not understand why there would be differences; it would be helpful to hold a workshop to understand the current legislation; that for clergy moving between dioceses there is an advantage in having the same professional standards; and that even with the same professional standards each diocese is in charge of its own implementation. It was further noted that there is a value in sharing the resources available instead of needing to duplicate these in each diocese.
> It was moved: Bishop Huggins, Seconded: Bishop McIntyre
>
> *That the Victorian Provincial Council agrees to form a subcommittee including Diocesan Bishops, Chancellors, Registrars and representatives of Professional Standards Committees to review the level of integration of Professional Standards management and make any recommendation as to closer integration of our work in this area.*
> *CARRIED*[17]

Despite this resolution, the minutes of the following meeting of Provincial Council reveal that the proverbial inertia and ineffectiveness that characterizes the Australian provinces had not entirely escaped Victoria. The sub-committee which had been established had not yet met, some frustration is evident with the minutes noting that '. . . where possible it is important to make processes work more speedily. A meeting will be arranged.'[18]

A number of other provincial projects had reported no progress, or expressed other tensions, including efforts to extend the scope of the Melbourne Anglican Foundation to the other provincial dioceses (providing shared legal services and a vehicle for receiving tax-deductible donations) and the relationship between the Melbourne-based provincial welfare-agency, Anglicare Victoria, and the regional dioceses. The Metropolitan gathered together some of this discontent and extended a call to a renewed provincial identity and cooperation:

> The Archbishop expressed his concern that there is now increasing fragmentation across the Province with the canon law of the dioceses no longer being in common. While there appears to be a wish for the dioceses to work together more closely, at the same time dioceses are

working independently on some key matters such as professional standards and episcopal standards. He stated that we have lost some things we once held in common and we should consider how to build the confidence to inspire ministry and mission across the Province.[19]

It would not be too much of a stretch to see this as a 'wake-up call', prompting an intensification of provincial efforts and structures to address particularly the issue of Professional Standards – but also the related issues of Episcopal Standards (bishops not being covered within the existing Professional Standards regimes) and Redress Schemes for complainants. In both 2014 and 2015 the Provincial Council met twice and these issues began to dominate the agenda.

In particular, there is a renewed impetus to pursue a provincial approach through the adoption of uniform legislation with the August 2014 meeting of the Provincial Council establishing a Victorian Provincial Working Group '. . . to undertake a review of Professional Standards across the Province with a view to:

1   Establishing a common Provincial Model Ordinance for Professional Standards for clergy and church workers.
2   Establishing a common Provincial Protocol for Professional Standards for clergy and church workers . . .'[20]

The Provincial Working Group, in its report to the Provincial Bishops' Meeting in February 2015, identified the need for consistency across the Province by examining the perspectives of a variety of stakeholders: including the challenge articulated by the Royal Commission 'not just to consider our own diocese, but to look at this issue holistically and our response as Anglican Church leaders,' as well as community expectations which do not differentiate between diocesan and sector organizations such as welfare agencies and schools when dealing with the 'Anglican Church', the need to create a consistent and straightforward process for complainants and respondents ensuring both procedural fairness and pastoral care, and also removing from individual bishops both liability and responsibility for investigating, adjudicating and determining complaints and consequences.[21]

This Provincial Working Group, chaired by the Bishop of Bendigo and including the Chancellors of the dioceses of Melbourne and Ballarat, the Registrars of the dioceses of Melbourne and Gippsland, and the Advocates of the dioceses of Bendigo and Wangaratta, as well as the Chair of Anglicare Victoria and an independent consultant, was extremely productive, meeting sixteen times between August 2014 and the 29 April 2016 when a proposed Uniform Act was considered and approved by the Provincial Council.[22] This uniform legislation, intended to be enacted across all diocesan synods in the province, has as a key concern the need to balance diocesan autonomy with provincial coherency and consistency:

15. The proposal represents a balancing of the interests of diocesan autonomy and the need for independence and to achieve consistency and economies of scale:

(a) On the one hand, Synod must enact the Uniform Act and reserves the right to repeal it. As at present, the Archbishop in Council must approve any applicable code of conduct for Church workers and regulations under the legislation. The Scheme Corporation must also consult with Bishop in Council when appointing the Director of Professional Standards of a diocese and its Professional Standards Committee; and

(b) On the other hand, the directors of the Scheme Corporation will appoint the office holders of the Office of Professional Standards and approve operating protocols.[23]

This approach deliberately resisted the forces of 'diocesanism' in proposing a uniform provincial response. The plurality of diocesan approaches previously pursued risked the further erosion of community confidence as well as an incoherent Anglican response in both reality and public perception. However, it was also felt impracticable to work a provincial response through some of the existing provincial structures. This would have entailed diocesan synods ceding jurisdiction and legislative authority to the Provincial Council in an unprecedented way, and asking the Province to legislate for them. The Provincial Council is not principally a legislative body and there exist only two current ordinances, one of which provides for its constitutional basis (*Ordinance for Re-Constituting the Province of Victoria 1979*) and the other, implemented in response to a requirement of the National Church Constitution, is the *Canonical Fitness of Bishops Ordinance 1979*.[24] For these reasons, as well as difficulties in extending the scope of members to whom legislation would be binding, the establishment of an independent corporation was preferred and, indeed, deemed to be necessary. The establishment of diocesan corporations had already taken place in every diocese of the Province in response to government pressures to establish accountable persons to whom church workers might be deemed 'employees' for the purposes of the *Workplace Injury Rehabilitation and Compensation Act 2013 (Vic)*.[25] The corporate approach, therefore, offers something of a more flexible and innovative means of overcoming some of the structural and constitutional impediments of the inherited provincial and diocesan polities. However the approach is still very much a provincial one; albeit reimagining the province into a corporate entity which offers the potential to overcome entrenched 'diocesanism' as well as being inclusive of non-diocesan ecclesial entities (such as schools and welfare agencies):

> The diocesan approach has its limitations. Under the *Church Constitution Act* 1854 (Vic), the legislation of each diocesan synod in Victoria is binding on members of the Church to the extent there provided. A corporate entity affiliated with the Church, be it a school or other entity is not 'a member'. For like reasons, a provincial ordinance would not bind them. The corporation approach would bind them on a contractual basis if they were members of the corporation. It would also bind the diocesan corporation of a diocese outside Victoria, such as, for example, the diocese of Tasmania [an extra-provincial diocese within the Anglican Church of Australia]. If the process was to bind those office holders of a participating body who were not members of the Church, that would have to be achieved by possibly a contractual term of appointment. It therefore offers a more contemporary and effective means to bind together different organisations within the Anglican community who desire to come together in a professional standards context.[26]

Despite this, there have still been delays in overcoming the perceived threat to diocesan independence and bringing the process to full fruition through the participation of all provincial dioceses. The dioceses of Bendigo and Melbourne, which have provided significant leadership over the past decade, have both enacted the Professional Standards Uniform Act by means of an Adoption Act in their diocesan synods, the provincial Scheme Corporation, Kooyoora Ltd, has been established with the corporations of those two diocese as inaugural members and the legislation took effect from 1 July 2017. However, the dioceses of Wangaratta and Gippsland have been hesitant in joining themselves fully to the scheme through the adoption of the Uniform Act, and instead have opted for the time being to draw on the corporation on a 'fee for service' basis.[27] The minutes of the 2016 Provincial Council reveal some of the reservations expressed by the dioceses of Gippsland and Ballarat concerning the set-up and operation of this provincial model, in particular that certain functions ought to be '. . . retained by the Bishop and the Diocese,' in order to avoid the perception of "outsourcing' the work rather than the Church being seen to bear the responsibility.'[28] Notwithstanding the continuing progress in Melbourne and Bendigo, the minutes of the most recent 2017 Provincial Council indicate that the other three provincial dioceses remain hesitant to commit themselves fully.[29]

Despite diocesan delays, the progress already made within the Province of Victoria to push forward a single provincial Scheme Corporation by means of uniform legislation demonstrates a commitment to protect the integrity of the Church's mission and ministry through prevention and accountability, restore community trust and respond with compassion and authenticity to the needs of both complainants and respondents. Not only does this response adequately address the recommendations of the Royal Commission, but it also epitomises the ecclesial integrity of the province to make manifest the One, Holy, Catholic and Apostolic Church. Provincial polity, then, is not just some convenient exercise in ecclesial bureaucracy, or one among many arbitrarily imposed strata of authority, but is instead a providential polity capable of evidencing the marks of ecclesial authenticity by which the purposes and promises of God are both executed and assured, and into which an embedded Christian identity may flourish as both bounded yet relationally defined.

Provincial Polity as Demonstrating the Four Marks of the Church

The creedal affirmation that the church is One, Holy, Catholic and Apostolic has as its chief concern the recognition and verification of the 'true' church, so that wherever these 'marks' or 'notes' may be discerned there may be no doubt that therein dwells the constant presence of the Holy Spirit in a communion which has a continuity that stretches both backward to its apostolic foundations, and forward to its eschatological fulfilment. In the most simplistic sense, to seek to discern the four creedal 'marks' is to seek verification that the church is indeed 'Church'.[30] The notes themselves are a mixture of simple affirmations, the most fundamental perhaps being that the church is 'Holy' because of the enduring presence within it of the Holy Spirit, and also more polemical distinctions, such as the assertion of apostolicity which was originally defended by Irenaeus and Tertullian as a guard against Gnosticism.[31] In contrast to an overly polemicised sectarianism, Avery Dulles has pointed toward the impact and significance of the Second Vatican Council, within a Roman Catholic context, which 'broke away from a merely apologetic approach to the four creedal attributes of the Church, and opened up for Catholics the possibility of using the notes in other ways.'[32] Dulles recasts the four 'marks', according to his schematic 'models' of the church, as a 'task for every Christian community.'[33] The 'marks' become, therefore, an expression of aspiration rather than simply descriptive: the visible community coming to display more and more the signs of the church which subsists already within it. Grounded in their confessional context, the marks are 'statements of hope' born of faith which inevitably move the church toward the imperative of action as 'messianic predicates.'[34] To express belief in the One, Holy, Catholic and Apostolic Church, as the Nicene Creed would have us do, is to call the church to become more itself.[35] Accordingly, the church's oneness is not necessarily marked out by external uniformity but an 'interior unity of mutual charity,' its holiness may not be visible when compromised by sin and scandal but nevertheless depends upon a 'lived holiness of an interior communion with God,' it is catholic not because of its numerical or geographical extent but rather its 'dynamic catholicity of a love reaching out to all and excluding none,' and its apostolicity is assured not through a narrowly interpreted juridical succession but the 'perdurance of the magnanimity of the spirit that was originally poured forth . . . at Pentecost.'[36] Understood according to this more generous interpretation, the four 'marks' assume a sacramental quality as signs within the visible church of the enduring gift of the Spirit in gathering and guiding the Christian community. These signs may be particularly discerned through a provincial polity, not as exclusive arbiters of ecclesial authenticity but rather as dependable characteristics which together reveal, from the inside out, the church becoming what it is called to be: united but not uniform, sanctified but not sanctimonious, embedded but not bound by context, and motivated by an apostolic mission that stretches not just forward to the accomplishment of God's Kingdom but also back to the inauguration of that purpose in Creation.

This conceptualisation of the four 'marks' avoids a destructive polemic of denouncing the ecclesial authenticity of the church 'beyond', according to a too narrowly defined and self-referential set of descriptors, while placing an emphasis on the means by which the church might recognize itself and be recognized by others. This recognition is enabled by a 'visibility proper to a sacrament as a bodily expression of a divine mystery [which is] fully discernible only through a kind of connaturality given by grace."[37] The 'marks', therefore, become the means by which the church is recognized.[38] However, this recognition is dependent upon their manifestation made available only by grace. The discernment of the 'marks' of the church is, then, not simply a crude empirical exercise, but a spiritual discipline undertaken by and through the church itself and subject ultimately to its eschatological fulfilment. This discernment is possible too with respect to each of the 'marks' as they relate to the recent resurgence of provincial polity within Victoria.

Provincial Polity and the Church's Unity

That the church is one, and may be recognized by its unity, has been a central concern of both the Royal Commission and the Province of

Victoria's response. Challenging the fractured 'diocesanism' which char-acterizes the Anglican Church of Australia, the Royal Commission has exposed the paucity of unity which has so eluded the National Church:

> Commissioner Fitzgerald: It seems astonishing that the Anglican Church is still not capable of putting aside relatively minor differences to come to a common approach. What is the final barrier, because it seems almost inexplicable to all of us sitting on the outside?[39]

The response to this challenge given in the evidence to the Commission is that diocesan autonomy remains the final barrier and even in Victoria, where the most advanced effort has been made to drive a unified provin-cial response, overcoming this deeply ingrained principle in the psyche of Australian Anglicanism remains the final hurdle to meeting the com-missioner's criticism even if only provincially and not nationally. Where the 'national church' has failed to embody the church's unity, because of the geographical, cultural, and constitutional impediments outlined earlier, the province at least offers a more immediate context in which a unity of purpose can be pursued. The model established by the Province of Victoria embodies this unity of purpose, enabled by the impact of personal relationships and regular fellowship, without overwhelming each diocese's own synodical processes and prerogatives. This balance has been described as characteristic of the working of the Holy Spirit in making manifest the unity of the church which is itself predicated on the indwelling of the Spirit as the 'principle of unity, therefore [presupposing] an initial unity, which he himself is already bringing about.'[40] Congar describes the work of the Spirit as bringing unity not 'by using pressure or by reducing the whole of the Church's life to a uniform pattern,' but instead by 'the more delicate way of communion.'[41]

Contrasting with Hegel's destructive dynamic of confrontation and enslavement in the recognition of self-consciousness in the other, the Holy Spirit works within the church to enliven 'one life animating many without doing violence to the inner experience of anyone.'[42] The unity of the church, rooted in Jesus' prayer that 'they may be one' (John 17:21), is not just an institutional coherence but a participation in the divine life and commitment to the divine purpose. This is an inherently relational unity, exemplified in provincial polity through the communion which exists and is channelled through bishops as they together represent the church to itself and, as president at the Eucharist, unite the gathered *ecclesia* with the church in every time and place to participate in the sacramental manifestation of the redemptive unity of heaven and earth achieved by Christ's incarnation, death and resurrection.[43] The unity of the church is then also, perhaps more fundamentally, a unity with Christ and by extension a unity with those whom Christ is especially bonded to: the poor, the oppressed and the sick.[44] In what may seem institutionally counter-intuitive, the unity of the church in its response to sexual abuse (and indeed all other manifestations of sinful exercises and abuses of power) can only be achieved when it turns away from over-riding concerns of self-preservation and protection to a true and Christ-like unity with, and preference for, those whom the church has harmed: 'Christian partisan support for the oppressed is intentional and its goal is to save the oppressor also.'[45]

Provincial Polity and the Church's Holiness

This indwelling and agency of the Spirit, and the unity of the church with the divine life and purpose, is also at the heart of the affirmation that the church is holy.[46] The holiness of the church as grounded in God's holiness and the integral and persistent presence of the Holy Spirit makes it 'an original holiness that has no analogy in previous history; it is objective and full, fount and source of every other personal holiness that is born in the church and is developed.'[47] This affirmation, of course, almost immediately gives rise to the charge that it cannot possibly be substantiated given the self-evident scandal of sin. The problem is fundamental to individual, not just ecclesial, Christian identity as even the new and redeemed life of the believer, bathed and baptized in grace at the outpouring of the Holy Spirit, does not entirely mitigate the sinful orientation of human nature even if, as Paul proclaims, it heralds freedom from slavery to sin and the working out of its destructive purpose in death (Romans 7:22-25). The only resolution to this dilemma, for both the individual and the church, is eschatological as we, with Paul, 'groan inwardly while we wait for adoption, the redemption of our bodies' (Romans 8:23). In the life of the church, as also in the spiritual pursuit of individual holiness, this struggle is a creative one: 'Purity and fullness are the two great themes which call for and give rise, in the church, to reforms and new creations.'[48] The promise and presence of the Spirit also brings an imperative toward holiness, sparking the creative tension between the persistent working of sin (Romans 7:20) and freedom from its occupation of our bodies – individual and corporate – with lives liberated to worship God and to share in the inheritance of Christ's Kingdom (Romans 8:15-17). Holiness is revealed in the triumph of the latter over the former, that is, through the cycle of repentance and reconciliation which witnesses to the working of the Spirit and the dawning of a new creation. Through the work of the

Royal Commission, the imperative toward holiness has been highlighted from outside the church, through the voice of the community:

> Commissioner Fitzgerald: . . . isn't it time for the Anglican Church to recognise that the community at large would like to see a common approach in relation to these matters and, in a sense based on the evidence we've seen, perhaps society deserves that?[49]

Nevertheless, the work of the Province of Victoria in anticipating and responding to the concerns of the Royal Commission attests to the working of holiness in the church through repentance and restoration. It is in the confession of its past that the church witnesses to the sanctification of its future, the dynamic between 'the *communio peccatorum* it acknowledges in the confession of guilt,' and the '*communio sanctorum* that it believes when it believes in the forgiveness of sin.'[50] Of course, evidence of this dynamic in demonstrating holiness is not exclusive to a provincial polity, but in this case it has been through provincial action that an effective effort has been made to witness to the holiness of God within the church by challenging an institutional culture that is too protective of reputation over repentance.

Provincial Polity and the Church's Catholicity

The catholicity of the church relates most closely to its unity, exhibiting its internal unity as the Body of Christ through the extent of its geographical, and also cultural and perhaps even political, reach. The church's catholicity is the means by which its local life is interrelated 'according to the whole' giving even the most isolated ecclesial context a 'universal extension' which is also 'incontestably an aspect of the mark of catholicity.'[51] While the church's unity is grounded in the fundamental, and more-or-less uncontroversial, priestly prayer that 'they may be one', the patristic origins of describing the church as 'catholic', 'to mark the unity of an uncorrupted people,'[52] are more polemical: perhaps analogous to the way in which the word 'orthodox' is used within contemporary Anglicanism to signify authenticity of Anglican witness and identity. To describe the church as 'catholic' still has polemic associations in some parts, not least in Australia's Diocese of Sydney, because of the word's conflated identification with the Roman Catholic Church in popular parlance.[53] This notwithstanding, Roman Catholic theology since the Second Vatican Council has been particularly concerned with broadening the conceptual framework in which catholicity might be understood, drawing on it to more closely define the relationship between *particular* and *local* churches within the catholicity of the whole:

> The *local* Church is the Church of God in a certain place, and the excellent definition of the diocese provided by the Second Vatican Council can be applied perfectly to that Church. The *particular* Church is the Church which presents a particular aspect, for example, in language (Basque, perhaps) or in the recruitment of its members (soldiers, for instance). It may perhaps be a diocese, part of a diocese, a group of dioceses or even a patriarchate (the Armenian Church, for example). This rediscovery and reassessment of local or particular Churches is the work and fruit of the Second Vatican Council and, as Karl Rahner called it, its most novel contribution.[54]

The tension between the nature of the church as *local* as well as *particular* is at the heart too of the conflict over identity raging within international Anglicanism. Whereas the Roman Catholic definition associates the *local* with the diocese, within international Anglicanism the dominance of the 'national church' model has pushed forward the autonomous member-church (erroneously designated as the 'province') as the complete and bounded unit of ecclesial polity containing and expressing the *local* church. An emphasis on this aspect of polity will stress the sufficiency of the *local* church's constitutionally bound and canonically regulated self-determination. Alternatively, an emphasis instead on the church as *particular* attempts to identify the qualifiers of Anglican identity through its cultural, theological, linguistic and historical traits and inheritance. Accordingly, Anglican catholicity has little to do with constitutional or canonical norms but instead may be discerned through a variety of contested and often self-appointed indicators: an adherence to its Reformation heritage, a liturgical commitment to the Book of Common Prayer, a historical (even if irregular) pedigree from the Church of England, or the perpetuation of a distinctive ethos or style which is deemed authentically Anglican. This clash between the understanding of the *local* and the *particular* in Anglican ecclesiology presents more simplistically in the seemingly irreconcilable contest between autonomy and interdependence. These two aspects of the church's catholicity – the concrete manifestation of the whole church within the local, and the transcendence of cultural and other characteristics in witness to a universal community – have become the battleground in Anglicanism's culture wars.

A rediscovery of provincial polity within Anglicanism has the potential to subvert this deadlock, and to provide some balance to the competing interests of autonomy and interdependence. This is evident in the provincial scheme for addressing Professional Standards in the Province of Victoria: providing a recognizable and consistent response to complainants, a streamlined system of redress and independent accountability under a common framework, while also protecting the canonical autonomy of dioceses which 'opt-in' to the scheme. The catholicity promoted through a provincial polity is not just the spatial or temporal extent of the church's witness, but a witness also to the ultimate and universal authority, or 'lordship', of Christ.[55] Catholicity, then, points beyond the borders of the church and its internal structures and polity to the eschatological accomplishment of Christ's assumption of all authority according to the mission of God the Father who is to be 'all in all' (1 Corinthians 15:24-28). Similarly, provincial polity ultimately points beyond itself and its own communion, to its communion with the living God which is the foundation of its interrelatedness. This eschatological dimension of catholicity, the participation of the church in the mission of God for which Christ was sent, equally underscores the apostolicity of the church.

Provincial Polity and the Church's Apostolicity

The eschatological and missional dimension of apostolicity is easily neglected in favour of a backward-looking apostolic witness. Clearly the apostolic nature of the church is related to its continuity and faithfulness to the tradition of the Apostles, it points back to a historical reality and a tangible tradition which bears out the authenticity of the 'message of Jesus and about Jesus' as well as the authority to bear it, granted to the Apostles, and those whom they appointed.[56] The surety of that tradition is guaranteed through the personal and intimate gesture of the *traditio* in the laying on of hands and the 'public and documented succession from the apostles onward through the drawing up of the lists of bishops.'[57] Such an emphasis rightly seeks to ensure that the church remains publicly accountable and the authority of its proclamation historically verifiable against the Gnosticism of appeals to a secret and self-appointed tradition.[58] Nevertheless, its over-emphasis sees the crude collapse of the apostolic character of the church into a narrowly defined 'apostolic succession' that distorts the corporate witness of the church catholic into a preoccupation with the legitimation of the authority and status of individuals. Metropolitical authority, particularly, is susceptible to this distortion of the church's apostolicity where it is reduced to conflating apostolic authority with the mere personal, and even canonical, credentials of archbishops.

However, a reclaiming of provincial polity can offer Anglicanism a more nuanced and developed understanding of its own share in the apostolicity of the church. This is an apostolicity that is forward looking, missional and eschatological. Provincial polity, with its foundations in relationality, and metropolitical authority, with its preference for the personal, tangible and verifiable, reflects an apostolicity that is able to 'fill in the space between the Alpha and Omega by ensuring that there is a continuity between the two and a substantial identity between the end and the beginning.'[59] Provincial polity provides a means, through the ordering of ecclesial relationships, by which the church can be consistently discernible and recognizable. The apostolicity which is inherent to metropolitical authority is not just a witness to ecclesial legitimacy but also the lived articulation within the church of its commission to proclaim and participate in the manifestation of God's future as well as assuring the promise of God's faithfulness and its own perseverance to that end.[60]

The exercise of all authority within the church, and so particularly metropolitical authority which represents both the corporate nature of the church's catholicity as well as the personal and tangible nature of apostolicity entrusted to it, is ultimately oriented toward the eschatological fulfilment of all authority under God. This balance is inherent to provincial polity: both the personal and the corporate, the individual and the institutional, is necessary for the church to inhabit both its catholicity and apostolicity. The need for this balance has been explored in relation to the developing nature of primacy within global Anglicanism, and its tendency to overly privilege personal relationships at the expense of meaningful ecclesial communion, and the critique of a trend toward the elevation and institutionalisation of the 'national church' in Anglican polity. This balance is apparent, however, in the Victorian provincial solution to Safeguarding, by its establishment of an independent corporation through which the province coordinates clearance for ministry as well as responds to complains of misconduct and abuse. Incorporation gives the province a 'personality' which can be held accountable and has clear lines of authority, but nevertheless stands as independent from the person of the bishop (or anyone else) within the dioceses. As well as a personal identity it also has institutional flexibility, able to gather different ecclesial bodies such as dioceses, schools and agencies, without crushing their autonomy or individual characteristics.

Understanding ecclesial identity as a 'body corporate' is not new: Paul's memorable description of the church as one body with many parts (1 Corinthians 12:12) speaks of a complex organism made up of a number of negotiated relationships headed by Christ, initiated through baptism, and united in the Spirit. Further, the Letters Patent of 1847 constituting William Broughton as Metropolitan of Australia and Bishop of Sydney made that office a body corporate in perpetuity, able to 'prosecute, claim, plead and be impleaded, defend and be defended, answer and be answered . . . in and upon all and singular causes, actions, suits, writs, and demands, real and personal, and mixed, as well spiritual as temporal, and in all other things, causes and matters whatsoever.'[61]

The strategy of the Province of Victoria in establishing a corporation is not necessarily to propose the widespread incorporation of provinces across Anglican polity, but it is an example of how one particular province has been able to effectively witness to the church's apostolic nature, as missional, eschatological, verifiable and responsible, by balancing the twin apostolic concerns of personal and institutional coherence in response to a particular and contemporary challenge.

Notes

1 Royal Commission into Institutional Responses to Child Sexual Abuse 2013b, 2.

2 Royal Commission into Institutional Responses to Child Sexual Abuse 2017b, 27053.

3 *Report of the Viability & Structures Task Force, and Other Materials Impinging on the Small Groups Discussion Program* 2014, 8–049.

4 This personal dimension refers not merely to the kind of personal accountability called for through the proceedings of the Royal Commission, but also the establishment of 'corporate bodies' within dioceses and provinces which make it possible for such responsibility and accountability to be appropriately located.

5 'Terms of Reference' 2017.

6 'Fast Facts' 2017.

7 'Case Study 52, Sydney' 2017.

8 The terms 'Provincial Synod' and 'Provincial Council' are, in the Constitution of the Anglican Church of Australia, used interchangeably (see Definitions under Section 74.1). This reflects a varied nomenclature across the provinces: New South Wales retains a Provincial Synod. The Victorian Provincial Synod was renamed as a Council in 1980, and its equivalent body in both Western Australia and South Australia is called a Provincial Council. In Queensland, legislation was passed by the Provincial Synod in 2000 creating an additional body, the Provincial Council, which is able to conduct almost all of the business of the Synod other than legislative.

9 The Constitution of the New South Wales Provincial Synod was recently amended, given the paucity of legislative business and the cost of its convening, to substantially reduce its size and quorum requirement while also introducing into the Constitution the possibility of convening 'Provincial Conferences'. The Synod was also reconstituted into three houses of bishops, clergy and lay representatives whereas previously clerical and lay representatives had voted as one house. See the Diocese of Sydney Ordinance (No. 41 of 2015), '*General Synod – New South Wales Provincial Synod Constitution Amendment Ratification Canon 2015* Assenting Ordinance 2015'.

10 *Anglican Church of Australia - Province of Victoria. Provincial Council Minutes* 2014.

11 Royal Commission into Institutional Responses to Child Sexual Abuse 2003; see also 2017a, 2.

12 Royal Commission into Institutional Responses to Child Sexual Abuse 2003, 2.

13 The historical development of this early settlement of colonial synodical governance is described in detail in Sharwood 2004.

14 Royal Commission into Institutional Responses to Child Sexual Abuse 2017a, 2–3.

15 *Anglican Church of Australia - Province of Victoria. Provincial Council Minutes* 2010.

16 *Anglican Church of Australia - Province of Victoria. Provincial Council Minutes* 2011.

17 *Anglican Church of Australia - Province of Victoria. Provincial Council Minutes* 2012.

18 *Anglican Church of Australia - Province of Victoria. Provincial Council Minutes* 2013.

19 *Anglican Church of Australia - Province of Victoria. Provincial Council Minutes* 2013.

20 *Anglican Church of Australia - Province of Victoria. Provincial Council Minutes* 2014.

21 Chair of the Provincial Working Group on Professional Standards 2015, 2–3.

22 Royal Commission into Institutional Responses to Child Sexual Abuse 2016, 2.

23 Royal Commission into Institutional Responses to Child Sexual Abuse 2016, 5.

24 Royal Commission into Institutional Responses to Child Sexual Abuse 2014, 2.

25 For more information see Explanatory Memorandum to the Melbourne Anglican Diocesan Corporation Bill presented to a Special Session of the 51st Synod of the Diocese of Melbourne in June 2015.

26 Royal Commission into Institutional Responses to Child Sexual Abuse 2014, 4.

27 *Anglican Church of Australia - Province of Victoria. Provincial Council Minutes* 2016.

28 *Anglican Church of Australia - Province of Victoria. Provincial Council Minutes* 2016.

29 *Anglican Church of Australia - Province of Victoria. Provincial Council Minutes* 2017.

30 Dulles 2002, 115.

31 Dulles 2002, 115.

32 Dulles 2002, 118.

33 Dulles 2002, 121.

34 Moltmann 1977, 339.

35 Dulles 2002, 121.

36 Dulles 2002, 122.

37 Dulles 2002, 125.

38 Di Beradino 2010, 54.

39 Royal Commission into Institutional Responses to Child Sexual Abuse 2017b, 27034.

40 Congar 1983, 2:15.

41 Congar 1983, 2:17.

42 Congar 1983, 2:17.

43 The scriptural and sacramental images employed particularly in the patristic period are helpfully summarized and collated in Di Beradino 2010, 55.

44 Moltmann 1977, 345.

45 Moltmann 1977, 352.

46 Di Beradino 2010, 55.

47 Di Beradino 2010, 54.

48 Congar 1983, 2:57.

49 Royal Commission into Institutional Responses to Child Sexual Abuse 2017b, 27034.

50 Moltmann 1977, 355.

51 Congar 1983, 2:24.

52 Ignatius of Antioch (To the Smyrneans 8.2) in relating the symbolism of the bishop as a centre of unity and holiness to his presidency of the Eucharist, attributes the term 'catholic' to the church in this context. See Di Beradino 2010, 55.

53 The Diocese of Sydney makes liturgical provision to substitute the word 'apostolic' for 'catholic' in the Nicene and Apostles' Creeds, 'because the popular, contemporary meaning generally describes the Roman Catholic Church, rather than the church which is 'according to the whole', the one true church in all places and at all times. Attempts to reflect the meaning of 'catholic' by such words as 'universal' have not been well received. The choice of 'apostolic' as a replacement for 'catholic' seeks to reflect the unity and orthodoxy of the church in its apostolic roots.' See Archbishop of Sydney's Liturgical Panel 2001.

54 Congar 1983, 2:26. Congar is referring particularly to the Second Vatican Council's document Lumen Gentium, paragraph 13.

55 Moltmann 1977, 338.

56 Di Beradino 2010, 55.

57 Di Beradino 2010, 56.

58 For Irenaeus on this aspect of apostolicity, see Di Beradino 2010, 58.

59 This description of the apostolic task is taken from Congar 1983, 2:39.

60 Moltmann 1977, 359.

61 'Letters Patent appointing Bishop Broughton Metropolitan of Australia, 25 June 1847' in Giles 1929, 234.

Conclusion

How do you solve the Anglican Communion?
How do you hold back GAFCON walking out?
How do you find a way to bring reunion?
An Anglican Covenant? A Primates' 'gathering'? A clout!

Many a thing the Primates want to tell her
Many a thing they prob'ly oughtn't say.
But then who is at the helm
Once you move beyond the Realm?
You might as well look to the Vicar of Bray!

Oh, how do you solve the Anglican Communion?
How do you seek to tread the middle way?
- With apologies to *The Sound of Music*

The typical reaction of those to whom I have explained that I am engaged in research on questions of international polity, identity, relatedness and authority within the Anglican Communion has been a bemused raised eyebrow, and an expression along the lines of 'oh yes, and how's that working out for you?' Their cynicism is perhaps justified, because ultimately at the heart of this endeavour is the vexed question: how do you solve the Anglican Communion? I cannot claim, through the preceding chapters, to have found the definitive and determinative answer, nor have I presented a crude 'blueprint' for easy and instant implementation. However, what has been achieved through this examination of metropolitical authority and provincial polity within Anglicanism is, in the first place, a careful conceptual and historical analysis of the development of 'the province' in Anglican polity, giving some clarity to its distinctiveness and demonstrating that, rather than having 'crept in' as the IASCUFO report *Towards a Symphony of Instruments* asserts, it has a complex and evolving pedigree which locates it broadly within the tradition of the church in both the 'Greek East' and the 'Latin West'. Particularly, the historical exploration of Part One has highlighted the inability of Anglicanism, when working from a 'national church' paradigm, to claim an ecclesial identity that is more than just the sum of its parts.

Secondly, through Parts Two and Three, this research has interrogated the increasingly unchallenged axiom within Anglican Studies that posits the 'national church' as the most complete and perfect form of ecclesial organization. Where once the ecclesial landscape within Anglicanism was characterized by the undulation of a complex geodiversity, it has, since the second half of the twentieth century, been flattened and homogenized. It is as if a monolithic façade has been retrofitted over the organic, and sometimes untidy and unsightly, features of the Anglican edifice, in order to present a Communion of uniform proportions where each 'national church' is slotted in like just another brick in the wall. Accordingly, attempts to respond to tensions and shifting foundations have focused on finding a 'coping stone' to set off and cap the edifice. Most recently the Primates have shown an eager readiness to bear this weight upon their own shoulders, and assert a kind of magisterial authority through pronouncements and 'communiques'. It might seem that the assertion of the 'shibboleth of autonomy' as integral to the identity of national churches within Anglicanism was in contradistinction to the increasing assumption of authority on the part of the Primates, and it is certainly true that proponents of the different 'camps' in current debates would be quick to champion the cause of one over the other according to their immediate outcomes. However, this research suggests that both the hegemony of the 'national church' and the dawning 'Age of the Primates' are related, as the latter is only the natural extension of a unitary, isolationist and atomised polity projected onto the international stage.

Instead, and finally, this research proposes a rediscovery of an authentic provincial polity in reimagining the nature of ecclesial polity within the Anglican Communion. This is to be, necessarily, something of an ongoing proposition and, indeed, represents a dramatic 'paradigm-shift' away from current accepted norms into unexplored territory. Part Four illustrates the recent potential shown by one province in the Anglican Church of Australia, as analogous to the Communion at large, to creatively negotiate the balance between autonomy and interdependence and witness to an ecclesial polity which manifestly demonstrates the church to be One, Holy, Catholic and Apostolic.

These three strands constitute the unique contribution of this project to the field of Anglican Studies and, more particularly within it, Anglican ecclesial polity: a detailed historical examination of the development of metropolitical authority and provincial polity within international Anglicanism; a double critique of the acceptance of the 'national church' as a fundamental unit of Anglican polity, as well as an increasingly unitary responsibility being claimed by the Primates for the exercise of authority within the Communion, as both symptomatic of a common 'flattened' ecclesiology; and, the proposal for a rediscovery of a properly 'provincial' polity for the Communion.

Alongside this stands a renewed call for greater theological reflection on questions of polity as the practical outworking of ecclesiology. The content of this project as well as its methodological approach has taken seriously its positioning as 'applied' theology, relating together the actual experience of the church through historical enquiry and archival research with the resources of theological, and sometimes interdisciplinary, insight. This dynamic of context, reflection and action has been followed at a macro level across the book: the historical examination of Part One setting up a 'thick description' and providing the context in which the contemporary questions of the place of metropolitical authority and provincial polity must be grounded; Parts Two and Three each offering more sustained theological reflection and critique of the critical questions that arise; and, Part Four offering a paradigm for proposed action. However, this dynamic is also worked out to some extent within the structure of Parts Two, Three and Four as they each contain chapters which, firstly, offer some general conceptual analysis and theological reflection and, secondly, relate this to some more specific piece of archival research or case study analysis. In addition, the archival research made possible by access to the archives of the Anglican Communion Office in London, and my involvement in cataloguing and digitising parts of their collection, represents a further contribution to the scholarly pursuit of Anglican Studies that has been an important outcome of this research.

In sum, this research provides an overarching historical and theological examination of the place of metropolitical authority and provincial polity within the Communion, raising some critical questions and challenging some of the assumptions and norms of Anglican ecclesial polity, as well as proposing an alternative paradigm for addressing the underlying ecclesiological challenges which threaten the integrity of Anglicanism, which some recapitulation here of the central narrative of each Part and Chapter will bear out.

Recapitulation

Part One, through its historical analysis, has sought to chart the lineage of provincial polity within Anglicanism, the language of which has become confused and bound up with the 'national church'. Chapter One identifies the roots of the province in the pattern of Roman civil administration existing in the first centuries of the Early Church, with elements of its relational characteristics finding expression in the Canons of Nicaea and Antioch before being firmly established by the fifth century and introduced into England with Augustine in 597. At the English Reformation the void of authority left by the break with Rome was filled by a powerful assertion of the Royal Supremacy which served to hold together the ecclesial edifice of the two English provinces in a single 'national church'. Chapter Two demonstrates that while the Royal Supremacy was able to serve the 'contained catholicity' of the English Church, wherever Anglicanism moved beyond these bounds and the Royal Supremacy was either found wanting (as in Scotland), thrust off (as in the United States) or pushed to contain more than a single nation (as in the 'United Church of England and Ireland') it proved insufficient and what results are largely unitary churches formed along national lines with, internally, various forms of adapted and abolished expressions of provincial polity and, internationally, only a vague relational identity as 'Anglican' but with no claim to be a 'Communion'. Chapter Three takes up the formation of something we might recognizably identify as the 'Anglican Communion' in the nineteenth century, following the expansion of the British Empire, where the Royal Supremacy again proves itself insufficient to hold together the burgeoning internationalism of Anglicanism. Instead, for the first time more intentional effort is made to imagine what a provincial polity might look like as autonomous churches relate across the British Empire and beyond it, looking to the Archbishop of Canterbury to minister in new ways and advocating self-government through synods and ecclesial expression by means of new 'pan-Anglican' for a such as the Lambeth Conferences.

Part Two examines the key definitional category of the 'national church' which has, since the twentieth century, supplanted any kind of meaningful provincial polity within the Communion. Chapter Four identifies the origins of this between 1900 and 1920 as there developed a profound belief in the providence of the 'nation' with little regard for a 'universal' church, and this was continued until after the Second World War as evidenced through the language of Lambeth Conference resolutions which show a marked shift toward 'nationalism' by 1930. Unsurprisingly the language of 'nationalism' as it relates to Anglican ecclesiology goes out of favour in 1948 and is replaced by the perhaps more neutral terminology of 'provinces': however, the patterning of the church along national lines remained, leading to a conflation of provincial and national church polities which remains confused. Furthermore, the Anglican conceptualisation of the 'national church' is crudely defined, and some reflection on how the concept of the 'nation' has developed in

International Relations helps to nuance its ecclesial employment and, in fact, turn us back to a more authentic provincial polity. Chapter Five sets out on a close reading of provincial constitutions to enable some discernment of how provincial polity might nevertheless be expressed (and be perhaps lying latent) within the foundational documents of national churches, a project enabled by extensive access to the archives of the Anglican Communion Office. There is a relatively well defined and consistent articulation of metropolitical authority within provinces, not least because of a push facilitated by the Anglican Communion Office in the 1960s and 70s toward autonomy and independence, but there is much greater diversity and vagueness in defining their place within the Anglican Communion and the role of the Archbishop of Canterbury in relation to their own internal polity. In short, there is generally no real reckoning for how provincial polity might operate inter-provincially.

Part Three examines the nature of primacy, the proliferation of which has become a peculiarly Anglican phenomenon since the second half of the twentieth century. It has also become the vehicle by which this accounting for how provinces ought to relate has been driven. Nevertheless, it is also a confused and underdeveloped concept which requires further exploration. Chapter Six explores the terminology of primacy, particularly the often-repeated tropes of *primus inter pares*, *prima sedes*, and 'primacy of honour', the interpretation of which is not so self-evident as sometimes supposed but, in fact, largely unhelpful and deeply contested, not least ecumenically. Ultimately, confusion over these terms point to the fundamental controversy over whether primacy is purely honorific or whether it has an inherent attendant authority. This has been an Anglican dilemma too since at least the dispute between York and Canterbury as Primates of 'England' and 'All England' respectively, and it is now being taken up afresh through the Primates' Meetings. Chapter Seven examines the antecedents of the Primates' Meetings: the Lambeth Consultative Body and the Advisory Council on Missionary Strategy. The replacement of these bodies by the Anglican Consultative Council in 1968 sets up a tension between that body and the Primates, which persists, chiefly over the question of which should exercise real authority and responsibility for the life of the Communion. The balance between these competing claims has been tipped toward the Primates since at least 1998 as the Primates have sought to exercise an 'enhanced' responsibility, most recently evidenced by an extraordinary assertion of authority at the 2016 Primates' Meeting.

Part Four turns to the case study of the Anglican Church of Australia, which has been called a 'microcosm' of the Communion. Chapter Eight tests this claim through an examination of the prevalence of 'diocesanism', in parallel to the claim for 'provincial autonomy' within the Communion, as the principal comparison drawn between the two. The power of 'diocesanism' bears out the claim that the Australian context provides something of a 'microcosm' which might prove instructive for the Communion. Chapter Nine then follows this with an exposition of a recent revival of provincial polity within the Australian church whereby the Province of Victoria has driven a response to issues of Professional Standards and Safeguarding that witnesses to an ecclesial polity that manifests the four 'marks' of the church: that it is one, in achieving a unified approach according to unity with the Divine purpose; that it is holy, in participating in the work of holiness through repentance and restoration; that it is catholic, in demonstrating the principles of recognizability, faithfulness and intensity of communion across the province while protecting the integrity of diocesan autonomy; and that it is apostolic, in balancing the 'corporate' and the 'personal' identity of the church, witnessing to its legitimacy, holding it accountable and furthering the proclamation of its mission.

Final Remarks

The Australian example gives some insight into how a provincial polity can creatively engage with contextual challenges, prioritize relationality, and witness to a vision of the church that is both holistic and locally grounded. However, the recovery of a provincial polity for the Communion is unlikely to achieve a neat and tidy ordering of the ecclesial household, and much less produce a simple and straightforward 'shop window' that can be easily represented with a logo, slogan and website. A recovery of provincial polity is to find the identity of the Communion in the myriad of relationships between and within its provinces, relationships not only between metropolitan archbishops but at every level, measured not just by their extent, but also by their intensity.

The call to recover a provincial polity is a call to messiness, confusion, complexity but, ultimately, authenticity. Martyn Percy is among those theologians calling for an embrace of this kind of vision for Anglicanism, reminding us that 'rich and dense ecclesial communities are also complex; so it is not so easy to be simple and clear, as some may hope.'[1] Percy further points out that the images Jesus invokes for the Kingdom of God are 'untidy': vines, 'a sprawling, knotted plant that requires patience and careful husbandry,' and mustard seeds, 'an ungainly sprawling shrub that can barely hold up a bird's nest.'[2] I am indebted to Martyn Percy for suggesting to me the image of a 'coping stone' as something of a key to unlocking the answer to the question, 'How do you solve the Anglican Communion?' A coping stone sets off and caps an edifice, not only aesthetically but also with practical effect: it holds the whole together, to cope is – after all – to bear up under the weight of something.

Instead, I might offer another masonry metaphor for a vision of Anglicanism that seeks to model a provincial polity. That is of a fan-vaulted ceiling, with ribs outstretched and interconnected, each balanced by the other, pushing out beyond the centre and drawing what is distant closer.[3] Of course, if not perfectly proportioned it can be a precariously untidy picture; with no small risk that the roof falls in! Nevertheless, its ultimate form is secured in the eschatological promise that all our relationships are held in Christ (2 Cor 5:1–5). Robert Runcie evoked the same analogy at the 1988 Lambeth Conference, reflecting on the pillars of Canterbury Cathedral:

> In their strength they seem to stand on their own feet, symbols of strong foundations and sturdy independence. Yet their strength is an illusion. Look up and you see the pillars converting into arches which are upheld, not by independence, but through inter-dependence.[4]

Reflecting on the vaulted ceiling of King's College Chapel in Cambridge, John Betjeman sets before us a vision of that which might be our ecclesiological hope:

> And with what rich precision the stonework soars and springs
> To fountain out a spreading vault – a shower that never falls . . .

May the ongoing discernment of the working out of Anglican polity, to which this research may make some contribution, continue to 'buttress with prayer this vaulted roof, so white and light and strong.'[5]

Notes

1 Percy 2012, 135.
2 Percy 2012, 135.
3 Percy does allude to this image in reference to the 'ecclesial canopy' of a Gothic cathedral described by John Milbank. Percy 2012, 16.
4 Runcie 1989, 23.
5 Betjeman 2005, 101.

Bibliography

General Works Cited

'A Conversation with the Archbishop of Canterbury'. 2015. *Council of Foreign Relations Website*. October 13. http://www.cfr.org/religion/conversation-archbishop-canterbury/p37093.

Abbott, William Henry. 1845. *A Practical Analysis of the Several Letters Patent of the Crown, Relating to the Bishopricks in the East Indies*. Calcutta: Bishop's College Press.

ACC-1 Limuru, 23 February to 5 March 1971: Preparatory Documents Circulated. 1971. ACC/C/1/1(a). Anglican Communion Office Archives.

ACC-8 Wales, 22 July to 3 August 1990: Preparatory Files. 1989. ACC/C/8/1(a). Anglican Communion Office Archives.

Acheson, Alan. 2002. *A History of the Church of Ireland 1691–2001*. Dublin: The Columba Press.

Adam, Peter. 2012. 'Communion, Covenant, Conflict and Cooperation'. *St Mark's Review*, no. 220 (May): 65–77.

Advisory Council on Missionary Strategy. 1963. *Mutual Responsibility and Interdependence in the Body of Christ*. London: SPCK.

Altham, Roger. 1717. *A Charge Deliver'd to the Clergy of the Arch-Deaconry of Middlesex: At His Primary Visitation*. London: printed for John Morphew near Stationers-Hall.

———. 1721. *Provincial Authority. The First External Settled Authority in the Church of Christ: A Sixth Charge Delivered to the Clergy of the Arch-Deaconry of Middlesex*. London: printed for George Strahan at the Golden Ball.

Anglican Church of Australia - Province of Victoria. Provincial Council Minutes. 2010.

———. *Anglican Church of Australia - Province of Victoria. Provincial Council Minutes.* 2011.

———. *Anglican Church of Australia - Province of Victoria. Provincial Council Minutes.* 2012.

———. *Anglican Church of Australia - Province of Victoria. Provincial Council Minutes.* 2013.

———. *Anglican Church of Australia - Province of Victoria. Provincial Council Minutes.* 2014.

———. *Anglican Church of Australia - Province of Victoria. Provincial Council Minutes.* 2016.

———. *Anglican Church of Australia - Province of Victoria. Provincial Council Minutes.* 2017.

Anglican Communion Legal Advisors' Consultation Report. 2002. Primates' Papers: 2002 Meeting Electronic Backup. Anglican Communion Office Archives.

———. *Anglican Communion Legal Advisors' Consultation Report*. 2016. http://www.acclawnet.co.uk/report.pdf.

Anglican Communion Office. 2016. 'What Is the Anglican Communion?' *Anglican Communion Website*. Accessed May 19. http://www.anglicancommunion.org/identity/about.aspx.

'Anglican 'hidden Treasure' Archives to Be Restored'. 2016. *Anglican Communion News Service*. Accessed July 28. http://www.anglicannews.org/news/2016/06/anglican-hidden-treasure-archives-to-be-restored.aspx.

Anglican-Roman Catholic International Commission. 1982. *The Final Report: Windsor, September 1981*. London: SPCK.

———. 1998. 'The Gift of Authority'. Palazzola, Italy.

Appellate Tribunal Opinion: Reference Concerning Diaconal and Lay Presidency. 1997. New South Wales: General Synod of the Anglican Church of Australia.

'Archbishop of Canterbury Calls for Primates' Gathering'. 2015. *Archbishop of Canterbury Website*. September 16. http://www.archbishopofcanterbury.org/articles.php/5613/archbishop-of-canterbury-calls-for-primates-gathering.

Archbishop of Sydney's Liturgical Panel. 2001. *Sunday Services: A Contemporary Liturgical Resource*. http://www.sundayservices.anglican.asn.au/.

'Article VIII: Φιλολογικὴ Καὶ Κριτικὴ Ἱστορία, &c.' 1859. *The Christian Remembrancer* 38 (106): 428–56.

Aspinall, Phillip. 2009. *Presidential Address to 32nd Provincial Synod*.

Australian Town and Country Journal. 1883. 'The New Bishop of Tasmania', September 8.

Avis, Paul. 2002a. *Anglicanism and the Christian Church: Theological Resources in Historical Perspective*. London: T & T Clark.

———. 2002b. 'The Church of England as a National Church'. *Law & Justice: The Christian Law Review* 149: 111.

———. 2006. *Beyond the Reformation? Authority, Primacy and Unity in the Conciliar Tradition*. London: T & T Clark.

———. 2007. *The Identity of Anglicanism: Essentials of Anglican Ecclesiology*. London: Bloomsbury.

———. 2014. *In Search of Authority: Anglican Theological Method from the Reformation to the Enlightenment*. London: Bloomsbury.

———. 2015. 'Editorial: From Ecclesiology to Ecclesiastical Polity'. *Ecclesiology* 11 (3): 285–88.

———. 2016. 'Polity and Polemics: The Function of Ecclesiastical Polity in Theology and Practice'. *Ecclesiastical Law Journal* 18 (1): 2–13.

Ballard, Paul. 2000. 'Pastoral and Practical Theology in Britain'. In *Blackwell Reader in Pastoral and Practical Theology*, edited by James Woodward and Stephen Pattison. Oxford: Blackwell.

Battle, Michael. 2015. 'Race, Spirituality and Reconciliation'. In *The Oxford Handbook of Anglican Studies*, edited by Mark D. Chapman, Sathianathan Clarke, and Martyn Percy. Oxford: Oxford University Press.

Bayne, Stephen. 1964. *An Anglican Turning Point: Documents and Interpretations*. Austin, TX: Church Historical Society.

Beach, Foley. 2015. 'Statement from Archbishop Beach on the Proposed Primates' Gathering'. *Anglican Church in North America Website*. September 16. http://anglicanchurch.net/?/main/page/1103.

———. 2016. 'Update from Archbishop Foley Beach on the Primates' Meeting 2016'. *Anglican Church in North America Website*. January 14. http://anglican-church.net/?/main/page/1164.

Beardsley, E. Edwards. 1881. *Life and Correspondence of the Right Reverend Samuel Seabury*. Boston, MA: Houghton, Mifflin and Company.

Beetham, David, and Christopher Lord. 1998. *Legitimacy and the European Union*. London: Longman.

Benson, Robert Louis. 1968. *Bishop-Elect: A Study in Medieval Ecclesiastical Office*. Princeton, NJ: Princeton University Press.

Bertie, David. 2000. *Scottish Episcopal Clergy, 1689–2000*. Edinburgh: T & T Clark.

Bethell, Denis. 1968. 'William of Corbeil and the Canterbury-York Dispute'. *The Journal of Ecclesiastical History* 19 (2): 145–59.

Betjeman, John. 2005. *Faith and Doubt of John Betjeman: An Anthology of Betjeman's Religious Verse*. Edited by Kevin Gardner. London: Continuum.

Bingham, Joseph. 1726. *The Works of the Learned Joseph Bingham*. Vol. 1. 2 vols. London: printed for Robert Knaplock.

Bingham, Richard, ed. 1834. *Origines Ecclesiasticae; or the Antiquities of the Christian Church, and Other Words, of the Rev. Joseph Bingham, MA*. Vol. 1. 8 vols. London: William Straker.

Blair, John. 2005. *The Church in Anglo-Saxon Society*. Oxford: Oxford University Press.

Blake, Garth. 2008. 'Diocesan Autonomy and National Coherence in the Anglican Church of Australia'. *Ecclesiastical Law Journal* 10 (1).

Bode, F. D. 1888. 'Centennial Fund'. *Newcastle Morning Herald and Miners' Advocate*, February 17.

Border, Ross. 1962. *Church and State in Australia 1788–1872: A Constitutional Study of The Church of England in Australia*. London: SPCK.

Bosher, Robert S. 1962. *The American Church and the Formation of the Anglican Communion, 1823–1853*. The M Dwight Johnson Memorial Lecture in Church History. Seabury-Western Theological Seminary.

Bradbury, Nicholas. 2000. 'Ecclesiology and Pastoral Theology'. In *Blackwell Reader in Pastoral and Practical Theology*, edited by James Woodward and Stephen Pattison. Oxford: Blackwell.

Brandt, James M. 2011. 'Historical Theology'. In *The Wiley-Blackwell Companion to Practical Theology*, edited by Bonnie J Miller-McLemor. Oxford: Wiley-Blackwell.

Brittain, Christopher Craig. 2015a. *A Plague on Both Their Houses: Liberal vs Conservative Christians and the Divorce of the Episcopal Church USA*. London: Bloomsbury.

———. 2015b. 'The Truth of the Gospel, the Gospel of 'Truthiness' and the Future of the Anglican Communion'. *ABC Religion & Ethics (Australian Broadcasting Corporation)*. June 1. http://www.abc.net.au/religion/articles/2015/05/29/4245098.htm.

———. 2016. 'The Primates's Dilemma: Game Theory and the Anglican Communion'. *Australian Broadcasting Commission: Religion and Ethics*, January 4.

Brooke, Christopher. 1958. 'The Archbishops of St David's, Llandaff and Caerleon-on-Usk'. In *Studies in the Early British Church*, edited by Nora Chadwick, Kathleen Hughes, Christopher Brooke, and Kenneth Jackson. Cambridge: Cambridge University Press.

Brooks, Nicholas P. 1984. *Early History of the Church of Canterbury*. Leicester University Press.

'Broughton Papers (Moase Collection): Correspondence and Other Papers of William Broughton, Bishop of Australia, 1836–1853'. University of Tasmania Library Special and Rare Materials Collection.

Brown, Andrew. 2015. 'Archbishop of Canterbury Plans to Loosen Ties of Divided Anglican Communion'. *The Guardian*, September 16.

Brown, Stewart J. 2001. *The National Churches of England, Ireland and Scotland 1801–46*. Oxford: Oxford University Press.

Bubbio, Paolo Diego. 2014. 'Hegel, the Trinity, and the 'I''. *International Journal for Philosophy of Religion* 76 (2): 129–50.

Calvani, Carlos. 2005. 'The Myth of Anglican Communion'. *Journal of Anglican Studies* 3 (1): 139.

Cameron, Gregory K. 2013. 'Locating the Anglican Communion in the History of Anglicanism'. In *The Wiley-Blackwell Companion to the Anglican Communion*, 1–14. John Wiley & Sons, Ltd.

Campbell, Alistair. 2000. 'The Nature of Practical Theology'. In *Blackwell Reader in Pastoral and Practical Theology*, edited by James Woodward and Stephen Pattison. Oxford: Blackwell.

'Case Study 52, Sydney'. 2017. *Royal Commission into Institutional Responses to Child Sexual Abuse Website*. March 17. http://www.childabuseroyal-commission.gov.au/case-study/d431df6f-2a52-4c87-a8d7-855fa865694a/case-study-52,-march-2017,-sydney.

'Celebrations as Sudan Becomes Anglican Communion's 39th Province'. 2017. *Anglican Communion News Service*. July 31. http://www.anglicannews.org/features/2017/07/celebrations-as-sudan-becomes-anglican-communions-39th-province.aspx.

Chadwick, William Owen. 1991. *Michael Ramsey: A Life*. Oxford: Oxford University Press.

Chair of the Provincial Working Group on Professional Standards. 2015. *Report to the Victorian Provincial Bishops' Conference*.

Chapman, Mark. 2010. *The Hope of Things to Come: Anglicanism and the Future*. London: Bloomsbury.

———. 2013a. 'American Catholicity and the National Church: The Legacy of William Reed Huntington'. *Sewanee Theological Review* 56 (Easter).

———. 2013b. 'The Church of England'. In *The Wiley-Blackwell Companion to the Anglican Communion*, 412–25. John Wiley & Sons, Ltd.

Chapman, Mark, Sathianathan Clarke, and Martyn Percy, eds. 2015. *The Oxford Handbook of Anglican Studies*. Oxford Handbooks in Religion and Theology. Oxford: Oxford University Press.

Churton, Edward. 1863. *Memoir of Joshua Watson*. Oxford: J. Henry and J. Parker.

Clarke, Henry Lowther. 1918. *The Constitutions of the General Provincial and Diocesan Synods of the Church of England in Australia, Together with an Introduction to the Constitutional History of the Said Church.* Melbourne, Vic: Church of England in Australia.

— — —. 1924. *Constitutional Church Government: In the Dominions beyond the Seas and in Other Parts of the Anglican Communion.* London: SPCK.

Colenso, John William. 1864. *Remarks upon the Recent Proceedings and Charge of Robert, Lord Bishop of Capetown and Metropolitan at His Primary Metropolitical Visitation of the Diocese of Natal.* London: Longmans, Green, and Co.

Collected Provincial Responses to Request of Anglican Executive Officer for Comment on Metropolitical Authority in Preparation for ACC-4. 1977. ACC/C/4/2(e). Anglican Communion Office Archives.

'Communique from the 2016 Primates' Meeting'. 2016. *Anglican Communion Website.* January 15. http://www.anglicancommunion.org/media/206035/communiqu%c3%a9_from_the_primates_meeting_2016.pdf.

Congar, Yves. 1983. *I Believe in the Holy Spirit.* Translated by David Smith. Vol. 2. New York, NY: The Seabury Press.

Conger, George. 2016. 'Blackout in Canterbury'. *Anglican Ink.* January 13. http://www.anglican.ink/article/blackout-canterbury.

Constitution of the Anglican Consultative Council. 2010. Certificate of Incorporation of a Limited Company, No. 7311767.

Cooper-White, Pamela. 2011. 'Suffering'. In *The Wiley-Blackwell Companion to Practical Theology,* edited by Bonnie J Miller-McLemor. Oxford: Wiley-Blackwell.

Covenant Design Group. 2007. *An Anglican Covenant: Preliminary Report.*

Cowdrey, H. E. J. 2003. *Lanfranc: Scholar, Monk, Archbishop.* Oxford: Oxford University Press.

Cox, R. D. 1987. *A Vision to Fulfil: Mutual Responsibility and Interdependence in the Anglican Communion.* Yale Divinity School.

Coxe, Arthur Cleveland. 1995. 'Constitutions of the Holy Apostles'. In *Ante-Nicene Fathers,* edited by Alexander Roberts and James Donaldson. Vol. 7. The Writings of the Fathers Down to AD 325. Peabody, MA: Hendrickson.

Cranmer, Frank. 2002. 'National Churches, Territoriality and Mission'. *Law & Justice: The Christian Law Review* 149: 157.

Craston, Colin. 1986. *Current and Emerging Issues within and between the Centres of Authority in the Anglican Communion.* In *Inter-Anglican Relationships: Inter-Anglican Organisations, Structures & Constitution.* ACC/INT-ANG/1(a). Anglican Communion Office Archives.

Creighton, Mandell, and Louise Creighton. 1901. *The Church and the Nation: Charges and Addresses.* London: Longmans, Green, and Co.

Crouter, Richard. 2005. *Friedrich Schleiermacher: Between Enlightenment and Romanticism.* Cambridge: Cambridge University Press.

Currie, Robert, Lee Horsley, and Alan D. Gilbert. 1977. *Churches and Church-Goers: Patterns of Church Growth in the British Isles.* Oxford: Oxford University Press.

Cushing, Kathleen G. 1998. *Papacy and Law in the Gregorian Revolution: The Canonistic Work of Anselm of Lucca.* Oxford: Clarendon Press.

Daley, Brian E. 1993. 'Position and Patronage in the Early Church: The Original Meaning of 'Primacy of Honour''. *The Journal of Theological Studies* 44 (2): 529–553.

Danaher, William J. 2011. 'Beyond Imagination:" Mutual Responsibility and Interdependence in the Body of Christ"(1963) and the Reinvention of Canadian Anglicanism'. *Anglican Theological Review* 93 (2): 219.

Davidson, Randall Thomas, ed. 1889. *The Lambeth Conferences of 1867, 1878, and 1888*. London: SPCK.

———, ed. 1907. *The Lambeth Conference of 1897*. London: SPCK.

———. 1920. *The Five Lambeth Conferences*. London: SPCK.

Davies, Madeleine. 2016. 'Primates' Ruling Is Not Binding - Says Canon Lawyer'. *Church Times*, January 19.

Davis, John. 1993. *Australian Anglicans and Their Constitution*. Canberra: Acorn Press.

Deep Engagement, Fresh Discovery: Report of the Anglican Communion 'Bible in the Life of the Church' Project. 2012. St Andrew's House, London: Anglican Communion Office.

Delivré, Fabrice. 2008. 'The Foundations of Primatial Claims in the Western Church (Eleventh–Thirteenth Centuries)'. *The Journal of Ecclesiastical History* 59 (3).

Deng, Daniel, Hilary Garang, Hilary Adeba, Ezekiel Kondo, Joseph Maker, Stephen Dokolo, Peter Munde, and Bismark Avokaya. 2015. 'Letter from the Province of the Episcopal Church of Sudan & South Sudan's House of Bishops.' *Anglican Ink*. November 28. http://www.anglican.ink/article/communique-sudanese-house-bishops-meeting.

Di Beradino, Angelo, ed. 2010. *We Believe in One Holy Catholic and Apostolic Church*. Ancient Christian Doctrine 5. Downers Grove, IL: InterVarsity Press.

Dickey, Brian. 2002. 'Secular Advance and Diocesan Response 1861–1900'. In *Anglicanism in Australia: A History*, edited by Bruce Kaye, Tom Frame, Colin Holden, and Geoffrey Treloar, 52–75. Melbourne, Vic: Melbourne University Press.

Doe, Norman. 1996. *The Legal Framework of the Church of England: A Critical Study in a Comparative Context*. Oxford: Oxford University Press.

———. 1998. *Canon Law in the Anglican Communion: A Worldwide Perspective*. Oxford: Oxford University Press.

———. 2002. 'The Notion of a National Church: A Juridical Framework'. *Law & Justice: The Christian Law Review* 149: 77.

———. 2008. 'The Contribution of Common Principles of Canon Law to Ecclesial Communion in Anglicanism'. *Ecclesiastical Law Journal* 10 (01).

———. 2013. *Christian Law: Common Principles*. Cambridge: Cambridge University Press.

Doll, P. M. 2012. 'Autonomy or Communion? The Passion of the Episcopal Church'. *Theology* 115 (6): 427–35.

Dougherty, Jane Elizabeth. 2001. 'Mr and Mrs England: The Act of Union as National Marriage'. In *Acts of Union: The Causes, Contexts and Consequences of the Act of Union*, edited by Dáire Keogh and Kevin Whelan. Dublin: Four Courts Press.

Douglas, Ian T., and Paul Zahl. 2005. *Understanding the Windsor Report: Two Leaders in the American Church Speak across the Divide*. New York, NY: Church Publishing.

Draper, Jonathan. 2003. *The Eye of the Storm: Bishop John William Colenso and the Crisis of Biblical Inspiration*. London: T & T Clark.

Driver, Jeffrey. 2009. 'Beyond Lambeth 2008 and ACC14: Tuning a Polity of Persuasion to the Twenty-First Century'. *Journal of Anglican Studies* 7 (2): 195–211.

———. 2014. *A Polity of Persuasion: Gift and Grief of Anglicanism*. Eugene, OR: Cascade Books.

Duggan, Joseph F. 2009. 'The Postcolonial Paradox: Becoming Less than Whole(s) Producing Parts That Exclude Other Parts'. *Journal of Anglican Studies* 7 (1): 67.

Dulles, Avery. 2002. *Models of the Church*. Expanded Edition. New York, NY: Doubleday.

Dyer, J. Mark. 2001. *The Ministry of Primacy: Primacy, Collegiality, Episcope*. Kanuga Primates' Meeting Files. Anglican Communion Office Archives.

Ecclesiastical Appeals Act. 1532. 24 Hen 8 c 12.

Eliot, T. S. 1931. *Thoughts after Lambeth*. London: Faber & Faber.

Evans, Peter. 1997. 'The Eclipse of the States? Reflections on Stateness in an Era of Globalization'. *World Politics* 50 (62): 70–71.

Eyton, Robert William. 1855. *Antiquities of Shropshire*. Vol. 2. 12 vols. London: John Russell Smith.

Facsimile Message from Archbishop of Canterbury to Members of the Drafting Group. 2001. Primates' Papers: 2001 Meeting Electronic Backup. Anglican Communion Office Archives.

'Fast Facts'. 2017. *Royal Commission into Institutional Responses to Child Sexual Abuse Website*. Accessed December 15. http://www.childabuseroyalcommission.gov.au/.

Fletcher, Brian. 2002. 'Anglicanism and the Shaping of Australian Society'. In *Anglicanism in Australia: A History*, edited by Bruce Kaye, Tom Frame, Colin Holden, and Geoffrey Treloar, 293–315. Melbourne, Vic: Melbourne University Press.

———. 2006. 'Memory and the Shaping of Australian Anglicanism'. In *Agendas for Australian Anglicanism: Essays in Honour of Bruce Kaye*, edited by Tom Frame and Geoffrey Treloar, 3–28. Adelaide, SA: ATF Press.

Fowler, Michael Ross, and Julie Marie Bunck. 1995. *Law, Power, and the Sovereign State: The Evolution and Application of the Concept of Sovereignty*. University Park, PA: Pennsylvania State University Press.

Fox, Edward. 1548. *The True Dyfferens Betwen Ye Regall Power and the Ecclesiasticall Power Translated out of Latyn by Henry Lord Stafforde*. Imprynted at London : In the Fletestret at ye signe of the Rose Garland by Wyllyam Copland.

Frame, Tom. 2002. 'Local Differences, Social and National Identity: 1930–1966'. In *Anglicanism in Australia: A History*, edited by Bruce Kaye, Tom Frame, Colin Holden, and Geoffrey Treloar, 100–123. Melbourne, Vic: Melbourne University Press.

———. 2006. 'The Dynamics and Difficulties of Debate in Australian Anglicanism'. In *Agendas for Australian Anglicanism: Essays in Honour of Bruce Kaye*, edited by Tom Frame and Geoffrey Treloar, 139–70. Adelaide, SA: ATF Press.

———. 2007. *Anglicans in Australia*. Sydney, NSW: University of New South Wales.

Frappell, Ruth. 2002. 'Imperial Fervour and Anglican Loyalty 1901–1929'. In *Anglicanism in Australia: A History*, edited by Bruce Kaye, Tom Frame, Colin Holden, and Geoffrey Treloar, 76–99. Melbourne, Vic: Melbourne University Press.

Frend, W. H. C. 1968. 'The Christianization of Roman Britain'. In *Christianity in Britain, 300–700*, edited by M. W. Barley and R. P. C. Hanson. Leicester: Leicester University Press.

Fuller, Thomas. 1837. *The Church History of Britain: From the Birth of Jesus Christ Until the Year 1648*. T. Tegg & Son.

Gee, Henry, and William John Hardy. 1896. *Documents Illustrative of English Church History*. London: Macmillan.

Gehring, David S. 2015. *Anglo-German Relations and the Protestant Cause: Elizabethan Foreign Policy and Pan-Protestantism*. Abingdon: Routledge.

George, Ian. 1989. *Comments on Draft Document 'The Anglican Communion: Identity and Authority' in Correspondence with Secretary General of the Anglican Consultative Council, Samuel Van Culin*. ACC/PM/4/1(a-i). Anglican Communion Office Archives.

Giles, R. A. 1929. *The Constitutional History of the Australian Church*. London: Skeffington & Son.

Goddard, Andrew. 2003. *True Union in the Body? A Contribution to the Discussion within the Anglican Communion Concerning the Public Blessing of Same-Sex Unions*. Grove Books.

———. 2013. 'The Anglican Communion Covenant'. In *The Wiley-Blackwell Companion to the Anglican Communion*, 119–33. John Wiley & Sons, Ltd.

———. 2015. 'From Communion to…Federation ?' *Fulcrum Anglican*. September 20. https://www.fulcrum-anglican.org.uk/articles/from-communion-to-federation/.

Goldie, Frederick. 1976. *A Short History of the Episcopal Church in Scotland: From the Restoration to the Present Time*. 2nd ed. Edinburgh: St Andrew Press.

Gomez, Drexel W., and Maurice W. Sinclair, eds. 2001. *To Mend the Net: Anglican Faith and Order for Renewed Mission*. Carrollton, TX: The Ekklesia Society.

Gordon, Alexander. 2004. 'Richard Mant (1776–1848)'. Edited by Karl S. Bottigheimer. *Oxford Dictionary of National Biography (Online Edn)*, Oxford University Press.

Granfield, Patrick. 1979. 'The Church as Societas Perfecta in the Schemata of Vatican I'. *Church History* 48 (4): 431.

Gray, Robert. 1867. *A Statement Relating to Facts Which Have Been Misunderstood, and to Questions Which Have Been Raised, in Connexion with the Consecration, Trial, and Excommunication of the Right Rev. Dr. Colenso*. 2nd ed. London: Rivingtons.

Groves, Philip Neil. 2010. 'A Model for Partnership: A Model of Partnership Distilled from the Relationship between Paul and the Philippian Church as a Tool to Examine the Partnership Programmes of the Anglican Communion and to Propose New Directions.' Unpublished PhD Dissertation, Birmingham: University of Birmingham.

Guardian Editorial. 2015. 'The Guardian View on the Anglican Communion: Catching up with Reality'. *The Guardian*, September 17.

Guidelines for the Creation of New Provinces and Dioceses: Resolutions Passed by the Anglican Consultative Council. Anglican Communion Office.

Gunton, Colin. 1991. *The Promise of Trinitarian Theology*. Edinburgh: T & T Clark.

Guy, Jeff. 1983. *The Heretic: A Study of the Life of John William Colenso 1814–1883*. Johannesburg: Raven Press.

Habermas, Jürgen. 1998. 'The European Nation-State: On the Past and Future of Sovereignty and Citizenship'. Translated by Ciaran Cronin. *Public Culture* 10 (2): 397–416.

Haggart, Alastair. 1983. *Primates' Meetings - History, Nature and Expectations*. ACC/PM/2(c). Anglican Communion Office Archives.

Hamid, David. 2002. 'Church, Communion of Churches and the Anglican Communion'. *Ecclesiastical Law Journal* 6 (31): 352–74.

Hammond, Herbert. 1988. 'The Church of England in South Africa and the Anglican Communion'. *Churchman* 102 (3): 251–58.

Handley, Stuart. 2004. 'Joseph Bingham'. *Oxford Dictionary of National Biography (Online Edn)*, Oxford University Press.

Harrison, G. B., ed. 1968. *The Letters of Queen Elizabeth*. New York, NY: Funk and Wagnalls.

Harvey, Margaret. 1993. *England, Rome and the Papacy 1417–1464: The Study of a Relationship*. Manchester: Manchester University Press.

Hassett, Miranda. 2004. 'Episcopal Dissidents, African Allies: The Anglican Communion and the Globalization of Dissent'. Chapel Hill, NC: University of North Carolina.

Hastings, Adrian. 1995. *The Shaping of Prophecy*. London: Geoffrey Chapman.

Healy, Nicholas. 2000. *Church, World, and the Christian Life: Practical-Prophetic Ecclesiology*. Cambridge: Cambridge University Press.

Heaney, Robert S. 2013. 'Views of Colonization Across the Anglican Communion'. In *The Wiley-Blackwell Companion to the Anglican Communion*, 726–38. John Wiley & Sons, Ltd.

Hefling, Charles. 2006. 'Scotland: Episcopalians and Nonjurors'. In *Oxford Guide to the Book of Common Prayer: A Worldwide Survey*, edited by Charles Hefling and Cynthia Shattuck. Oxford: Oxford University Press.

Hegel, Georg Wilhelm Friedrich. 1977. *Phenomenology of Spirit*. Translated by A. V. Miller. Oxford: Oxford University Press.

Henry VIII. 1532. *A Glasse of the Truthe*. London: Thomas Berthelet.

Henson, Hensley. 1950. *Retrospect of an Unimportant Life*. Vol. 2. London: Oxford University Press.

Hilliard, David. 2002. 'Pluralism and New Alignments in Society and Church 1967 to the Present'. In *Anglicanism in Australia: A History*, edited by Bruce Kaye, Tom Frame, Colin Holden, and Geoffrey Treloar, 124–48. Melbourne, Vic: Melbourne University Press.

———. 2006. 'Diocese, Tribes and Factions: Disunity and Unity in Australian Anglicanism'. In *Agendas for Australian Anglicanism: Essays in Honour of Bruce Kaye*, edited by Tom Frame and Geoffrey Treloar, 57–81. Adelaide, SA: ATF Press.

Hiltner, Seward. 2000. 'Meaning and Importance of Pastoral Theology'. In *Blackwell Reader in Pastoral and Practical Theology*, edited by James Woodward and Stephen Pattison. Oxford: Blackwell.

Hinchliff, Peter. 1963. *The Anglican Church in South Africa: An Account of the History and Development of the Church of the Province of South Africa*. London: Darton, Longman & Todd.

Holden, Colin. 1997. *Ritualist on a Tricycle - Frederick Goldsmith: Church, Nationalism and Society in Western Australia, 1880–1920*. Nedlands, WA: University of Western Australia Press.

Holy Women, Holy Men: Celebrating the Saints. 2010. New York, NY: Church Publishing.

House of Commons' Paper. 1832. *Report from the Select Committee on the Affairs of the East India Company, with Minutes of Evidence in Six Parts and an Appendix and Index to Each*. No. 734, 735(I-VI).

———. 1833. *Further Papers Regarding the East India Company's Charter*. No. 549.

———. 1850a. *Copies or Extracts of Despatches Relative to the Establishment of Episcopal Sees in Australia*. No. 174.

———. 1850b. *Ecclesiastical Jurisdiction (Australian Colonies)*. No. 175.

———. 1863. *Synodical Action (Ireland)*. No. 258.

Humphries, Mark. 2006. *Early Christianity*. London: Routledge.

Huntington, William Reed. 1899. *A National Church*. New York, NY: Charles Scribner's Sons.

Idowu-Fearon, Josiah. 2017. 'The Ties That Bind Our Anglican Communion Family'. *Anglican Communion News Service*. December 14. http://www.anglicannews.org/blogs/2017/12/the-ties-that-bind-our-anglican-communion-family.aspx.

Inter-Anglican Standing Commission on Unity, Faith and Order. 2012. *Towards a Symphony of Instruments: Report to ACC-15*.

Inter-Anglican Theological and Doctrinal Commission. 1986. 'For the Sake of the Kingdom: God's Church and the New Creation'. London: Published for the Anglican Consultative Council by Church House.

Jefferies, Henry A. 2004. 'George Cromer'. *Oxford Dictionary of National Biography (Online Edn)*, Oxford University Press.

Jensen, Michael P. 2012. *Sydney Anglicanism: An Apology*. Eugene, OR: Wipf & Stock.

Jensen, Peter, and Eliud Wabukala. 2016. 'Statement on the Canterbury 2016 Primates' Gathering'. *GAFCON Website*. January 14. https://www.gafcon.org/events/canterbury-2016.

Joint International Commission for the Theological Dialogue between the Roman Catholic Church and the Orthodox Church. 2007. 'Ecclesiological and Canonical Consequences of the Sacramental Nature of the Church: Ecclesial Communion, Conciliarity and Authority'. Ravenna.

———. 2016. 'Synodality and Primacy during the First Millenium: Towards a Common Understanding in Service to the Unity of the Church'. Chieti.

Joyce, James Wayland. 1869. *The Crisis in the Church of Ireland: A Letter to the Lord Bishop of Derry on the Constitution of Diocesan and Provincial Synods, with the Ancient Forms of Proceeding*. Dublin: Hodges, Foster and Co.

Kaye, Bruce. 1995. 'The Baggage of William Grant Broughton: The First Bishop of Australia as Hanoverian High Churchman'. *Pacifica* 8: 291–314.

———. 2002. 'The Emergence and Character of Australian Anglican Identity'. In *Anglicanism in Australia: A History*, edited by Bruce Kaye, Tom Frame, Colin Holden, and Geoffrey Treloar, 154–76. Melbourne, Vic: Melbourne University Press.

———. 2003. 'The Strange Birth of Anglican Synods in Australia and the 1850 Bishops' Conference'. *Journal of Religious History* 27 (2): 177–197.

Kemp, Eric Waldram. 1961. *Counsel and Consent: Aspects of the Government of the Church as Exemplified in the History of the English Provincial Synods*. Bampton Lectures 1960. London: SPCK.

Knowles, David. 1970. *The Episcopal Colleagues of Archbishop Thomas Becket.* Cambridge: Cambridge University Press.

Koffeman, Leo J. 2014. *In Order to Serve: An Ecumenical Introduction to Church Polity.* Zurich: LIT Verlag.

―――. 2015. 'The Ecumenical Potential of Church Polity'. *Ecclesiastical Law Journal* 17 (2): 182–93.

Krasnoff, Larry. 2008. *Hegel's 'Phenomenology of Spirit': An Introduction.* Cambridge: Cambridge University Press.

Kuehn, Evan F. 2008. 'Instruments of Faith and Unity in Canon Law: The Church of Nigeria Constitutional Revision of 2005'. *Ecclesiastical Law Journal* 10 (2).

Lambeth Commission on Communion. 2004. *The Windsor Report.* London: Anglican Communion Office.

Lambeth Conference. 1948. *The Lambeth Conference 1948: The Encyclical Letter from the Bishops Together with Resolutions and Reports.* London: SPCK.

―――. 1968. *The Lambeth Conference 1968.* London: SPCK.

―――. 1978. *The Report of the Lambeth Conference 1978.* London: Church Information Office.

Lambeth Consultative Body. 1963. *Minutes of Meeting Held at Huron College, London, Ontario.* ACC/LCB/1(c). Anglican Communion Office Archives.

Lambeth Consultative Body & Executive Officer, Papers Relating to Formation of 'Consultative Body' and Appointment of Executive Officer, 1958 to 1960. ACC/LCB/1(a). Anglican Communion Office Archives.

Lambeth Consultative Body and Advisory Council on Missionary Strategy. 1964. *Minutes of Joint Meeting, the 'Meeting of Metropolitans', Held at St Augustine's College, Canterbury.* ACC/LCB/1(c). Anglican Communion Office Archives.

Lambeth Palace: Press Release. 2013. 'Justin Welby Confirmed as Archbishop of Canterbury at St Paul's Cathedral'. *Archbishop of Canterbury Website.* February 4. http://www.archbishopofcanterbury.org/articles.php/5014/justin-welby-confirmed-as-archbishop-of-canterbury-at-st-pauls-cathedral.

Langham, Mark. 2015. 'Too Early to Call Time on the Anglican Communion'. *The Tablet*, September 17.

Lartey, Emmanuel. 2000. 'Practical Theology as a Theological Form'. In *Blackwell Reader in Pastoral and Practical Theology*, edited by James Woodward and Stephen Pattison. Oxford: Blackwell.

Laughlin, Martin. 2004. *The Idea of Public Law.* Oxford: Oxford University Press.

'Law & Justice: The Christian Law Review'. 2002 149.

Lenski, Noel. 2010. 'Tetrarchy'. *Oxford Encyclopedia of Ancient Greece and Rome.* Oxford: Oxford University Press.

Levi, Leone. 1868. *Annals of British Legislation: Digest of Blue Books.* Vol. 4. London: Smith, Elder & Co.

Living Church Editorial. 2015. 'Primatial Option for the Covenant'. *The Living Church*, November 30.

MacCulloch, Diarmaid. 1995. *The Reign of Henry VIII: Politics, Policy and Piety.* Palgrave Macmillan.

MacDougall, Scott. 2015. *More than Communion : Imagining an Eschatological Ecclesiology.* London: T & T Clark.

Macneil, Sarah. 2006. 'Body Image: Ecclesiology and Governance in Changing Times'. In *'Wonderful and Confessedly Strange': Australian Essays in Anglican*

Ecclesiology, edited by Bruce Kaye, Sarah Macneil, and Heather Thomson, 201–22. Hindmarsh: ATF Press.

Mager, Robert. 2011. 'Action Theories'. In *The Wiley-Blackwell Companion to Practical Theology*, edited by Bonnie J Miller-McLemor. Oxford: Wiley-Blackwell.

Maginn, Christopher. 2018. 'Continuity and Change: 1470–1550'. In *The Cambridge History of Ireland*, edited by Brendan Smith, 1:300–328. Cambridge University Press.

Makower, Felix. 1895. *The Constitutional History and Constitution of the Church of England*. London: Swan Sonnenschein & Co.

Mant, Richard. 1840. *History of the Church of Ireland*. Vol. 1. London: John W. Parker.

Maritain, Jacques. 1951. *Man and the State*. Chicago, IL: University of Chicago Press.

Mason, J. F. A. 2004. 'Richard de Belmeis'. *Oxford Dictionary of National Biography (Online Edn)*, Oxford University Press.

Mather, F. C. 1992. *High Church Prophet*. Oxford University Press.

McCullough, Peter. 2014. ''Anglicanism' and the Origins of the Church of England'. *Ecclesiastical Law Journal* 16 (03): 319–34.

McGiffert, Arthur Chusman, trans. 1995. 'Eusebius: Church History from A.D. 1–324'. In *Nicene and Post-Nicene Fathers*. Vol. 1. A Select Library of the Christian Church 2. Peabody, MA: Hendrickson.

McGowan, Andrew. 2016. 'Primacy and Communion'. *Journal of Anglican Studies* 14 (1): 1–7.

McGrade, Arthur Stephen, ed. 2013. *Richard Hooker: Of the Laws of Ecclesiastical Polity*. Vol. 1. 3 vols. Oxford: Oxford University Press.

McPherson, James. 1994. 'Anglican Episcopacy in Australia: Reflections on Theory and Practice'. In *Episcopacy: Views from the Antipodes. Essays on Episcopal Ministry Presented to the Primate, Archbishop Keith Rayner, on the 25th Anniversary of His Consecration as Bishop.*, edited by Alan Cadwallader, 75–90. North Adelaide, SA: Anglican Board of Christian Education.

Meyers, Ruth. 2015. 'Bishops Accept 'Statement of Clarification' about Marriage'. *The Episcopal Church Website*. July 6. http://www.episcopalchurch.org/posts/sclm/bishops-accept-statement-clarification-about-marriage.

Micklem, Philip Arthur. 1921. *Principles of Church Organization: With Special Reference to the Church of England in Australia*. London: SPCK.

Miller-McLemor, Bonnie J. 2011. 'The Contributions of Practical Theology'. In *The Wiley-Blackwell Companion to Practical Theology*, edited by Bonnie J. Miller-McLemor. Oxford: Wiley-Blackwell.

'Minutes of Proceedings of a Meeting of the Metropolitan and Suffragan Bishops of the Province of Australasia, Held in Sydney, October 1 to November 1, 1850'. 1924. In *Constitutional Church Government*, by Henry Lowther Clarke. London: SPCK.

Moltmann, Jürgen. 1977. *The Church in the Power of the Spirit*. Translated by Margaret Kohl. London: SCM Press.

Montgomery, Henry Hutchinson. 1920. *Preliminary Paper on Problems Connected with Provincial Organization*. London: H.B. Skinner & Co.

Moorman, John R. H. 1980. *A History of the Church in England*. London: Adam & Charles Black.

Moses, Sarah. 2015. 'The Ethics of 'Recognition': Rowan Williams's Approach to Moral Discernment in the Christian Community'. *Journal of the Society of Christian Ethics* 35 (1): 147–65.

Moxon, David. 2016. *'Global, Regional, Local' in a Communion Ecclesiology*. Private document supplied by author.

National Anglican Centre - a Brochure Prepared for General Synod. 1985. ACC/CH/PROV/1(e). Anglican Communion Office Archives.

Neale, John Mason. 1863. *Essays on Liturgiology and Church History: With an Appendix on Liturgical Quotations from the Apostolic Fathers by Gerard Moultrie*. London: Saunders, Otley.

Nicholson, Graham David. 1977. 'The Nature and Function of Historical Argument in the Henrician Reformation'. Unpublished PhD Dissertation, Cambridge: University of Cambridge.

Norman, Edward. 1999. 'Authority in the Anglican Communion'. *Ecclesiastical Law Journal* 5 (24): 172–187.

Norman, James. 1953. *John Oliver North Queensland*. Melbourne, Vic: General Board of Religious Education of the Church of England in Australia.

Ntagali, Stanley. 2016. *Letter to the Bishops, Clergy and Lay Leaders of the Church of Uganda*, January 6. Published on the Anglican Ink online blog and news service.

Ohmae, Kenichi. 2008. *The End of the Nation State: The Rise of Regional Economies*. London: Harper Collins.

Ould, David. 2015. 'Archbishop of Canterbury Calls Critical Primates' Meeting'. *Davidould.Net*. September 18. http://davidould.net/archbishop-of-canterbury-calls-critical-primates-meeting/.

———. 2016. 'Portents, Prophecy and Predictions - What Will Happen at the Primates' Meeting?' *Davidould.Net*. January 9. http://davidould.net/portends-prophecy-and-predictions-what-will-happen-at-the-primates-meeting/.

Pabst, Adrian. 2010. 'Modern Sovereignty in Question: Theology, Democracy and Capitalism'. *Modern Theology* 26 (4): 570–602.

Palmer, Edwin James. 1930. 'The Anglican Communion: Its Ideal and Future. LC 1930 Agenda IV(A)'. In *Lambeth Conference: Documents Circulated to the Bishops*. London: Lambeth Palace.

Palmer, William. 1838. *A Treatise on the Church of Christ*. Vol. 2. 2 vols. London: J. G. & F. Rivington.

Pancirolus, Guido. 1608. *Notitia Utraque Dignitatum, Cum Orientis, Tum Occidentis, Ultra Arcadii Honoriique Tempora*. Lyon: Ioannes de Gabiano.

Papers for Primates' Meeting - Canterbury 2016. 2015. Anglican Communion Office. Primates' Papers. Anglican Communion Office Archives.

Pattison, Stephen. 2000. 'Some Straw for the Bricks: A Basic Introduction to Theological Reflection'. In *Blackwell Reader in Pastoral and Practical Theology*, edited by James Woodward and Stephen Pattison. Oxford: Blackwell.

Percival, Henry. 1995. 'The Seven Ecumenical Councils'. In *Nicene and Post-Nicene Fathers*, edited by Philip Schaff and Henry Wace. Vol. 14. A Select Library of the Christian Church 2. Peabody, MA: Hendrickson.

Percy, Martyn. 2001. *The Salt of the Earth: Religious Resilience in a Secular Age*. Sheffield: Sheffield Academic Press.

———. 2004. 'Joking Apart: Exploring Comedy and Irony in Anglican Polity'. *Ecclesiology* 1 (1): 75–86.

———. 2005. *Engaging with Contemporary Culture: Christianity, Theology and the Concrete Church*. Burlington, VT: Routledge.

———. 2010. *Shaping the Church: The Promise of Implicit Theology*. Burlington, VT: Routledge.

———. 2012. *The Ecclesial Canopy: Faith, Hope, Charity*. Burlington, VT: Routledge.

———. 2013. *Anglicanism: Confidence, Commitment and Communion*. Burlington, VT: Ashgate.

———. 2015. 'Diversity Not Divorce: Anglicans Must Aim for a Broad Church If They Can't Agree'. *The Conversation*, September 18.

———. 2016a. *On Not Rearranging the Deckchairs on the Titanic - A Commentary on Reform and Renewal in the Church of England*. Modern Church.

———. 2016b. 'Emergent Archiepiscopal Leadership within the Anglican Communion'. *Journal of Anglican Studies* 14 (1): 46–70.

Perry, Charles. 1850. *Diary Entry - 3 October*. Diocese of Melbourne Archives.

'Peter Jensen Speaks to GAFCON Supporters - End of Day 1'. 2016. *Davidould. Net*. January 12. http://davidould.net/peter-jensen-speaks-to-gafcon-supporters-end-of-day-1/.

Phidas, Vlassios. 2006. 'Papal Primacy and Patriarchal Pentarchy in the Orthodox Tradition'. In *The Petrine Ministry: Catholics and Orthodox in Dialogue. Academic Symposium Held at the Pontifical Council for Promoting Christian Unity*, edited by Walter Kasper, 65–82. New York, NY: Newman Press.

Pickard, Stephen. 2013. 'Gifts of Communion: Recovering an Anglican Approach to the 'Instruments of Unity''. *Journal of Anglican Studies* 11 (2): 233–55.

Podmore, Colin. 2008. 'A Tale of Two Churches: The Ecclesiologies of The Episcopal Church and the Church of England Compared'. *Ecclesiastical Law Journal* 10 (1).

———. 2009. *The Governance of the Church of England and the Anglican Communion*. GS Misc 910.

———. 2010. 'Two Streams Mingling: The American Episcopal Church in the Anglican Communion'. *Journal of Anglican Studies*, September, 1–26.

Porter, Muriel. 2011. *Sydney Anglicans and the Threat to World Anglicanism: The Sydney Experiment*. Burlington, VT: Ashgate.

Presler, Titus. 2013. 'The History of Mission in the Anglican Communion'. In *The Wiley-Blackwell Companion to the Anglican Communion*, 15–32. John Wiley & Sons, Ltd.

Press Conference Following Primates' Gathering. 2016. Recorded Periscope Broadcast. Canterbury.

Prichard, Robert W. 2013. 'The Lambeth Conferences'. In *The Wiley-Blackwell Companion to the Anglican Communion*, 91–104. John Wiley & Sons, Ltd.

'Primates 2016: Archbishop of Canterbury's Address'. 2016. *Vanguard Nigeria Website*. January 11. http://www.vanguardngr.com/2016/01/primates-2016-archbishop-of-canterburys-address/.

Primates' Meeting 2002: Action Plan. For Internal Use. 2002. Primates' Papers: 2002 Meeting Electronic Backup. Anglican Communion Office Archives.

Primates' Meetings: Informal Meeting of Primates - Nairobi. 1975. ACC/PM/1(a). Anglican Communion Office Archives.

Primates' Meetings: Primates' Meeting, Ely - Agenda and Minutes. 1979. ACC/PM/1(c). Anglican Communion Office Archives.

Primates' Meetings: Selected Documents. 1978. ACC/PM/1(c). Anglican Communion Office Archives.

Primates' Meetings: Small Group of Primates Meeting. 1978. ACC/PM/1(b). Anglican Communion Office Archives.

Provincial Constitutions of New South Wales, Victoria, Queensland and Western Australia. 1967. Constitutional Collection. Anglican Communion Office Archives.

Randall, Michael. 2008. *The Gargantuan Polity: On the Individual and the Community in the French Renaissance*. University of Toronto Press.

Raven, Charles. 2015. 'To Mend the Net?' *GAFCON Website*. December 16. https://www.gafcon.org/news/to-mend-the-net.

Rayner, Keith. 1962. 'The History of the Church of England in Queensland'. Unpublished PhD Dissertation, Brisbane: University of Queensland.

———. 2006a. 'Historical and Global Contexts'. In *'Wonderful and Confessedly Strange': Australian Essays in Anglican Ecclesiology*, edited by Bruce Kaye, Sarah Macneil, and Heather Thomson. Hindmarsh: ATF Press.

———. 2006b. 'The Idea of a National Church in Australian Anglicanism'. In *Agendas for Australian Anglicanism: Essays in Honour of Bruce Kaye*, edited by Tom Frame and Geoffrey Treloar, 29–56. Adelaide, SA: ATF Press.

Rees, John. 1998. 'The Anglican Communion: Does It Exist?' *Ecclesiastical Law Journal* 5 (22): 14–17.

Report from the Meeting of the Standing Committee of 6-7 April, 2016 to the 16th Meeting of the Anglican Consultative Council. 2016. Http://www.anglicancommunion.org/media/229078/SC-Report-to-ACC16.pdf.

Report of the Viability & Structures Task Force, and Other Materials Impinging on the Small Groups Discussion Program. 2014. Sydney, NSW: Standing Committee of the General Synod of the Anglican Church of Australia.

Report of the Working Party Appointed by the Primates of the Anglican Communion on Women and the Episcopate. 1987. ACC/LC/5/3/1a. Anglican Communion Office Archives.

'Response from the Secretary General of the Anglican Communion to the Archbishop of Canterbury's Call for a Special Primates' Meeting in January 2016'. 2016. *Anglican Communion News Service*. September 16. http://www.anglicannews.org/news/2015/09/response-from-the-secretary-general-of-the-anglican-communion-to-the-archbishop-of-canterburys-call-for-a-special-primates-meeting-in-january-2016.aspx.

Rex, Richard. 2003. 'Redating Henry VIII's A Glasse of the Truthe'. *The Library* 4 (1): 16–27.

———. 2006. *Henry VIII and the English Reformation*. New York, NY: Palgrave Macmillan.

Reynolds, Roger E. 1995. 'The Organisation, Law and Liturgy of the Western Church, 700–900'. In *The New Cambridge Medieval History*, edited by Rosamond McKitterick, 2:587–621. Cambridge: Cambridge University Press.

Ring, Diane M. 2008. 'What's at Stake in the Sovereignty Debate: International Tax and the Nation-State'. *Virginia Journal of International Law* 49: 155.

'Roman Catholic Code of Canon Law'. 2016. Accessed October 13. http://www.vatican.va/archive/eng1104/_index.htm.

Ross, Alexander John. 2013. "Naked Autonomy' or 'Clothed Communion': What Place Is There for Provincial Autonomy in Worldwide Anglicanism and Its

Continued Existence?' Unpublished MTh Dissertation, Oxford: University of Oxford.

Royal Commission into Institutional Responses to Child Sexual Abuse. 2003. *Victorian Provincial Legal Committee: Commentary on a Proposed Scheme to Deal Uniformly with Problems Arising from Sexual Abuse*. Case Study 36, January 2016. Document ID: ANG.0147.001.0306.

———. 2013a. *Public Inquiry into the Response of the Diocese of Grafton of the Anglican Church to Claims of Child Sexual Abuse at the North Coast Children's Home: Submissions on Behalf of Archbishop Phillip Aspinall, Mr Martin Drevikovsky and Mr Rodney McLary*. Case Study 3, November 2013. Document ID: SUBM.1003.006.0001.

———. 2013b. *Statement of Archbishop Phillip Aspinall, in the Matter of Anglican Diocese of Grafton North Coast Children's Home*. Case Study 52, March 2017. Document ID: STAT.0078.001.0001_R.

———. 2014. *Professional Standards Working Group - Province of Victoria. Options for Implementing a Model Professional Standards Scheme*. Case Study 36, January 2016. Document ID: ANG.0147.001.0924.

———. 2016. *Anglican Dioceses of Melbourne: Professional Standards Uniform Act Adoption Bill 2016. Explanatory Memorandum*. Case Study 52, March 2017. Document ID: STAT.1297.001.0097.

———. 2017a. *Statement of Michael Warner Shand QC*. Case Study 52, March 2017. Document ID: STAT.1326.001.0001.

———. 2017b. *Public Hearing Transcript (Day 262)*. Case Study 52.

Runcie, Robert. 1989. *The Unity We Seek*. London: Darton, Longman & Todd.

Sachs, William L. 2013. 'The Emergence of the Anglican Communion in the Nineteenth and Twentieth Centuries'. In *The Wiley-Blackwell Companion to the Anglican Communion*, 33–44. John Wiley & Sons, Ltd.

Sadgrove, Joanna, Robert M. Vanderbeck, Kevin Ward, Gill Valentine, and Johan Andersson. 2010. 'Constructing the Boundaries of Anglican Orthodoxy: An Analysis of the Global Anglican Future Conference (GAFCON)'. *Religion* 40 (3): 193–206.

Schaff, Philip, ed. 1995. 'Homilies on the Epistles of St Paul the Apostle to Timothy, Titus, and Philemon'. In *Nicene and Post-Nicene Fathers*, by The Oxford Translation, with additional notes. Vol. 13. A Select Library of the Christian Church 1. Peabody, MA: Hendrickson.

Schilderman, Hans. 2011. 'Quantitative Method'. In *The Wiley-Blackwell Companion to Practical Theology*, edited by Bonnie J Miller-McLemor. Oxford: Wiley-Blackwell.

Schleiermacher, Friedrich. 1988. *Christian Caring: Selections from Practical Theology*. Edited by James O. Duke and Howard Stone. Philadelphia: Fortress Press.

Schmitt, Francis Salesius. 1968. *S. Anselmi Cantuariensis Archiepiscopi Opera Omnia*. Vol. 2. Stuttgart-Bad Cannstatt: Friedrich Frommann.

Sellar, A. M. 1907. *Bede's Ecclesiastical History of England: A Revised Translation with Introduction, Life and Notes*. London: George Bell & Sons.

Sharwood, Robin. 2004. *'To Strive, to Seek, to Find, and Not to Yield' - The Making of the (Victoria) Church of England Act 1854*. Vol. September 2005. Trinity Papers 29. The Sidney Smith Lecture for 2004, delivered at Trinity College Melbourne.

Shaw, George Peter. 1970. 'William Grant Broughton and His Early Years in New South Wales'. Unpublished PhD Dissertation, Canberra: Australian National University.

Shaw, Richard. 2016. 'When Did Augustine of Canterbury Die?' *The Journal of Ecclesiastical History* 67 (3): 473–91.

Skinner, John. 1788. *An Ecclesiastical History of Scotland*. Vol. 2. Printed for T. Evans and R.N. Cheyne.

Smith, Brian. 2013. 'The Scottish Episcopal Church'. In *The Wiley-Blackwell Companion to the Anglican Communion*, 441–51. Chichester: John Wiley & Sons.

Smith, E A. 2009. 'Act of Union (Ireland)'. In *Oxford Companion to British History*, edited by John Cannon. Oxford University Press.

Smith, Saumarez. 1900. 'Anglican General Synod - Quinquennial Session. Presidential Address'. *The Sydney Morning Herald*, August 29, Second edition.

Smith, William, and Samuel Cheetham. 1875. *A Dictionary of Christian Antiquities: Being a Continuation of the 'Dictionary of the Bible'*. 2 vols. London.

Southey, Nicholas. 1998. 'Robert Gray and His Legacy to the Church of the Province of Southern Africa'. In *Change and Challenge: Essays Commemorating the 150th Anniversary of the Arrival of Robert Gray as First Bishop of Cape Town (20 February 1848)*, edited by John Suggit and Mandy Goedhals, 18–25. Marshalltown, SA: CPSA Publishing Committee.

Starkie, Andrew. 2007. *The Church of England and the Bangorian Controversy 1716–1721*. Studies in Modern British Religious History. Woodbridge, UK: Boydell & Brewer.

Statement Concerning Lay Presidency, Agreed by Primates and Distributed by John Peterson, 30 March. 2000. Primates' Papers: 2000 Meeting Electronic Backup. Anglican Communion Office Archives.

'Statement from Primates'. 2016. *Anglican Communion News Service*. January 14. http://www.anglicannews.org/news/2016/01/statement-from-primates-2016.aspx.

'Statement on the Primates' Meeting'. 2016. *Changing Attitude Scotland*. January 14. http://www.changingattitudescotland.org.uk/statement-on-the-primates-meeting-2016-from-changing-attitude-scotland/.

Stephens, Christopher William Barrow. 2015. *Canon Law and Episcopal Authority: The Canons of Antioch and Serdica*. Oxford: Oxford University Press.

Stevenson, James, and W H C Frend, eds. 1989. *Creeds, Councils and Controversies*. Revised. London: SPCK.

Story, J. 2012. 'Bede, Willibrord and the Letters of Pope Honorius I on the Genesis of the Archbishopric of York'. *The English Historical Review* 127 (527): 783–818.

Strong, Rowan. 2007. *Anglicanism and the British Empire, c.1700–1850*. Oxford: Oxford University Press.

Stubbs, William. 1858. *Registrum Sacrum Anglicanum: An Attempt to Exhibit the Course of Episcopal Succession in England*. Oxford: Oxford University Press.

Sykes, Stephen. 1978. *The Integrity of Anglicanism*. London: Mowbrays.

— — —, ed. 1981. *Authority in the Anglican Communion: Essays Presented to Bishop John Howe*. London: Chameleon Press.

Tanner, Norman P. 1990. *Decrees of the Ecumenical Councils*. London: Sheed & Ward.

Temple, William. 1915. *Church and Nation: The Bishop Paddock Lectures for 1914–15. Delivered at the General Theological Seminary, New York*. London: Macmillan.

'Terms of Reference'. 2017. *Royal Commission into Institutional Responses to Child Sexual Abuse Website*. Accessed May 17. http://www.childabuseroyalcommission.gov.au/about-us/terms-of-reference.

Thacker, Alan. 2008. 'Gallic or Greek? Archbishops in England from Theodore to Ecgberht'. In *Frankland: The Franks and the World of the Early Middle Ages*, edited by P. Fouracre and D. Ganz, 44–69. Manchester.

The Anglican Communion Covenant. 2009. Anglican Communion Office.

The Anglican Communion Office: A Brief Guide. 2017. Anglican Communion Office.

The Argus. 1904. 'Church of England - Proposed Ecclesiastical Province', July 29.

The Colonial Church Chronicle and Missionary Journal. 1849. Vol. 2, July 1848–June 1849. 28 vols. London: Francis and John Rivington.

———. *The Colonial Church Chronicle and Missionary Journal*. 1853. Vol. 6, July 1852–June 1853. 28 vols. London: Francis and John Rivington.

The Time Is Now: Anglican Consultative Council First Meeting. Limuru, Kenya. 1971. SPCK. ACC/C/1/2. Anglican Communion Office Archives.

The Truth Shall Make You Free: The Lambeth Conference 1988, the Reports, Resolutions, Pastoral Letters from the Bishops. 1988. London: Church House Publishing.

Thiry, Leon. 1981. 'Nation, State, Sovereignty and Self-Determination'. *Peace Research* 13 (1): 15–20.

Thomas, Philip H. E. 2002. 'The Evolution of the Primates: Anglicanism, Primacy and Conciliarity'. *International Journal for the Study of the Christian Church* 2 (2): 79–95.

———. 2004. 'Unity and Concord: An Early Anglican 'Communion''. *Journal of Anglican Studies* 2 (1): 9.

Thomson, Janice E. 1995. 'State Sovereignty in International Relations: Bridging the Gap between Theory and Empirical Research'. *International Studies Quarterly* 39 (2): 213.

Tierney, Stephen. 2005. 'Reframing Sovereignty? Sub-State National Societies and Contemporary Challenges to the Nation-State'. *International and Comparative Law Quarterly* 54 (01): 161–183.

Tindal Hart, Arthur. 1986. *Ebor: A History of the Archbishops of York*. York: The Ebor Press.

To Set Our Hope on Christ: A Response to the Invitation of Windsor Report ¶135. 2005. New York, NY: Office of Communication, Episcopal Church Centre.

Tolliday, P. W. 2008. 'Being Anglican in Australia Today'. In *Okumene Der Zekunft: Hermeneutische Perspektiven Und Die Suche Nach Identitat*. Frankfurt, Germany: Verlag Otto Lembeck.

Turner, Frank M. 2009. 'The Imagined Community of the Anglican Communion'. *Episcopal Cafe*. September 9. http://www.episcopalcafe.com/the_imagined_community_of_the_anglican_communion/.

Vatican Council, Edward H Peters, and Gregory Baum. 1966. *De Ecclesia: The Constitution on the Church of Vatican Council Ii Proclaimed by Pope Paul VI, November 21, 1964*. Glen Rock, NJ: Paulist Press.

Vatican Council, and George H Tavard. 1966. *De Divina Revelatione: The Dogmatic Constitution on Divine Revelation of Vatican Council, Promulgated by Pope Paul VI, November 18, 1965*. Glen Rock, NJ: Paulist Press.

Vialart, Charles. 1641. *Geographia Sacra, Sive, Notitia Antiqua Episcopatuum Ecclesiæ Universæ: Ex Conciliis, Patribus, Historia Ecclesiastica, & Geographis Antiquis Excerpta*. Lutetiæ Parisiorum: Melchioris Tavernier.

Warren, Max. 1984. *The Functions of a National Church*. Latimer Series 19. Oxford: Latimer House.

WCC Commission on Faith and Order. 1982. *Baptism, Eucharist and Ministry*. Geneva: World Council of Churches.

Welby, Justin. 2016. 'The Cost and the Joy of Unity – Reflections on the Primates' Meeting in Canterbury'. *Archbishop of Canterbury Website*. January 21. http://www.archbishopofcanterbury.org/blog.php/26/the-cost-and-the-joy-of-unity-reflections-on-the-primates-meeting-in-canterbury.

Whalon, Pierre W. 2011. 'The Tale Needs Re-Telling: A Reply to Colin Podmore's 'A Tale of Two Churches''. *Theology* 114 (1): 3–12.

White, Edwin Augustin, and Jackson A. Dykman. 1997. *Annotated Constitution and Canons for the Government of the Protestant Episcopal Church of the United States of America Otherwise Known as The Episcopal Church*. 1981 Edition, Combined Volumes. New York, NY: Church Publishing Incorporated.

White, William. 1782. *The Case of the Episcopal Churches in the United States Considered*. Philadelphia: Printed by David C. Claypool.

Wilkins, John. 2005. 'Back from the Brink? The Windsor Report on the Anglican Communion'. *Ecclesiology* 1 (3): 101–7.

Williams, Rowan. 1997. 'Interiority and Epiphany: A Reading in New Testament Ethics'. In *Spirituality and Social Embodiment*, edited by L. Gregory Jones and James J. Buckley, 29–51. Oxford: Blackwell.

— — —. 1999. 'On Making Moral Decisions'. *Anglican Theological Review* 81 (2).

— — —. 2005. 'One Holy Catholic and Apostolic Church: Archbishop's Address to the 3rd Global South to South Encounter Ain Al Sukhna, Egypt'. *Dr Rowan Williams: 104th Archbishop of Canterbury. Archived Website*. October 28. http://rowanwilliams.archbishopofcanterbury.org/articles.php/1675/one-holy-catholic-and-apostolic-church.

— — —. 2007. 'The Archbishop's 2007 Advent Letter to Primates'. *Dr Rowan Williams: 104th Archbishop of Canterbury. Archived Website*. December 14. http://rowanwilliams.archbishopofcanterbury.org/articles.php/631/the-archbishops-advent-letter-to-primates-2007.

— — —. 2008a. 'Rome, Constantinople, and Canterbury: Mother Churches? Message from the Archbishop to a Conference on Primacy, Sponsored by the Fellowship of St Alban and St Sergius at St Vladimir's Seminar, New York.' *Dr Rowan Williams: 104th Archbishop of Canterbury. Archived Website*. June 5. http://rowanwilliams.archbishopofcanterbury.org/articles.php/1357/rome-constantinople-and-canterbury-mother-churches.

— — —. 2008b. 'A Common Word and Future Christian-Muslim Engagement: Opening Address, in Emmanuel College, Cambridge, of a Conference Entitled 'A Common Word and Future Christian-Muslim Engagement'.' *Dr Rowan Williams: 104th Archbishop of Canterbury. Archived Website*. October 12. http://rowanwilliams.archbishopofcanterbury.org/articles.php/1040/a-common-word-and-future-christian-muslim-engagement.

Wondra, Ellen K. 2005. "The Highest Degree of Communion Possible': Initial Reflections on the Windsor Report 2004'. *Anglican Theological Review* 87 (2): 193.

———. 2016. 'The Importance of Moral Authority: Reflection on Current Events in the Anglican Communion'. *Anglican Theological Review* 98 (3): 533–43.

Woodward, James, and Stephen Pattison, eds. 2000. *Blackwell Reader in Pastoral and Practical Theology*. Oxford: Blackwell.

Wordsworth, Christopher. 1865. *On the Judicial Functions of Metropolitans, and on the Appeal of Bishop Colenso*. London: Rivingtons.

Working Papers for the Lambeth Conference 1988: Prepared at the Saint Augustine's Seminar Held at Blackheath, London, England. 29 July - 7 August. 1987. Divinity School Library, Reference: PAM WOR. University of Cambridge.

Wyatt, Ransome. 1937. *The History of the Diocese of Goulburn*. Sydney, NSW: Edgar Bragg & Sons.

Ypi, Lea. 2013. 'What's Wrong with Colonialism'. *Philosophy & Public Affairs* 41 (2): 158–191.

Yudha, Thianto. 2006. 'Baptismal Practice and Trinitarian Belief in Joseph Bingham's Origines Ecclesiasticae: A Study in the Historical and Theological Contexts of Patristic Scholarship at the Close of the Era of Orthodoxy'. Unpublished PhD Dissertation, Grand Rapids, MI: Calvin Theological Seminary.

Zink, Jesse. 2011. 'Changing World, Changing Church: Stephen Bayne and 'Mutual Responsibility and Interdependence''. *Anglican Theological Review* 93 (2): 243.

Index